D0758329

REDIRECTING EDUCATION

IN TWO VOLUMES

———

VOLUME TWO

EUROPE AND CANADA

REDIRECTING EDUCATION

EDITED BY

REXFORD G. TUGWELL

AND

LEON H. KEYSERLING

WITHDRAWN
UTSA LIBRARIES

VOLUME TWO

EUROPE AND CANADA

Essay Index Reprint Series

BOOKS FOR LIBRARIES PRESS
FREEPORT, NEW YORK

Copyright © 1935 by Columbia University Press

Reprinted 1971 by arrangement

INTERNATIONAL STANDARD BOOK NUMBER:
0-8369-2031-7

LIBRARY OF CONGRESS CATALOG CARD NUMBER:
74-128323

PRINTED IN THE UNITED STATES OF AMERICA

PREFACE

About fifteen years ago a group of teachers in Columbia College began an experiment which is bearing fruit today. They decided that the artificial boundaries separating the various social sciences made it difficult to bring all of these disciplines to bear at once upon the insistent problems of our times. They organized a course which is taught coöperatively by specialists drawn from many fields, and which considers issues such as law administration, price regulation, population distribution—to take but a few of many—not as problems of sociology or history or government or economics, but as public questions calling for whatever aid knowledge has to offer.

This experiment has had very broad results. When the various social sciences came to be considered as instrumentalities rather than in purely scholastic terms, it became possible, indeed necessary, to reëvaluate the contribution which each might make toward the attainment of social objectives. Thus the disciplines themselves took on new characteristics. Along with this, the projectors of the experiment began to think in still wider terms. What was the purpose of the liaison course? What is the function of American education today? Obviously, the answer to these questions involves more than a statement of the nature and possibilities of the social sciences themselves. There must be a consideration of the educational machinery, and of the great outside world and of the constant interaction between the two. Such considerations were stimulated by the Columbia project, and the results have been published in the previous volume of this work, which deals with the problems of college education in the United States.

Naturally enough, when thoughtful men begin to think about the social objectives of education and the means of attaining these objectives, they want to survey what other countries are doing with their schools. Furthermore, particular countries are certain to draw attention. Russia, Italy, and France are important because they present definite social objectives in education resulting from clearly defined

political ideals: Communism, Fascism and *laissez faire*. Germany,
where the sands are shifting daily, England, and Canada are worthy
of study because of the similarity between their problems and our
own: these countries find, as we do, that educational systems which reflect nineteenth-century society are losing contact with a changing
world. Danish education affords a telling example of what definite
social objectives in education may accomplish, at least in a small
homogeneous nation with an admirable social organization.

Thus the small experiment of a group of social scientists has taken
on wider and wider implications until the seven foreign studies contained in this volume have been made. While each of the contributors
has been animated by association with the original project for improving American education, each is unusually qualified to write on
the topic he has chosen. The author of the essay on Russian education is a native of that country who has spent the major portion of
his life there; the same is true of one of the contributors on French
education and of the specialist in Danish education. The writer on
Canadian and English Universities is a native of the former country
and a graduate of Oxford. The analysis of the German system is the
result of a year of study in that country as a Cutting Fellow from
Columbia. The essay on Italian education is the work of the co-author,
with Herbert W. Schneider, of one of the most competent and best
known books on Fascism, *Making the Fascist State*. Thus each con-
tributor combines specialized knowledge of his subject with the central point of reference to be found in the coöperative American interest out of which all of these inquiries arose. It is this unique situation which should commend these essays to the American reader.

WASHINGTON, D.C.   REXFORD G. TUGWELL
January 25, 1935   LEON H. KEYSERLING

CONTENTS

GERMAN EDUCATION IN THE REPUBLIC

AND IN THE THIRD REICH

BY

HORACE TAYLOR

EDUCATION IN ENGLAND

BY

J. BARTLET BREBNER

SOCIAL OBJECTIVES IN DANISH EDUCATION

BY

JOHN H. WUORINEN

EDUCATION IN CANADA

BY

J. BARTLET BREBNER

GERMAN EDUCATION IN THE REPUBLIC AND IN THE THIRD REICH

BY

HORACE TAYLOR

I

GERMAN IDEAS AND INSTITUTIONS

Both the past and the future are more orderly and more coherent than the present. Through history we can view the past only as a set of processes which led up to something, and which, for this reason, contained implicitly the meaning which our minds discover and express. Through prediction and planning the future is revealed as a logical fulfillment of whatever trends or purposes we may have in mind. The bewilderment of the present comes from the double failure of the past to continue and of the future to arrive.

An axiom of fascism—which is by no means peculiar to it—is that past, present, and future are a continuum. The national character has grown in the past, and is cultivated in the present, so that it will bear a desired fruit in the future. The work of dictatorship is that of assisting nature by grafting and pruning. A real appreciation of the past must perplex and embarrass a dictator. It must cause him to consider whether the methods he uses and the objectives which he serves are consistent with the collective habits and values of his nation. The test of dictatorship is here. An honored fascist, Machiavelli, says of dictators: "He will be successful who directs his actions according to the spirit of the times, and he whose actions do not accord with the times will not be successful."

In the present unsettled state of affairs in Germany, the aims and consequences of particular immediate policies are impossible to estimate in detail. Many of the day-to-day measures which apply to education belong properly to the second or third order of expedients. In the welter of verbal change, the only purposes and objectives which can have any lasting influence are those which are consistent with German habits of thoughts and with the broad lines of institutional change. For German ideas and habits are not less inert than those of other nations; and in Germany, as elsewhere, there is change.

In this chapter the explicit objectives which are served by education in Germany will be discussed, not so much in their own terms, as in relation to their setting in German ideas and institutions.[1]

1. *Contradictions in German Modes of Thought*

Any inquiry into the conditions which go to shape the trend of educational affairs in Germany is confronted at the outset with a confusion of apparently opposing tendencies and conflicting principles, which seems to reduce any characterization of Germany, the German people, or German education, to a baffling set of contradictions. It is necessary that a way be threaded among the broader forms of these contradictions, simply in order that their implications to the subject of this discussion may be clear.

Reference should be made, in the first place, to habitual modes of thought. Rationalism is the chief intellectual bent in Germany, not only in the formal sense represented, for example, by Kant's metaphysics, but also in the sense that it is a habit of German people to think categorically and to proceed from a priori premises to their conclusions. The process is fixed and widely prevalent, although the cement which joins premise and conclusion may be either logic or sophistry. It is commonly observed also that Germans are habitually downright and matter-of-fact. They approach their problems in a workmanlike fashion which probably is not surpassed by the people of any other nation, and their persistence in the face of obstacles has almost no modern parallel. Their scholarship and their refined inventiveness afford countless instances of this trait. Thus, to take a recent example, when the Treaty of Versailles forbade Germany to have warships of more than ten thousand tons' displacement, the Germans proceeded to build more effective ships of that tonnage than ever before had been conceived.

The matter-of-factness exhibited by Germans in their ordinary affairs often suggests—at least to foreign observers—an essentially materialistic and practical attitude of mind. Such judgments, however, are vigorously and resentfully denied by the Germans themselves, and the very terms in which the denials are cast are likely to

[1] For the opportunity to study the teaching of the social sciences in Germany, on which study the present chapter is largely based, I am indebted to a grant from the Council for Research in the Social Sciences of Columbia University.

carry conviction. For most Germans, if they thought about the matter at all, probably would find no inconsistency in possessing mental habits which are at once rationalistic and matter-of-fact. These conditions appear, indeed, to be as reasonable as the two sides of a coin. Here is a country in which each individual is virtually compelled, by tradition, by education, by status, even by a language rich in abstractions, to be the conscious creator of a *Weltanschauung*. With rather more completeness, and vastly more tidiness, this serves its possessor, be he metaphysician or peasant, in much the same fashion as the controlling ideas which we loosely call a "philosophy of life." Between the inner sanctions and the outer experience there is no essential friction. Lines of conduct are referred back to the conceptual premises, and the premises themselves are subject to greater or less modification by experience. Thus the rationalism which, in general, characterizes the German people, appears to exist by virtue of, rather than in opposition to, the matter-of-fact traits of these same people.

Another apparent contradiction—which, however, seems to impose no burden of vindication on the Germans themselves—is their concern with matters of pressing immediacy, and their absorption, at the same time, in tradition. It is not necessary to stress the interest of Germans in practical and immediate affairs; the facts of the case are notorious. But the range of German tradition, and its place in widely shared habits of thought, has an equally significant bearing on the intellectual traits and tendencies of the German people.

When the Roman state lacked the stability and dignity which comes from authentic tradition, Vergil endowed his city with a majestic epic. With no more substantial material than myth and symbolism, he convincingly tied the destiny of Rome to the heroism of ancient Troy. In similar vein, Plutarch sought—by biographical analogy between the great Greeks and the often merely conspicuous Romans—to appropriate for Rome the grand dimensions of the Hellenic legend. In the case of Germany, there has been no necessity for such invention. Excepting only the fountainheads in Greece and Italy, there is probably no other western country which exceeds Germany in the abundance and richness of its tradition. Every town and village has its heroes, its legends, its songs, its myths, its often

impressive history. The territory of the present Reich has been unified politically for only sixty years. Yet much of it was for centuries
Roman, and for even more centuries an important segment of the
Holy Roman Empire. Extending beyond its own political history
are its cultural roots in Greece and its Christian Hebraism. This
background is common to most countries of the West, yet it is doubtful if it exists elsewhere in such profusion of conscious detail. Peculiarly Germany's own are the numerous national heroes, whose
special place in German habits of thought will be detailed at another
point in this discussion.

In spite of its wealth of tradition—in part, perhaps, because of
it—there has not existed in Germany that degree of internal and total
cohesiveness which usually is found in the politically powerful nation
state. Such unity and centralization as has existed was imposed originally from the top instead of springing impulsively from a common
aspiration of the common people. Since the origin of the Reich, the
full force of its statecraft and its authority has been devoted to keeping intact a country in which separatism has never been far beneath.
the surface. Catholicism versus Protestantism, agrarianism versus in-
dustrialism are conflicts which have been drawn along geographical
lines, and which have been strengthened by the diversity of local tradition. Single-minded individualism on the part of the bulk of the
people has added a persistent·disruptive power. The forces which
appear to have been most potent in preserving the integrity of Germany are economic necessity and an acute consciousness of hereditary
national enmities. The classic formulations of these forces are, respectively, the "national economy" conceptions of Friedrich List
and the impassioned appeal to German patriotism of Fichte's "Ad-
dresses to the German Nation." Such matters of comparative expediency do not serve, however, as competent substitutes for a widely
spread consciousness of national destiny and faith in national ideals.
Such an interpretation implies, among other things, that the genius
of Fichte consisted, not in stirring the souls of Germans with a
sudden realization of cultural and traditional nationalism, but rather
in prophesying to a defeated and despairing people the inevitable
trend of political affairs.

One reason that tradition along national lines has not succeeded in creating a stable and spiritually unified state may lie in the failure of this larger tradition to remain within the national limits. In addition to their concern with cultural origins in antiquity, Germans long have shown a lively interest in affairs beyond their own borders. The most conspicuous modern instance is the Industrial Revolution in Germany, which was borrowed, in its early phases, from England (and refined and improved with characteristic German thoroughness) and, in its later phases, from the United States (and again refined and improved). Such borrowings of material apparatus characterize the whole of Germany's economic development, and appear to run back as far as the neolithic period.[2] Of the less materialistic elements of culture, Germany has produced a vast domestic supply. And yet she has adopted, and made her own through habituation, all of those things of foreign origin which have, for one reason or another, caught her fancy. During the cosmopolitan movement of the eighteenth century, many cultivated Germans adopted French manners and tastes and also the French language, and affected to despise their national language and all else purely German. But for the later phases of the Napoleonic episode, these cosmopolitan Germans might never have discovered dignity and worth in their national culture.

In numerous particulars this gift of absorption shows itself at the present time. The Volsunga Saga was accepted and revered as a German epic long before it was raised to musical immortality by Richard Wagner. England's greatest dramatist appears to be held in higher regard in Germany than in his native land (this disproportion being indeed so marked that there should be a reproach to Englishmen, rather than a gibe at Germans, in Bernard Shaw's reference to "*unser* Shakespeare"). And this high esteem in which Shakespeare is held among Germans seems to be due, not to any classic universality in his works, but rather to the "essentially German" character of his art. In the field of intellectual creation, Germany has an independent record which is unsurpassed by any modern nation. But in the great variety of other elements which go to make a culture and a national habit of thought, her people have borrowed widely, and

[2] Cf. Thorstein Veblen, *Imperial Germany and the Industrial Revolution*, New York, The Macmillan Co., 1915, pp. 11-49.

have adopted as "German," whatever may have appealed to their
fancy. Neither such a habit of borrowing, nor its fruits, go to make
a genuinely national tradition. Germans are, in this respect, emi-
nently qualified to become "citizens of the world."

This suggests another set of contradictions in the current trend of
German affairs: the growing force of political centralization, and the
tendencies toward particularism and separatism. Whatever the
mechanics of nationalism may be, a nation must consist of a unity of
individuals along socio-psychological lines, the unifying element
being national consciousness. That tradition fails to supply such a
consciousness, in the case of Germany, is a negative phase of the
matter. On the positive side there have been strong forces working
toward political disintegration. One such force has been the resent-
ment felt by smaller states (both before and after the revolution of
1919) toward the hegemony of Prussia. Another has been the discon-
tent of several of the provinces within Prussia itself, which, between
1919 and 1933, led to movements toward separating these sections from
Prussia and creating out of them new states within the structure of the
Reich. Professor Hugo Preuss, the chief author of the republican constitution, was sharply conscious of this latter tendency. In Paragraph
11 of the first draft of the constitution (which was omitted from the
final instrument) he wrote:

The German people may form new autonomous republics within
the *Reich* without consideration of the state boundaries until now in
existence, insofar as the tribal nature of the inhabitants, the economic
conditions, and the historic relations warrant the formation of such
states. Newly formed autonomous republics must comprise at least
two million inhabitants.[3]

The attitude of Bavarians toward a centralized government dom-
inated by Prussia is shown in the "Memorandum on the Revision
of the Weimar Constitution," which was presented in 1924 by the
government of Bavaria to the government of the Reich. A brief extract shows its tenor:

Culture pertains to the state. German culture has grown and blos-
somed from the soil of the German tribes (*Stämme*) and their state
organizations. The spirit of the people, which varied according to
their tribe and their state form, was the soil which nourished it. De-

[3] Quoted by Herbert Kraus, *Germany in Transition*, p. 201.

centralization, not centralization, has stamped German culture with its individuality. . . . The Bavarian people wish to remain the masters of their own souls, and the masters of the soul of their state. . . .[4]

The final set of contradictions which we shall consider here goes behind such matters as mass national consciousness and factional political differences, and refers to the motives of individual Germans. The two sets of uniformities indicated here have quite opposite effects on social behavior. The adaptability to discipline of the German people makes for definiteness in social relationships. The intense individualism of the same people is a force moving always in the direction of anarchy. This paradox of German character has challenged countless students of German affairs. Veblen offers an ingenious account of the causes of individualism among Germans in terms of the early mixture of tribes and peoples which has gone to make the racial composition of the Baltic-North Sea littoral. His thesis is that:

Their hybrid composition gives an extremely large facility for the acceptance of novel ideas from outside, together with a wide range of adaptation in all the arts of life, both in technological matters and as regards the scheme of civil and social institutions and the currency of religious and intellectual conceptions. At the same time the same individual variability of the hybrid acts to hinder any given scheme or system of accepted use and wont from attaining a definite stability. . . . Therefore, in a population of this character, any comprehensive scheme of use and wont, of knowledge and belief, will in effect necessarily be in some degree provisional; it will necessarily rest on acceptance (in some part concessive acceptance) by a majority of the individuals concerned, rather than on a uniform and unqualified spontaneous consensus of the entire population that lives under its rule. The acceptance accorded such a standard scheme by this effective majority is also necessarily in some appreciable measure an acceptance by consent rather than by free initiative.[5]

If an individualistic predisposition is biologically determined, or is a product of racial mixing, it is, of course, a fixed element of German character. Veblen points out that the discipline which binds the German social organization is, on the other hand, unstable and contingent. His view, which runs in terms of coercion and habituation coming from feudal times, is that the authority of the "terri-

[4] *Ibid.*
[5] Veblen, *op. cit.*, pp. 52 f.

torial state" has descended from earlier princely prerogative. "The
concept is visibly of feudal derivation, and the habit of mind which
makes it a practicable form of political organization is the feudal
habit of personal subservience to a personal master."[6] Clearly such a
"habit of mind" cannot be maintained indefinitely, after the conditions which gave rise to it have ceased to exist. On this score, however,
there is much more that might be said. To the habit of subservience
should be added the matter-of-factness which causes Germans—in-
dividualists though they be—to act together in an emergency and to
be conscious of common dangers and common aspirations where the
rest of the world is concerned.

One of the expressions of German individualism warrants a brief
mention. That is the deep-rooted and widespread "great man tradition." Perhaps there is a partial explanation here of the failure of the
German people to be collectively stirred by tradition. Germany has
no epic which embraces the German nation; she has instead great
men. And these great men of Germany do not lend themselves to
belittling and "debunking" by smaller and meaner men; they have
the statures and the potency of heroes. It is significant, too, that
these great men stood apart from crowds, and so maintained their
clarity of view and their independence of mind. Such men were Bar-
barossa, Melanchthon, Luther, Lessing, Kant, Frederick the Great,
Goethe, Schiller, Fichte, Hegel, Nietzsche, Bach, Beethoven,
Wagner—but no real enumeration is possible here. The works of
these men, like the men themselves, were steeped in individualism.
Luther sought to base religion upon the moral consciousness and
responsibility of the Christian man. And Goethe speaks through
Faust to say:

> Yes! To this thought I hold with firm persistence;
> The last result of wisdom stamps it true:
> He only wins his freedom and existence
> Who daily conquers them anew.

The traits of mind which have been presented here in the form of
apparently opposing tendencies and conflicting principles are among

---

[6] It should be borne in mind that Germany is not far removed from the forms
of feudalism. There were serfs in Prussia until the reforms initiated by Stein were
completed in 1807-13. And, until the revolution of 1918, employers had certain
legal rights to punish their domestic servants.

the important "givens" from which any system of social objectives in Germany must proceed. Without prejudice to the facts of the present investigation, it should be pointed out here that such "contradictions" as these seem peculiarly congenial to German minds. Some of their most profound intellectual accomplishments have consisted in resolving anomalies, and in illuminating the struggle between opposing forces. Thus the organizing conception of Hegel's *Philosophy of History* is a dialectical interplay of antagonistic principles. In *Faust* and *Wilhelm Meister*, Goethe wrote, not German epics, but epics of the human spirit torn between good and evil. To a similar end, Luther sought[7] to differentiate soul and body by elaborating the paradox of St. Paul: "A Christian is free lord over all things and subject to no man; a Christian is a bounden servant in all things and subject to everyone."

2. *German Education and Political Changes*

There probably are no people who traditionally have set higher store by education than the Germans. One evidence of this is the deference which has been paid to persons of recognized learning. Such official designations as doctoral degrees and professoral titles have for centuries been highly respected as marks of intellectual achievement. It is significant that the chief work of writing the constitution of republican Germany was entrusted, not to a professional political leader, but to a professor of political science. The same attitude has been shown repeatedly in the appointment of people of academic rank to ministerial posts both in the Reich and in the various states.

The motive to education, while springing from the individual's desire for understanding, is given inevitable form and direction by the social values of each time and place. Thus Paulsen, the German philosopher, was led to the generalization that "in ancient times the individual was educated for the State, in the middle ages for the Church, and in modern times for himself." In this regard—and with equal reference to the numerous generalizations to which I have been driven by the shortness of this chapter—it should be pointed out that broad statements about a subject as complex as the present one may

[7] In *The Freedom of a Christian Man.*

obscure important deviations in detail. It is broadly true that the cultivation of the individual's capacities for self-realization has been the focus of educational policy since the Renaissance. This is a field, however, in which habit is especially strong, and it is probable that education ranks next to religion as a preservative of the ideas, forms, and values of the past. Thus, while the political and economic institutions of Germany have undergone, since the World War, a series of "breaks with the past," there were, prior to the Fascist régime, no comparably sudden and far-reaching changes in the content of education. The changes which have occurred in the more conspicuous cases of politics and economics have been to a large extent the result of fortuitous circumstance. In regard to newer educational policies, it appears that positive action has followed, rather than preceded, the political and economic changes which have occurred.

The policies of the earlier republican government and of the present dictatorship are not the first instances in Germany's recent history in which the state has attempted to use the public educational system as a vindication for itself and for its policies. In the earlier cases there were such gifted forecasters as Fichte and Bismarck to predict the run of affairs, and to carry conviction to the public at large. And, in these cases, certain social and political principles were fostered by education in such a thoroughgoing fashion as to make it appear that important historical events were direct fulfillments of ideas. Thus the abortive—albeit prophetic—attempt of 1848 to unify Germany was brought about directly by the efforts of university professors. And the common saying that "the war of 1870 was won by German schoolmasters" is a fair statement of secondary cause. The economic and political strengthening of the empire, which was the chief aim of Reich policy between 1871 and 1914, was given its spiritual and intellectual emphasis by the schools. In the case of the union of Germany, the practical motives were those of economic expediency and political necessity. The separate German states could not reach a high state of industrial efficiency with their limited areas and resources. And the Napoleonic wars had taught the people of these states that they could not, independently and severally, cope with the powerful nation states which were their neighbors. After union had been accomplished, the tasks of economic expansion—

industrial, commercial, imperialistic—and of achieving an impregnable political position among the nations, were taken up with characteristic German downrightness.

But Germans, taken collectively, demand more congenial reasons than "expediency" or "necessity" in which to clothe their actions. What was required was a controlling principle to serve as moral vindication for the necessary and inevitable trend of events. The abstract phases of this principle were offered by Fichte and Hegel and their followers, and were elaborated by numerous workers in the fields of art, literature, science, and history. This was the principle of *Kultur,* of the almost mystical significance of the German state, of the innate moral superiority of all things German,[8] of the cultural mission to the rest of the world which was Germany's by racial preordination and by historical inevitability. This principle is properly to be regarded as a national philosophy rather than as a warmly emotional national tradition. It was proclaimed by intellectuals to "the common man" during a hundred years.

Any faith they may have had in this principle was dispelled for most Germans by the events of the World War, and it was contradicted and cast out by the Weimar constitution of the German Republic. Much energy has been spent in reviving it since the campaign headed by Herr Hitler commenced. The vigorous fascist movement in Germany, however, does not draw its force from the principle of *Kultur.* More substantial grounds for "fascism," or "Hitlerism," are to be found in the desperate economic straits of the postwar period, and in the widely shared belief that these difficulties have been due to the terms of peace which were forced upon Germany by her enemies. It was a shrewd political sense which led Herr Hitler, before he became chancellor, to evade a positive economic program, and to make his campaign one of impassioned opposition to the payment of reparations, to the possession by Poland of the "Corridor" and Upper Silesia, to financial domination by foreign creditors, to the "theft" of Germany's former colonies, to the military weakness of Germany before powerful unfriendly neighbors, to the "sole war guilt" clause of the Versailles Treaty. These antipathies are shared

[8] To be consistent with long habituation, these necessarily included all of the things which had been absorbed through borrowing.

by virtually the entire population of Germany. By comparison to
these matters, the program of "purification" is itself of little consequence. "Aryanism," and its corollary "anti-Semiticism" are abstractions such as are congenial to German habits of thought. They
serve, at the same time, to create energy in action. The action may
be trifling but the concentrated energy is necessary to larger political
ends. The present nationalistic ardor in Germany appears to be due
to experience rather than to any political philosophy or any national
creed. *Kultur*—to the extent that it is regenerated—can only serve
as a vindication for expediency. In relation to German fascism, it
will be an effect rather than a cause.

3. *Types of Schools and Qualifications of Teachers*

The popular antipathy toward existing conditions from which the
German fascist movement drew its strength was shaped politically
through opposition to the policies of the republican government.
Responsibility for the entire list of grievances—reparations, "war
guilt," and so forth—was laid upon the dominant parties, especially
the Social Democrats. All of the ills of Germany, including the
devastating economic depression, were said by fascist leaders to be
due to the weak and pacifistic government which was established by
the democratic Weimar constitution. The revolution of 1918, out
of which the Weimar constitution was born, has been described by
these same leaders as an un-German act, and as a "stab in the back
to the Fatherland." The constitution of the German Republic has
been set aside,[9] and its place has been taken by a one-party dictatorship. But the principles set forth by this constitution, and the institutions which were established in conformity with it, represent
a fairly stable starting place for the study of present objectives and
methods. As regards current educational objectives, they can be understood only against the background from which they emerged. That
background is the educational organization and policies which were
established by the earlier republican government.

A large section of the constitution of the German Republic
(Articles 142 to 150) was devoted to the subject of public education.
Art and science and their teaching were declared to be free from all

[9] It probably will be officially repealed in the near future.

restrictions, and the Reich pledged its support to them. The education of youth was to be carried on through public agencies. Teachers were made public officers, and their qualifications in training and education were specified for the entire Reich. The administration of schools was assigned to the several states, with the required acquiescence of the localities. All children were compelled to attend school until the age of eighteen. No payment could be required for attendance at common schools (*Volksschulen*) or continuation schools (*Fortbildungsschulen*). States were required to construct their educational systems organically and comprehensively, using the primary schools (*Grundschulen*) as a basis for all more advanced and specialized study. Economic or social status of parents, or religious beliefs, could not prevent the acceptance of a child in a particular school. Public means were to be provided by Reich, states, and localities to assist qualified children of poor parents to attend the secondary and higher schools. Private schools were placed under strict supervision of the states; their standards were to be as high as those of the public schools, and they were not allowed to select students according to the wealth of their parents. Private elementary schools were permitted only for the children of minority groups whose beliefs and principles were not served by public schools in the community. Citizenship, and also international conciliation, were to be taught and fostered in all schools, and every student was to be given a copy of the constitution at the end of his attendance at school. Religion was to be taught in all except the "free thought" (*weltliche*) schools.

These provisions sum up the control over education which was exercised by the republican Reich. The carrying out of these express statements of principle was made the duty of each of the various German states. Aside from the fact that no state could have a law or a regulation affecting education which contravened the principles set forth above, the Reich had no direct control over education. Its government issued guides (*Richtlinien*) to the states concerning educational matters, but the observance of them was not mandatory. The freedom thus enjoyed by the states, led to some divergence among them as to educational emphasis, but did not cause any differences in systematic organization. The same plan and organization were followed throughout Germany.[10] The flexibility afforded to the various states by the constitution enabled the states to adapt their educational programs to their respective needs and to the values and traditions peculiar to their own people. Since the dictatorship of the National Socialist party has deprived the states of self-government, all matters pertaining to education will be determined by the government of the Reich: i.e., the National Socialist party. The instructions of the central government to the political divisions will be mandatory. They also will be arbitrary, in the sense that they will not be limited by any constitutional rights of states.

The charts on page 17 show the standard plan of educational organization.[11] Although the Nazi dictatorship has changed educational emphasis in many important ways—which will be indicated later in this discussion—the organization of the German school system has not yet been changed in any material sense.

The basis of the entire German system of education is the *Grundschule,* which comprises the first four years of the common school, or *Volksschule.* Every German child who is of sound mind and body is required by law to enroll in the *Grundschule* at the age of six. Here the child is given instruction in German, arithmetic, singing, drawing, religion, gymnastics, manual training and *Heimatkunde,* which comprises German manners and traditions and also local geography.

At the end of the four years of *Grundschule,* a number of possibilities present themselves. A child may, upon passing an examination, be admitted to one of the various types of *höhere Schulen* or of *mittlere Schulen* (indicated, respectively, at the right and left sides of the charts). Or he may continue for four more years in the *Volksschule.* The latter course is the one pursued by most students.[12] These

[10] The most complete account of differences in educational regulations among the several states under the Republic is Eugen Löffler's *Das öffentliche Bildungswesen in Deutschland,* Berlin, 1931. A convenient graphic chart of administrative organization in each state is contained in an appendix.

[11] These charts and also the curricular tables which follow are taken from the article by August Wilhelm Fehling, "Education for Business in Germany," *Journal of Political Economy,* October, 1926.

[12] According to the German school census of 1932, there were 7,590,000 students enrolled in public *Volksschulen,* and 50,000 in private schools of the same grade. 1,655,000 graduates of *Volksschulen* were continuing their studies in the various

CHART 1
GERMAN SCHOOL SYSTEM FOR BOYS

School Year	Various Types of Vocational and Continuation Schools	Universities and Professional Colleges of University Rank	School Year
13			13
12			12
11		*Aufbauschule, Type of Deutsche Oberschule* — *Aufbauschule, Type of Oberrealschule* — *Deutsche Oberschule* — *Oberrealschule; Realschule* — *Realgymnasium; Realprogymnasium* — *Gymnasium; Progymnasium*	11
10			10
9	*Various Types of Mittelschule*		9
8			8
7			7
6	*Volksschule*		6
5			5
4			4
3	*Grundschule*		3
2			2
1			1

CHART 2
GERMAN SCHOOL SYSTEM FOR GIRLS

School Year	Various Types of Vocational and Continuation Schools	Universities and Professional Colleges of University Rank	School Year
13			13
12		*Aufbauschule, Type of Oberrealschule* — *Aufbauschule, Type of Deutsche Oberschule* — *Deutsche Oberschule* — *Realgymnasium* — *Gymnasium* — *Oberlyceum, Type of Oberrealschule* — *Oberlyceum* — *Frauenschule*	12
11			11
10			10
9	*Various Types of Mittelschule*		9
8			8
7			7
6	*Volksschule*	*Lyceum*	6
5			5
4			4
3	*Grundschule*		3
2			2
1			1

last four years of the *Volksschule* continue the study begun in the first four. The chief emphasis is on German literature and culture, and also on those matters of knowledge which are needed in ordinary life. At the end of their *Volksschule* training (ordinarily at fourteen years of age) boys and girls may take employment, but are required by law to study for three years more in part-time vocational schools. Their training here centers on the learning of a trade, but also involves study of history, civics, and elementary economics.

The four general types of *höhere Schulen* are differentiated chiefly by the emphasis laid on the study of languages. Each type of curriculum, for the full nine years of study, is shown in the accompanying tables. The oldest of the *höhere Schulen* is the humanistic *Gymnasium,* in which Latin and Greek are the subjects of major importance. The classical emphasis given here originated centuries ago, and its chief revision consists in the shift from religious to humantisic interest which was the center of bitter controversy until fairly recent times in Germany. The first movement away from this rigorous classicism in secondary education came with the establishment of the *Realgymnasium,* which had its beginning in Prussia with the issuance of the "Order of Studies" of 1859. The omission of Greek from the requirements of this school, and the inclusion of a larger study of modern language, were looked upon, at that time, as a high accomplishment in "realistic" education. A still further drift away from classicism and in the direction of scientific study was accomplished somewhat later with the establishment of the *Oberrealschule.* Both of these more modern types of schools, however, remained long under the ban of educators, many of whom condemned them bitterly for their deviations from traditional standards. The practical handicap that their graduates would not be admitted to the universities prevented these schools from becoming popular, and caused the *Gymnasium* to retain a virtual monopoly in secondary education. In 1890 the emperor set himself in strong opposition to the traditional modes of education in the *Gymnasium,* which he declared to be neither national nor modern in character. This protest, added to a wide popular dissatisfaction, led to the School Reform

types of continuation and trade schools. There were 230,000 attending *mittlere Schulen,* and 787,000 in the *höhere Schulen. Statistisches Jahrbuch,* 1933.

TABLE I

FIELDS OF STUDY AND HOURS PER WEEK IN THE GERMAN GYMNASIUM AND REALGYMNASIUM FOR THE NINE SCHOOL YEARS[a]

SUBJECT	SCHOOL YEAR								
	I	II	III	IV	V	VI	VII	VIII	IX
Religion	2 (2)	2 (2)	2 (2)	2 (2)	2 (2)	2 (2)	2 (2)	2 (2)	2 (2)
German	5 (5)	4 (4)	3 (3)	3 (3)	3 (3)	3 (3)	4 (4)	3 (3)	3 (3)
Latin	7 (7)	7 (7)	7 (7)	6 (4)	6 (4)	5 (3)	5 (3)	5 (3)	5 (3)
Greek	...	...	...	6	6	6	6	6	6
French	...	...	3 (3)	2 (4)	2 (4)	2 (4)	2 (4)	2 (4)	2 (4)
English	...	...	...	(4)	(4)	(3)	(3)	(3)	(3)
History	...	1 (1)	2 (2)	2 (2)	2 (3)	3 (3)	3 (3)	3 (3)	3 (3)
Geography	2 (2)	2 (2)	2 (2)	1 (2)	1 (1)	1 (1)	1 (1)	1 (1)	1 (1)
Mathematics	4 (4)	4 (4)	4 (4)	3 (4)	3 (4)	4 (4)	3 (4)	4 (4)	4 (4)
Natural science	2 (2)	2 (2)	2 (2)	2 (2)	2 (2)	2 (4)	2 (3)	2 (4)	2 (4)
Drawing	2 (2)	2 (2)	2 (2)	2 (2)	2 (2)	1 (2)	1 (2)	1 (2)	1 (2)
Singing	2 (2)	2 (2)	...	...	...	...	...	...	...

[a] Figures for *Realgymnasium* are in parentheses.

TABLE II

FIELDS OF STUDY AND HOURS PER WEEK IN THE GERMAN OBERREALSCHULE AND DEUTSCHE OBERSCHULE FOR THE NINE SCHOOL YEARS[a]

SUBJECT	SCHOOL YEAR								
	I	II	III	IV	V	VI	VII	VIII	IX
Religion	2 (2)	2 (2)	2 (2)	2 (2)	2 (2)	2 (2)	2 (2)	2 (2)	2 (2)
German	6 (6)	5 (5)	5 (5)	3 (5)	3 (5)	3 (5)	4 (5)	4 (4)	4 (4)
First foreign language[b]	6 (6)	6 (6)	6 (6)	5 (6)	5 (6)	3 (4)	3 (3)	3 (3)	3 (3)
Second foreign language	...	...	...	5	5	3 (4)	3 (4)	3 (4)	3 (4)
History	...	1 (1)	3 (3)	3 (3)	3 (3)	3 (3)	3 (4)	3 (4)	3 (4)
Geography	2 (2)	2 (2)	2 (2)	2 (2)	1 (2)	2 (2)	1 (2)	1 (2)	1 (2)
Mathematics	4 (4)	4 (4)	5 (5)	4 (4)	4 (4)	6 (4)	6 (4)	5 (4)	5 (4)
Natural science	2 (2)	2 (2)	2 (2)	2 (4)	3 (4)	6 (4)	6 (4)	6 (4)	6 (4)
Drawing	2 (2)	2 (2)	2 (2)	2 (2)	2 (2)	2 (2)	2 (2)	2 (2)	2 (2)
Singing	2 (2)	2 (2)	...	...	...	...	...	...	...

[a] Figures for *deutsche Oberschule* are in parentheses.
[b] The two foreign languages at the *Oberrealschule* are always modern ones, mostly English and French. The first foreign language at the *deutsche Oberschule* is usually English; the second one, either Latin or a second modern one.

of 1901 by which the semi and non-classical schools were placed on an equal footing with the *Gymnasium,* including the right of graduates to enter the universities.

The youngest type of school, the *deutsche Oberschule,* has been in existence only a few years. It is a direct result of recommendations made by a conference of German educators, in 1920, that a new type of secondary school be created in which chief emphasis would be laid upon the whole range of German culture, its language, science, art, philosphy, and religion. This new school was given the same rank and privileges as the older types of *höhere Schulen.* It has not yet, however, attained the same prestige in the estimation of the people, and, to the present time, enrollment in schools of this type remains relatively small. The chronology of the various *höhere Schulen* which is given here is intended to show the drift of educational content in these schools, and also to indicate the "age" or "modernity" of the several curricular plans.

This division of the *höhere Schulen* into four fairly specific types (which included the retention intact of the three existing types) was the work of the important conference of 1920 referred to above. Its explicit purpose was to care for individual differences in tastes and aptitudes among students. It also was clearly stated that specialization in one of the four cultural fields, represented by the four curricular plans, would be of larger educational benefit than a wider range of study which would seek to encompass all, or most, of these fields. In practice, an even greater variety of choices is afforded to students. Ceaseless experimentation in educational content has been going on for the past decade. The result is that there exist many deviations, of greater or less degree, from the four types, none of which is large enough, however, to violate the central purpose of the type to which the school belongs. With reference to these deviations, there exist, in Berlin alone, upwards of thirty different curricular plans in *höhere Schulen.* Another variant is in the existence, in places which cannot afford a full equipment of nine-year schools, of six-year prototypes of the *höhere Schulen.* The more common of the prototype schools are called: *Progymnasium, Realprogymnasium,* and *Realschule;* there is no special name for the prototype of the *deutsche Oberschule.*

A feature of the school system which gives it still further flexibility is the *Aufbauschule*. By means of it, a student may, before finishing the *Volksschule*, change his educational plans and enter upon a course preparatory to a university or other institution of that rank. This opportunity is open only to students of marked ability. The various types of *mittlere Schulen* have points of similarity to the more modern *höhere Schulen*, but are more "practical" in their purpose. Their courses extend over six years, and are intended to train students for business or agriculture, or for public or private administrative or clerical work.

The *höhere Schulen* for girls do not differ fundamentally from those for boys, although they offer an even wider variety of types. Since 1901, the secondary education of girls has been of equal rank with that of boys, in the sense that it gives to girl students the right of admission to universities upon passing an *abiturenten* examination.[13] This right was very rarely used until the postwar period. The *Lyceum* (or *Mädchenrealschule* or *Mädchenschule* as it is named in some of the states) furnishes a fairly unified basis for secondary education. It inclines to the *Realschule* type of curriculum, although local variations exist. The specialization along lines of different interests comes with the higher forms of schools which follow the *Lyceum*.

In April, 1933, the national government issued a decree demanding that the curricular plans of all *höhere Schulen* be restored to what they were before the Republic. The practical effect of this is to lay greater stress on the study of German literature, history, and geography than has been done since 1919. Since the Nazi *coup d'état* there has been much discussion of "unifying" the *höhere Schulen* by reducing the number of types to one or two. Although no official plan has been announced, it is probable that some such "unification" will occur in the near future.[14]

No summary of educational trends in the German schools would

[13] As will be shown at a later point in this paper, the right of women to enter universities has been seriously restricted by the Nazi government. The restriction, however, is not due to any inferior status of secondary schools for girls.

[14] See John W. Taylor, "Education in the New Germany," *International Education Review*, Vol. III (1933-34), No. 3. This article is the most complete recent account of legislation affecting education during the Nazi régime.

be complete without some mention of the qualifications and training of teachers. These have, for a long time, been uniformly high in all of the states, although some differences in requirements have existed. The qualifications and status of teachers in the *höhere Schulen* of Prussia were first officially defined by the installation, in 1810, of the *examen pro facultate docendi*. This examination, which was required of all teachers in the secondary schools, elevated this branch of educational work to the level of an independent profession. Before that time almost all of the teachers in the secondary schools had been clergymen, it having been assumed that they were best fitted to give instruction in the classics. The professionalizing of secondary-school teachers has gone forward steadily until today each candidate for a position must hold a doctoral degree and be experienced through practice teaching before becoming eligible for examination.

The qualifications demanded of elementary school teachers have been increased at an equal rate. In the second quarter of the nineteenth century, there gradually grew up in Prussia a number of training schools in which the principles of Pestalozzi were taught to candidates for teaching positions in the elementary schools. Thus, these schools were, in Paulsen's words, "taken over by trained teachers from the hands of third-rate tailors and disabled soldiers." At present, teachers in the elementary schools are required to have completed a course in one of the *höhere Schulen* and to have studied for two years at a university or in a normal school especially designed for their training.[15] During the Republic, both elementary- and secondary-school teachers were officials of the state, and appointed for life. By these means the states of Germany developed a highly professionalized and competent body of teachers. Since the Fascist régime commenced, all heads of schools (public and private) known to be communists, socialists, liberals, or Jews have been dismissed or compelled to resign. Many public-school teachers also have been removed,[16] and some of the few private "progressive" schools have

[15] These new training schools for elementary teachers (*pädagogische Akademien*) have been established in several cities of Germany since the war.

[16] The appointment of public-school teachers was influenced by politics, even before the advent of Herr Hitler. For some time it has been well known that new appointments as teachers went chiefly to candidates whose political views were agreeable to the government of the state concerned.

been permitted to remain open only on condition that they appoint Fascists to all of their teaching positions.

The trend toward official indoctrination of teachers-in-training has been led by Prussia. An order of the Prussian Ministry of Education of April 20, 1933, converted the *pädagogische Akademien* into a new set of institutions called *Hochschulen für Lehrerbildung*. These new schools "are to express the cultural purposes of the National Socialist party, which has recognized in educational policy a significant political weapon."[17]

The universities of Germany for a century or more were devoted to the learned professions and to science. The concentration on scientific pursuits commenced, in 1810, with the establishment of the University of Berlin, and spread rapidly to the other universities of Germany. Thus the educational work of the universities followed lines of specialization in research which set the pattern followed by the most important American graduate schools. The fields of investigation covered by the universities are divided among four faculties: law, medicine, theology, and philosophy. The first three of these, as their names imply, provide professional training to their students; the fourth traditionally has been concerned with the pursuit of learning as an end in itself, and, through specialized lectures and seminars, has encompassed the whole range of the humanities and pure sciences. The faculty of philosophy is itself a professional school, however, to the extent that it trains teachers for the secondary schools and laboratory experts for the various fields of science.

Through long tradition and well established precedent, the German universities had—until the Nazi régime—been self-governing in the sense that their faculties had virtually complete control over the selection of their own members. For generations their most jealously guarded rights have been those of *Lernfreiheit* (the right of a student to follow his own inclinations as to his field of study, his selection of courses and seminars, his line of specialization within his field) and *Lehrfreiheit* (the freedom of a professor to conduct his courses according to his own preferences, to lecture on any phase of his subject that he might choose, to express any opinions that he

[17] See Joachim Haupt, *Neuordnung im Schulwesen und Hochschulwesen*, Berlin, 1933, p. 22.

might hold with reference to his subject). Until quite recently these traditional liberties were so well established, and self-government was so complete, that there was little positive control over educational policies except that exercised by faculties, or over educational content except the dispositions of individual professors.[18] Thus the universities of Germany have, in the past, maintained a degree of academic freedom which has not been surpassed in any country. In the present, academic freedom appears to have reached its lowest ebb in Germany. A member of a university faculty is entitled to hold only those views and beliefs which are approved by the National Socialist party, and to have only "Aryan" blood in his veins. In support of these principles, the Nazis have ousted hundreds of university teachers of all ranks.

A struggle between faculties and state governments for control of the universities had commenced before the Nazi régime. During the Republic, the governments of several states had imposed a partial "reform" upon the universities, despite the vigorous opposition of many professors in the fields which were affected. This was done by the establishment of "state examinations" in certain subjects, which might be taken by students after two or three years in the university and without their being compelled to complete the study required by the faculties for the doctoral examination. These examinations continue to be used under the Nazi régime. They are intended to test the fitness of candidates for work in certain fairly practical fields. They also are prescribed for all students in stipulated fields of study, before those students may be examined for a doctoral degree. The original purpose of this prescription was to maintain uniformly high standards of university study which was an official

---

[18] Self-government had become greatly weakened during the later years of the Republic. Political considerations weighed heavily with the Ministries of Education of various states. The traditional method by which members were elected to university faculties was complicated, but certain. If a vacancy existed, the members of the faculty concerned would choose a list of candidates acceptable to it. This list would be transmitted to the Minister of Education. The Minister had no choice but to appoint one of the people named on the list. Even before the Nazi dictatorship, this rule was not being strictly observed. There are cases on record in which the Minister of Education refused to appoint any person named on a list, and notified the faculty concerned that it could have a person named by him—or no one.

recognition of the overcrowding, and of the severe strain on the morale of the universities in the postwar period.[19] An important consequence of these "state examinations," however, and also of the degrees which they confer, is the official sanction which they give to education for practical ends.[20]

The emergence, during the past century, of specialized and advanced fields of applied science has led, in Germany, to the creation of a variety of institutions of university grade which are devoted exclusively to serving one or another of these specialized fields. By this means the traditional four faculties of the universities have been preserved and protected against the vocational elaboration of university study such as has occurred in the United States.[21] There are now in Germany ten *technische Hochschulen* (institutes of technology), five *handels Hochschulen* (colleges of commerce), four *landwirtschaftliche Hochschulen* (agricultural colleges), two *tierarztliche Hochschulen* (colleges of veterinary medicine), two *Forsthochschulen* (colleges of forestry) and two *Bergakademien* (schools of mines). These institutions, especially the *technische Hochschulen*, have been of the greatest importance to Germany's economic development. They are, each and severally, devoted to the training of experts in their respective fields of applied science.

Besides the systematic public agencies for education which have been outlined above there are a large number of special public schools

[19] An article of mine, "The Teaching of Economics in Germany," *Columbia University Quarterly*, September, 1932, pp. 259-95, describes the degree of *Diplomvolkswirt* (graduate economist) awarded by state examination to university students, and the similar degrees, *Diplomkaufmann* (graduate in business) and *Diplomhandelslehrer* (graduate teacher of commerce) awarded to students in the colleges of business

[20] A more recent "reform" in Prussia, which went into effect in the spring semester of 1932, applies only to the teaching of law, political science, and economics. It was worked out jointly by the Prussian *Ministerium für Wissenschaft, Kunst und Volksbildung* and a committee of professors representing the faculties of law in the universities. The main end of this "reform" is to provide a system of tutors, and by other means to individualize the instruction of students. A summary of this "reform," is given in my article referred to above.

[21] A tendency in this direction is to be observed, however, in the two newest Prussian universities at Cologne and Frankfurt. In each of these cases a fifth faculty was created through the inclusion of an already existing college of commerce in the organization of the university.

devoted to serving particular interests. The principal classes of these are the schools of art and music and the higher continuation schools, which supplement the compulsory range of vocational education by offering optional advanced training in various trades and handicrafts. During the Republic, the schools of these various classes served to foster the artistic, occupational and intellectual interests of such persons as cared to attend them. Since the establishment of the Nazi dictatorship, they are used—like all other schools in Germany—to entrench the dominant party and to support its policies.[22]

[22] The principal type of school for general and non-occupational adult education under the Republic—the *Volkshochschule*—has been discontinued by the Nazis. The fact that these schools were established by the republican government was sufficient ground for their elimination by the present régime.

II

NATIONAL SOCIALISM AND THE GERMAN SCHOOL SYSTEM

The German Republic is dead, and appears to be beyond any hope of revival. Whatever turn political affairs may take, it is hardly conceivable that the Weimar constitution will become again the basic law of Germany, or that the old parties of the center will return and regain control. All of the social objectives of the republican régime have been superseded by the creed of German fascism. The new objectives—although they appeal for vindication to the entire range of German history from Wotan to Weimar—have no background beyond the emotional storm and stress of the postwar period. The institutions of the old monarchy have not been restored, any more than those of the Republic have been continued. Yet the present "official" history of Germany moves directly from the *Kaisertum* to the Nazi dictatorship. The period from 1918 to 1933 was "un-German" (and hence, according to Fascist principle, unhistorical), except that the Fascist movement grew from Hitler's first activities in 1919 to the *coup d'état* of 1933. The historical "emptiness" of that period is shown by the fact that its "great men" are not such figures as Friedrich Ebert, Walther Rathenau, Gustav Stresemann, or Max Weber. Next to Hitler himself, the official heroes of this gap in history are Schlageter, a young German patriot who was executed by the French for inciting a revolt in the Ruhr, and Horst Wessel, a Nazi labor organizer who was murdered by communist rivals.

1. The Contrast of Republican and Nazi Objectives

In spite of protestations by the National Socialists, it was the period from 1918 to 1933 which gave birth and direction to German fascism. The events of that period are well-known phases of recent history; but their broader consequences to political trends must be explicitly indicated.

The defeat of 1918 brought an end to the *Kaisertum,* the nobility, the great army—all that embodiment of grandeur and those symbols of national greatness to which popular allegiance had been given. The war, the inflation, and the ensuing chronic depression almost completely destroyed the middle class which for decades had been the solid foundation of economic and political life. Throughout the period, the people of Germany were harassed and humiliated by the terms of peace written at Versailles. In the face of general bewilderment, order and direction in social affairs was given by a constitution written by democrats and moderate socialists. Under constitutional government—that is, until Brüning's "government by decree"—such stability as existed was created chiefly by the trade-unionists of the Social Democratic party and the Catholics of the Center. The former party was, until 1932, the strongest single political group. It directed the revolution, had the largest share in preparing the constitution, and was a member, or an ally, of every majority coalition in the republican Reichstag. The Centrist party was an important participant in every coalition government from the beginning of the Republic. These two parties were humanitarian in their aims; they compelled the state to assume large responsibilities for the welfare of citizens—especially of the laboring classes—and created a great system of social institutions to aid and support the needy. The republican government attempted the impossible double task of dealing amicably and pacifically with the nations which were oppressing Germany, and of promoting domestic serenity and social order. Any stability which it was able to create was insubstantial indeed by comparison to the power of the old monarchy, and to the enterprise and obvious solvency of the old middle class. It was insubstantial also by comparison to that achieved by the concentrated power of the present dictatorship.

In this chapter, our interest in the republican government and its policies is due to the fact that they furnish the background for any study of the Nazi régime. It should be borne in mind that the German fascist movement was fundamentally negative in character. It summed up and motivated the widespread antipathies of the German people. Revolutions always aspire to a completely fresh start; yet they always are limited, at some point or other, by the conditions from which they sprang and by the historical backgrounds to which they are unwilling heirs.

The democratization of education was regarded as a major objective by the republican government of Germany. The general lines which were followed to this end were indicated in the constitutional provisions summarized above. The social implications of this aim, and the practical consequences of its fulfillment, dip deeply into the lives of the German people. Under the old monarchist régime there was little democracy in education in any of the German states; the educational system, on the contrary, was used as a major support for the system of social stratification which existed in those times. Free education through *Volksschulen* and trade schools has long been a feature of German education. The wealthier and more aristocratic classes, however, almost never exposed their children to the association with children of poorer and less distinguished families which attendance at the common schools entailed. Those who lived in the country ordinarily employed tutors for their sons and daughters, while in the towns and cities these classes were served by exclusive private schools. By these means the children of the higher and middle classes often were prepared for admission to the *höhere Schulen* in three years instead of the prescribed four. But the important social effect of this system was that it perpetuated and strengthened the existing class lines.

In the same way access to the *höhere Schulen,* and, through them, to the institutions of university grade was, before the establishment of the Republic, almost invariably an exclusive right of the same privileged classes. The charges for tuition in these schools were prohibitively high except for people with relatively large incomes. And the school authorities had full power to reject any applicant for admission to a given school. These arrangements not only prevented the democratic mingling of the youth of the land; they also made it virtually impossible for a son of poor parents to enter the learned professions, to attain high rank in the bureaucracies of the states or the empire, or to secure that training which is essential to the scholar or the scientist. The highest public officials in charge of educational administration, and also the teachers in the *höhere Schulen* themselves, were beneficiaries of this exclusive system, which may have given it added strength.

The republican régime almost completely eliminated these class discriminations. Parents were required to send their children to the free *Grundschulen*.[23] Admission to the *höhere Schulen* was based almost entirely upon the passing of an examination. The expense of secondary education was adjusted to the ability of parents to pay. In some states this was done through making the charges proportionate to the income taxes paid by parents; in others a flat charge was made, but exemptions were granted to parents who were unable to pay these amounts. Matriculation in a university, or institution of similar rank, required that the student pass the difficult *abiturenten* examination which is given at the end of the course in each of the *höhere Schulen*. A further democratization of university education was brought about by the admission of especially able *Volksschule* students to the *Aufbauschulen,* which gave them the same opportunity to enter a university as was enjoyed by students in the *höhere Schulen*. Tuition charges in German universities are much lower than those of endowed universities in the United States, and the states also provide free tuition to numerous needy students.

To a marked degree, these arrangements replaced wealth with ability as a basis for educational preferment. They also took account of individual tastes and aptitudes through widening the range of educational choice.

The Nazi régime has continued the policy of not discriminating on the basis of wealth or social class. The former liberty enjoyed by all members of the community in school affairs has, however, been severely limited. The famous *numerus Clausus,* which was promulgated for the Reich in April, 1933, reduces the proportion of Jewish students admitted to the *höhere Schulen* and the universities to one and a half percent of the students admitted.[24] This regulation was explained as an attempt to prevent overcrowding of the learned professions and unemployment of the educated classes.[25] An-

[23] Except in the cases of a few minority groups, which were permitted by the constitution to maintain schools to serve their own beliefs or principles.

[24] In the summer semester of 1932 more than four percent of the students in the universities were of the Jewish religion. A larger proportion than this would be classified as Jewish according to Nazi standards of race. Cf. *More Facts*, International Student Service, Geneva, June, 1933.

[25] It is estimated that there were 60,000 university graduates unemployed in 1933.

other stated purpose was to protect against "excessive foreign elements" (*Überfremdung*) in German schools and universities.

Admission to universities was sharply restricted by a decree of December 28, 1933, issued by the Minister of the Interior, Dr. Wilhelm Frick. It limits matriculations in 1934 to 15,000, with only one woman student to each ten men students. In 1933 there were 24,700 matriculates, of whom 4,400, or seventeen percent, were women. The avowed purpose of this restriction is both to eliminate "mediocre" students and to provide greater facilities for "highly gifted" students. The special restriction on women matriculates is consistent with the policy of the Prussian Ministry of Education that there should be for German girls "less learning and more body-building."[26]

During the Empire and the Republic, education in Germany was liberalized by the allocation of authority to the several states. The absence of centralization enabled each state to adapt its educational emphasis to its own cultural traditions and values. Thus the teaching of literature, history, art, and so forth, in Bavaria differed from the teaching of the same subjects in Saxony, for the reason that each state entertained its own views and tastes. By act of the Reichstag in January, 1934, the state governments were abolished and were succeeded by provincial administrative bodies. Thus there are no longer any states (in the political sense) in Germany. This means, among other things, that educational content and emphasis is made uniform for the entire Reich. The completely centralized control which now exists marks the political accomplishment of the Nazi program of *Gleichschaltung,* or enforced uniformity.[27] According to this formula, all Germans are to be made to act alike and think alike. Their modes of acting and thinking will be prescribed by the central government: i.e., the National Socialist party.

Until 1919, the study of religion was required in all German schools. The constitution of the Republic also provided for compulsory religious instruction in all except the "free thought" (*welt-*

[26] An Associated Press dispatch reported in *School and Society,* January 6, 1934.
[27] *"Gleichschaltung"* is a difficult conception for anyone not acquainted with Germany and the German language. The best description of it in English is, in my judgment, the article by Harold Callender in the *New York Times Magazine,* January 28, 1934.

liche) schools. Separate courses in religion were offered to students of Catholic, Protestant, and Jewish faiths. In practice, however, formal religious teaching had given way in many cases to courses in *Lebenskunde,* or non-religious moral instruction. This occurred principally in schools situated in the more radical working-class sections of industrial cities. The Nazis have reintroduced compulsory instruction in religion and have banned *Lebenskunde* from all schools. Since official Christianity in Germany has been taken away from both the Catholic and the Protestant churches, and since the Jews do not count, the liberty of choosing among even three different offerings no longer exists. Observers in Germany state that much "religious" instruction consists in explaining the Nazi movement in terms of God's will.[28] As for *Lebenskunde*—it represents a liberalism and a lack of discipline which do not square with Fascist thought.[29]

Another liberalist objective of the republican régime consisted in promoting the physical well-being of the people. Commencing with physical training and instruction in the care of the body in the schools, the program reached out to include the entire community. The Prussian government established in Berlin a *Hochschule für Leibesübung* which was devoted to educating experts in physical culture. Almost every town had facilities for exercise and for training people of all ages in athletic sports. The purpose in all this included more than the cultivation of strong bodies—although the importance of health was recognized. By this means it was sought also to build up a spirit of voluntary coöperation and habits of self-reliance among the people. The breakdown of liberalism during the Republic was reflected in the partially successful attempts of both Fascists and Socialists to organize societies for sports and physical training and thus to capture the energy and enthusiasm of these activities for political ends. In spite of these attempts, most of the sports and physical-culture societies remained independent. The independent groups were promoted and served by a national non-partisan organization, the *Reichsausschusz für Leibesübungen.*

[28] See, for example, "Education Under Hitler," by Vivian Ogilvie, *New Statesman and Nation*, June 3, 1933.

[29] For the official Nazi position, see the pamphlet, *Der Neubau des deutschen Schulwesens*, by Dr. W. Hartnacke, Leipzig, 1933.

The sports and physical-culture movement has now been made a part of the Nazi organization, and is made to serve Nazi ends. The *Reichsausschusz* has been dissolved. The national government has introduced the *Führerprinzip*—a euphemism for dictatorship. It has appointed as *Reichssportkomissar* a former army officer, Herr von Tschammer und Osten. A system of supervisors has been established to keep control of sport and physical-culture organizations. No such organization is permitted to exist except under the supervision of the *Komissar*.[30]

Within the schools the Nazi régime has laid a greater emphasis upon physical training than upon intellectual activities of students. The kind of thinking which lies behind this movement could not be more clearly demonstrated than by Führer Hitler himself:

Of first importance in the national educational plan is not the cramming in of mere knowledge, but the development of fundamentally sound bodies. . . . In a national state the school must set aside considerably more time for physical training. There is no point in loading a young mind with ballast of which only the incidentals instead of the essentials remain.[31]

An important provision of the republican constitution was that relating to the instruction of all children in *Staatsbürgerkunde,* or citizenship. Article 148 declared that:

Consciousness of citizenship, personal and occupational industriousness in the spirit of the German people, and reconciliation among the people, are to be striven for in all the schools. . . . Citizenship and occupational training are fields of instruction in the schools.

This statement of principle was interpreted by republican educational authorities to mean that young people should be brought, through the schools, to a consciousness of the interests and activities of the community and of their own parts in these affairs, to an understanding of the rights and obligations of citizens, and to an enlightened love of country.

There was not developed, during the Republic, any standardized plan or method for instruction in *Staatsbürgerkunde*. Great variations existed among the schools of different states, and even among different schools in the same state. The constitution itself, with em-

[30] Cf. communication by Joseph S. Roncek in *School and Society,* August 26, 1933.

[31] Adolf Hitler, *Mein Kampf,* pp. 452, 454 of the one-volume edition.

phasis on the organization and functions of the Reich, was studied
quite generally in the *Volksschulen*. In the continuation schools,
there were courses in *Staatsbürgerkunde* which comprised civics and
elementary economics on the descriptive level.

It is especially noteworthy that the *höhere Schulen*—the schools
devoted explicitly to the training of future leaders in the community
—had no coördinated plan or system for education in *Staatsbürgerkunde*. Some of these schools maintained courses of that name, dealing chiefly with political and economic organization, which met once
or twice a week during the final year of study. Many of them, however, gave no specialized instruction in citizenship. A common educational theory which obtained in schools of this grade was that
Staatsbürgerkunde should be a composite result drawn out of the
entire process of education, rather than a subject for particularized
instruction. According to this view all of those things which a student studied contributed to his comprehension of his place in the
social scheme, to his knowledge of his rights and duties as a citizen,
and to his understanding of social and national affairs. It is clear
that the study of history contributed definitely to these ends, especially in its more advanced phases where the currents of European
history were focused upon the cultural and political development
of Germany. The same ends were served by courses in *Erdkunde,*
or physical and human geography, which had reached a high development in many of the *höhere Schulen*. There also were some
results along this general line which were sought through the study
of foreign languages. Beyond these clearly related fields of study,
there was much faith in German literature, especially in the classics,
as contributing to education in citizenship.

The very liberalism which animated the German Republic stood
in the way of official indoctrination through the schools. Liberalism
gives a rationale to certain habitual modes of social conduct, but
it cannot provide (or, perhaps, even permit) a purposive and consolidated program of social action. As postwar conditions failed to
provide the economic and political security desired by the German
people, as the best efforts of the liberal republican government merely
demonstrated its own futility, as emotions were stirred by fear and
desperation, the German people came to demand stronger meat than

liberalism. Under these conditions, liberalistic *Staatsbürgerkunde* in the schools became an empty gesture. Students read the constitution with their lips, but their minds absorbed fascism through their feelings. The textbooks which were used were, in general, consistent with the tenets of liberalism.[32] The ideas of students were not.

The official position of the schools in regard to social objectives was, in the period just prior to the war, definitely opposed to the basic tenets of democracy and liberalism which were contained in the constitution of republican Germany.[33] This condition alone was sufficient to impair very greatly the principle of "non-partisan instruction" which was urged by educational leaders. Many teachers of the older generation lived through the changes brought by war and revolution without thereby undergoing any revision of their social or political thinking. The teachers who commenced their work after 1918 were themselves susceptible to the strong currents and counter currents of German politics. It is hardly to be expected that the teaching of politics and economics will not be colored by the views of the teacher, or to assume that his personal bias will be consistent with the avowed objectives of the community. There was the further fact that thousands of young people in Germany, lacking the stabilizing effect of a memory of pre-war conditions, and facing an empty future, were driven to desperate political and economic views. The failure to achieve the ends which were aspired to through training in *Staatsbürgerkunde* was recognized by many republican educational leaders. Much of the best literature dealing with the sub-

[32] For an account of practice in the teaching of *Staatsbürgerkunde*, and for a summary analysis of some of the textbooks in this subject which are used in elementary and continuation schools, see my article referred to in note 19 above.

[33] The positive program of indoctrinating students in the schools along conservative lines was initiated by the former Kaiser Wilhelm II. In a decree of 1889, he stated that he was determined "to make the several grades of schools useful, in order to combat the spread of socialistic and communistic ideas." This was followed by a ministerial decree, ordering that, through the study of history, religion, and other subjects, students should be taught to distinguish between the errors of social-democracy and "that which is true, real, and possible in the world." The Kaiser expressed these views in person at the School Conference of 1890. For a detailed account, see Eduard Spranger, *Fünfundzwanzig Jahre deutscher Erziehungspolitik* (Berlin, 1916), especially the introductory chapter.

ject consisted of wishful thinking and statements of what ought to be done.[34]

One of the ends to be served by the republican system of education, as explicitly stated in the constitution, was the promotion of international conciliation. In so far as purposive study of foreign cultures, and of the institutions of foreign countries, may be regarded as a fundamental means to this end, the schools of the Republic must be credited with a large accomplishment. It is doubtful if the educational system of any other country has been as deeply concerned with such alien matters as was the case in Germany. This probably was due, in the first instance, to the strong traditional interests of Germans in affairs beyond their own borders, which was discussed at an earlier point in this chapter. During the Republic, there was a marked stimulation of this interest, due to the postwar conditions in Germany, and to the new position which she occupied among the nations. As citizens of a young republic, her people had an interest in the forms of democracy as they existed in other countries. As a debtor nation, Germany sought to improve her trade position by studying the most economical uses of her resources, and much of this study was of methods of production in other industrial countries. As severely penalized losers in the war, the Germans also had a pressing interest in the domestic and international politics of their former enemies.

These interests were served, in various ways, by all of the different types of schools, from the study of *Erdkunde* in the *Volksschulen* to the numerous researches in foreign affairs which were carried forward in the institutions of university grade. In the upper classes of the *höhere Schulen* the study of foreign languages was "correlated" with the study of the history, government, law, social institutions, and so forth, of the countries whose languages were studied. Such "correlation" was also maintained in the study of German, history, *Erdkunde* and political geography. It is difficult to measure very exactly the content of "world affairs" in the curricular plans of the var-

[34] See, for example, *Staatsbürgerliche Erziehung*, edited by F. Lampe and G. H. Francke, Breslau, 1926; "Staatsbürgerliche Erziehung," by Fritz Wuessing, in the volume *Wesen und Wege der Schulreform*, edited by Adolf Grimme, Berlin, 1930; the articles by Wilhelm Ziegler, Rudolf Laun, and Richard Oehlert in the February and March, 1931, issues of the *Zeitschrift für Politik*.

ious types of schools. One investigator estimated, in 1930, that the study of what may properly be called "world politics" ranged from eleven percent to eighteen percent of the total study in the *höhere Schulen,* and that the study of subjects related to "world politics" constituted from twenty-seven percent to fifty-four percent of the total.[35] In 1932, there were, in the twenty-three universities of Germany, two hundred and fourteen seminars and institutes devoted to the study of foreign countries.[36]

The government of the Republic sought to promote international *rapprochement* as a German policy through the emphasis on international studies in the schools. These liberalistic aims did not succeed any more than liberalistic *Staatsbürgerkunde* succeeded—and for the same reasons. One striking evidence of failure was the rise of the new "science" of *Geopolitik* ("geographical politics" as distinguished from "political geography"). This became a field for study and research in several universities, from whence it filtered to the general public and the schools. Its central thesis was that Germans were *"ein Volk ohne Raum"* (a nation without space). It offered a technical demonstration (as if any were needed) of the absurdity of the Versailles treaty, and a technical argument for Germany's need of larger territory.

The confusion which applied to the study of both *Staatsbürgerkunde* and international affairs during the Republic does not exist under the Nazi régime. Instruction in these matters does not proceed from the viewpoint of either liberalism or world-citizenship. The attitude and the aim are explicitly and solely those of German fascism. An example of this is the introduction of *Rassekunde* (science of races), as a subject of instruction in the elementary schools.[37]

---

[35] Theodore Arldt, *Weltpolitik im Unterricht,* Berlin, 1930.

[36] W. M. von Staa, "Die auslandkundlichen Institute der deutschen Universitäten," *Inter Nationes,* April, 1932. For an account of work in this field by institutions of university grade, see also the composite volume, *Weltpolitische Bildungsarbeit an Preussischen Hochschulen,* Berlin, 1926.

[37] Such instruction conforms with the plans of the *Führer* himself: "The complete educational program of the national state must find its achievement in impressing indelibly upon the heart and mind of the youth entrusted to it the instinctive consciousness of race. No boy and no girl must leave school without the keenest consciousness of the necessity of purity of blood." Adolf Hitler, *Mein Kampf,* p. 475 of the one-volume edition.

Through this study it is demonstrated that culture is a creation of race, and that the highest culture is that of the Aryan race.

A more thoroughgoing example of the same principle is the instructions for the guidance of writers of history textbooks, issued by the Minister of the Interior in July, 1933.[38] It is required that all phases and epochs of history be presented as fulfillment of the Aryan race, especially in its Germanic embodiment.

Historical instruction at all levels must interweave the idea of the hero in its German expression, associated with the idea of the leader in our day. . . . The idea of the hero leads directly to a heroic world viewpoint which is characteristic of us as a German people, and of no other, and permits us to derive ever new power in the struggle for national self-determination in the midst of a hostile world.

There follow detailed instructions as to ways of giving effect to this purpose for each period of history. The most recent past will be treated in history textbooks according to the following formula:

The last two decades of our times must constitute a major feature in the study of history. The terrible experience of the World War with the vigorous struggle of the German people against a world of enemies, the disintegration of our power of resistance through unpatriotic forces, the humiliation of our people through the Dictate of Versailles, and the later breakdown of the liberal-Marxist philosophy, must be dealt with in much detail as the slow awakening of the nation from the Ruhr conflict up to the emergence of the National Socialist ideal of freedom and up to the restoration of German national unity on the day of Potsdam.

One of the strongest liberal aims expressed in the republican "school reform" was that of removing the traditional authoritarian relationship of teacher to pupil in the elementary and secondary schools. On the positive side, and as a substitute for authoritarianism, there was steady insistence from leaders of the reform that teachers and pupils should form friendly communities in which there should be complete freedom of thought and opinion, based

---

"It is, in short, the task of a national state to see to it that a world history shall sometime be written in which the race question shall be placed in the dominant position." *Ibid.*, p. 468.

[38] These regulations have been translated by I. L. Kandel. See his article "Nationalism, Patriotism and Education in Germany," *The Kadelpian Review*, January, 1934. This is the first order of its kind issued by the national government. Other regulations, applying to other fields of study, will follow.

on mutual respect and trust. Such a plan as this had been the aim of the German Youth Movement ever since its inception in 1902. In this regard, therefore, the effective working of the reform was made to depend largely on the desire of pupils themselves for such ideal community life, rather than exclusively on school organization or on the attitudes of teachers.

The Youth Movement in Germany commenced as a revolt of boys and girls, especially of students in the *höhere Schulen,* against the materialism, intellectualism, and formalism of the schools. The movement had attained great size and prominence before the beginning of the World War, and the misery and futility of the war itself intensified the distaste of these young people for the idols of their elders. They sought to find new beauty in nature and new values in themselves, although their expression—necessarily perhaps—took the form of negative agnosticism toward the going system of ideas and morals, as well as of positive views of their own.[39] They sought to cultivate, through companionship with one another in long walking-trips, through fêtes and mystic ceremonies, through group discussion, an "inner light" which would illuminate the good and the beautiful, which would enable them to be tolerant and to foster social justice, and which would give a moral and aesthetic focus for their enthusiasm. They also elected their own officers and practiced self-government, and the subordination of self to the ends of the group.

It was the aim of educational leaders in republican Germany to capture this enthusiasm and these ideals, and to organize them through school communities. Some formal accomplishments in this direction were made. And the authoritarianism among teachers was not as great, perhaps, as it was in pre-war times. There appear, however, to have been several hindrances which worked against any complete absorption of these principles in the schools. One was the force of the traditions of discipline and intellectualism. Another,

[39] The positive ideals of the German Youth Movement are, to a large extent, expressed through symbolism and ritualism. This mystical quality may explain the scarcity of substantial literature dealing with this subject. A helpful account of the influence of the Youth Movement in the *höhere Schulen* is the article by Karl Syneken in *Wesen und Wege der Schulreform,* edited by Adolf Grimme, Berlin, 1930.

which grew *pari passu* with the decline of the Republic, was the disintegration of the Youth Movement itself. Because of the unstable economic and political conditions in Germany, a number of the political parties organized youth movements of their own which were concerned with the practical realities of Germany's situation, and which offered a rich harvest to the party organizations. The Youth Movement proper did much for the moral development and the idealism of its members. It did not, however, direct or cause any far-reaching moral or idealistic rejuvenation of the schools.[40] The enthusiasm and high moral conviction of the Youth Movement were captured to a large extent by the National Socialist party, rather than by the social objectives of the Republic.

The only important movement of young Germans today is through the official Fascist organization, Hitler Youth. In the interests of this organization, an order of the Prussian Minister of Education, in 1933, made available the three former military academies at Plön, Köslin, and Potsdam. They will train boys and young men to become militant leaders of National Socialism. Students will wear the Hitler uniform. In these schools "there is no neutrality and no private citizenship. There is only one controlling idea—the national idea; only one scientific theory—the organic; only one political purpose—that of National Socialism."[41]

2. *Vocational Education in the Republic and in the Third Reich*

During the German Republic chief educational stress was laid upon vocational training. This contributed directly to the material and social ambitions of individuals, and only indirectly to the service of the community. This relationship of schools, individuals, and

[40] Objectives which were rather closely analogous to those of the Youth Movement had an important part in the work of some of the "experimental" schools of the republican period. These schools, which existed in rather wide variety, are not described in this review; in the light of the present, they appear to have been "traces" rather than "trends." An adequate descriptive literature exists in English. They are briefly described in Stephen P. Cabot, *Secondary Education in Germany, France, England and Denmark* (Harvard Bulletins in Education, No. 15), Cambridge, 1930; and more fully in Thomas Alexander and Beryl Parker's, *The New Education in the German Republic*, New York, 1929.

[41] Cf. Joachim Haupt, *Neuordnung im Schulwesen und Hochschulwesen*, Berlin, 1933, p. 24.

community is common to all democratic countries. In the Third Reich individuals are not expected to entertain personal ambitions, but are urged—even commanded—to subordinate their personal ambitions to the good of the Fatherland. This tenet of fascist doctrine is given effect through fascist methods. The control of the national government over subjects of instruction, over teachers, over admission of students to all grades of schools, and over the entrance of people to numerous occupations, adds force to the principle. The "service to the nation" which is expected of people of all ranks and callings is defined by the state—that is to say, by the National Socialist party.

In regard to vocational training the policies of the Republic were consistent with the broader liberalistic position which has been described. It was aimed to cultivate whatever abilities or capacities the individual students might possess. This was to be done in the terms in which the several capacities and abilities presented themselves, rather than by reference to an ulterior or extraneous principle. From this point of view it was more important that a bricklayer be skilled in his craft, or that a philosopher be competent and learned, and that the status of each be the highest for which he was by nature fitted, than that either of them be a Christian, a gentleman, or a member of a particular party. This does not mean, of course, that religion, personal conduct, and political inclinations were regarded as of no educational importance. But so far as the schools were concerned, more stress was laid upon effective adjustment of the individual to his environment and to his station in society than upon his indoctrination with the faiths of his people or the aims of his state. Such an educational purpose caters to, and fosters, a strong individualism. In time of stress this may be a source of weakness to a liberal government.

The principle of educating individuals to be effective workers in the practical affairs of the community is by no means a new one in Germany. It derives, in fact, from the system of apprenticeship for younger workers which has obtained in Germany from the times of powerful craft guilds in northern Europe.[42] In imperial Germany

[42] Even the compulsory feature of public education is quite old in Germany. As early as 1619 the school regulations of the little state of Weimar required all

this principle was employed in ways which fostered a system of status by virtually compelling young people to be trained for a station in life not greatly different from that occupied by their parents. In this way the best abilities of the individual might be brought to serve the interests of the community only when those abilities happened to coincide with the proprieties of caste. In republican Germany these limitations were at least formally removed; the gap between the "educated" and "uneducated" classes was bridged, and personal ambition held full sway.

Although this democratization of education released individual talents and abilities from the shackles of status, it added greatly to the upsetting of social conditions which occurred in the postwar period. The *Umschichtung* (rearrangement of classes), which created deep concern among upper- and middle-class Germans, was due to the war, the revolution, the inflation, the persistent depression—and to the democratizating of education. This observation does not, in any sense, deny that Germany might ultimately have benefited from a system which made ability rather than rank the basis for educational (and finally for vocational and social) preferment. It must be indicated, however, as one of the conditions which aggravated internal instability during the Republic, and which thus helped to inhibit far-reaching and settled social objectives.

The emphasis laid by the republican educational system on vocational and professional training contributed, in the broader social sense, to the development of skill and ability in performing the work of the community. To each person, it implied, in the narrower individualistic sense, ways and means of attaining a particular economic and social status. This stood out quite clearly in the cases of the *Volksschulen,* the *Fortbildungsschulen,* the *Mittelschulen,* and the technical institutions of university grade. In these schools the student was educated for a certain occupation, and for the station in life fixed by that occupation.

The same principle held, somewhat less conspicuously, in the case of the more purely academic sequence of *höhere Schulen* and uni-

---

children between six and twelve years of age to attend the elementary schools. The *Schul-Methodus* of Ernst the Pious of Gotha adopted the same principle in 1642. In the following century all Protestant states followed these examples.

versities. Three of the four faculties in the universities are training schools for the professions of law, medicine, and the ministry. And even the faculty of philosophy, while dedicated nominally to the service of science and scholarship as ends in themselves, has a strong professional bearing on account of its work in training teachers. During the Republic, a university degree was required of those who wished to enter many of the fields of public service, just as an official certificate of proficiency was necessary to the worker at a trade or a handicraft. The bureaucratic posts of the Reich and the states were divided between two classes of public servants: the *gebildete* (educated—meaning holders of doctoral degrees) and the *ungebildete* (uneducated) officials.

The professional value of higher education has long been marked in Germany, and the prominence of *"Brotwissenschaft"* (bread-science) as a subject of university study has been a matter of controversy among German educators and critics for several decades.[43] Many of the university "reformers" of the republican period referred with approval to Fichte's principle of reserving the universities for those who aspire to knowledge for its own sake, or who look forward to entering the highest branches of service to the state.[44] No real move in this direction took place, however, in the years of

[43] Hoffmann von Fallersleben summed up the leaning to *"Brotwissenschaft"* in the lines:

"Gelt und Brot, und Brot und Gelt
So schreit die Welt;
Das ist die einzige Mannichfältigkeit
In dem langweiligen Liede unserer Zeit.
Das ist das einzig Universelle
Unserer Universitaten—
Dies reimt sich nicht, ist aber doch wahr,
Und wer's nicht glaubt, dem wird's mit der Zeit noch klar."

In this connection, see John Hutchison's appendix to his translation of Johannes Conrad's *The German Universities for the Last Fifty Years*, 1885.

[44] The social end to be sought through education was somewhat similarly stated by King Friedrich Wilhelm III: "The state must recover through spiritual [*geistige*] powers what it has lost in physical." The foundation of the University of Berlin, in 1810, and its dedication to the service of pure science, was widely acclaimed as the realization of this ideal, as well as of Fichte's program, so far as higher education was concerned. The same dominant purpose was rapidly adopted by other universities of Germany, and remained in control for several decades. The *"Brotwissenschaft"* attitude is a wide deviation from this earlier principle.

the Republic; the democratization of all branches of education clearly led to an opposite effect. The universities became over-crowded, and there grew up a large "over-supply" of university graduates unable to find employment suited to their educational attainments. The high social esteem which traditionally has gone with the title of doctor probably contributed to the overcrowding of the learned professions—a tendency which may have gained im-petus from the fairly recent abolition of titles of hereditary nobility in a country in which titles long have been held in high regard.[45]

The individualistic motives implied here undoubtedly served to promote the great industrial advance which has taken place in Ger-many since 1870. They also were generated and stimulated by this same industrial advance. In this regard it should be borne in mind that the Industrial Revolution commenced in England, and that the part played by Germany consisted in adopting and improving the industrial methods. For such a part as this, Germany affords strong evidence of the benefit to be gained from training experts in tech-nology, in administration, and also for the service of the state.[46]

[45] These same individualistic motives were bitterly denounced by Fichte, in his *Reden an die deutsche Nation,* 1808, because of their incompatibility with his system of social idealism. Thus he declared, in the second of the *Reden:* "Man can will only what he loves; his love is the sole and at the same time the infallible motive of his will and of all his vital impulses and actions. Hitherto, in its educa-tion of the social man the art of the State assumed, as a sure and infallible prin-ciple, that everyone loves and wills his own material welfare. To this natural love it artificially linked, by means of the motives of fear and hope, that good will which it desired, namely, interest in the common weal. Anyone who has become outwardly a harmless or even useful citizen as a result of such a system of educa-tion remains, nevertheless, inwardly a bad man; for badness consists essentially in loving solely one's own material welfare and in being influenced only by the motives of fear or hope for that welfare. . . . In place of that love of self, with which nothing for our good can be connected any longer, we must set up and establish in the hearts of all those whom we wish to reckon among our nation that other kind of love, which is concerned directly with the good, simply as such and for its own sake."

[46] The most recent phase of the assistance given to economic development by higher education is the support, by institutions of university rank—especially by *technische Hochschulen*—of the "rationalization" of German industry. The not-able expansion of courses and seminars in *Betriebswirtschaftslehre* (management economics) in *technische Hochschulen* and *Handelshochschulen* is a conspicuous instance of this support. This training is described in my article, "The Teaching of Economics in Germany," *Columbia University Quarterly,* September, 1932.

Under the Third Reich, the services which individuals may render to the community and to the state are not permitted to follow solely from individual motives. In principle each person is required to subordinate his own interests to those of the Fatherland, as defined by the dominant party. Under existing conditions, acceptance of this principle is of more importance than technical competency. On even stronger grounds, it is more important than vocational qualifications gained through education. Many of the persons inducted to high positions in the public service are most distinguished by their ardor as Nazis.[47]

According to the highest authorities, the motivation and orientation of education in Nazi Germany are political. Thus, Ernst Krieck, Rector of the University of Frankfurt and chief Nazi educational philosopher:

The beginning of the national school reform took place with the influx of the national revolutionary movement in the school room. Therefore the political victory of the movement will open wide the flood gates.[48]

As to the orientation of education in the Nazi state, there is this word from Dr. Wilhelm Frick, Minister of the Interior, highest official of German schools:

The German school has to educate the political man, who, in all thoughts and dealings, is rooted, serving and self-sacrificing, in his people, and who is united at heart and inseparably with the history and the fate of his country. Only through a German education of the coming generation, uniform in all essentials, can the work of regeneration be completed and insured for all future time.[49]

It is this political character of education which is to give a cultural pattern to a great spiritual upheaval of the German nation. Again Herr Krieck:

On the political and social side of the total task which National Socialism, as advocate of the revolutionary principle, has to fulfill,

[47] A conspicuous instance of this is Herr Ernst Krieck, the recognized leader of Nazi educational thought. He was called by the Prussian Ministry of Education to a professorship in the University of Frankfurt and was, at the same time, appointed rector of that university. Herr Krieck does not hold a regular academic degree.

[48] Ernest Krieck, *Nationalpolitische Erziehung*, Leipzig, 1933, p. 113. This is the most authoritative single book on Nazi education.

[49] An address to the Ministers of Education of the German states, May 9, 1933.

comes the embodying of a new culture. The task is completely grasped, even though its fulfillment is distant. . . . It is a world-plan (*Weltbild*), appropriate to the content and goal of the National Socialist movement, to branch out through new creations into the realm of poetry and art, of science and philosophy, which will render in the victory of National Socialism its important share in accomplishing the greatest task of our time.[50]

Such is the conception of the Nazi Renaissance. It is to be expected that an educator would view the Nazi principle in education as "embodying a new culture." To the political leader the same principle permeates all pursuits of the mind and the spirit—but to an immediately practical end.

In science, also, the state perceives a means to the furtherance of its national pride. Not only world history, but also total cultural history, must be taught from this standpoint.[51]

3. *The Uncertainty of the Future*

History does not prove the moral worth of institutions or of ideas; it merely relates, in a systematic fashion, social changes which have occurred. The doctrines and objectives of the Third Reich are in no absolute sense "better" or "worse" than those of the Republic. Simply as an alternative to existing conditions, they became preferable to a large body of well organized and skillfully led Germans. To most of the rest of the world, doctrines and objectives of the Third Reich seem dangerous to peace—even to civilization. They are, to these non-Nazis, distinctly "worse" than those of the Republic.

The immediate conflict of preferences cannot be resolved. It is not possible to turn back in time and change the currents of affairs by damming up their sources. The republican régime in Germany tried sincerely and courageously to promote the ends of liberalism and peace. During the Republic more and more Germans came to feel that Germany was wronged in her political and economic relations with the rest of the world. The economic pinch was expressed through a progressive proletarization of large masses of German people. They demanded a dictatorial central government to check this process and to represent Germany aggressively before

[50] Ernst Krieck, *op. cit.*, p. 46.   [51] Adolf Hitler, *op. cit.*, p. 473.

other nations. The Third Reich is dangerous. So is a wounded tiger, driven and at bay. To this danger the hunter himself has contributed.

It follows from this that the teaching of fascist doctrine in the schools is not a primary cause of fascism in Germany. It is rather an expression of fascism, and a method which fascists are using in their effort to entrench themselves and their policies. The same method has been applied to all other general agencies of information and opinion—newspapers, radio, churches.

How effectively the German schools are serving the social objectives for which they stand cannot be estimated. The cultivation of consistent habits of thought and action in millions of people requires a long time. The future offers little certainty and numerous contingencies. These include economic and political relations with foreign countries, and also the maintenance of a strong single-mindedness within Germany. In the Third Reich there is one party and one leadership. It is probable that more people are driven than are led. Early in 1933 there were sixteen parties represented in the Reichstag. These differences in regard to policy have been driven underground; it can hardly be inferred that they have ceased to exist. Most of them probably are present, in one degree or another, within the National Socialist party itself. Serious dissension has been averted thus far by the masterful strategy of Herr Hitler. Single-mindedness has been abetted by revolutionary zeal and mob spirit. But Germans are, by temperament and habit, rational people. The long pull which lies ahead must be motivated by conviction rather than hysteria. It seems probable that stronger grounds than race-consciousness will be required for such conviction.

Economics might provide the grounds. Western societies have seen a widespread abandonment of their avowed principles—individualism, liberalism, internationalism. This has not been entirely an emotional revulsion. But fascism is only one expression of this abandonment. If the economic situation in Germany becomes more difficult for the mass of the people, authority and discipline will face a supreme test. Fascism is a logical outcome of the recent past; a united opposition may, with equal logic, grow in the future.

These are some of the broader contingencies confronting the political organization which directs education in Germany. The present social objectives in German education are sharply drawn by the hand of a strong government. Straight lines can be drawn only so long as the ground does not shake.

EDUCATION IN ENGLAND

BY

J. BARTLET BREBNER

III

THE EVOLUTION OF ENGLISH SOCIETY

Presumably education is always at the crossroads as traditional ways are confronted by changing circumstance. In England,[1] however, the necessity for choice of roads is perhaps more trying than elsewhere because the pathway from past society and education has been so confidently trodden and so generally esteemed. The victors of the great social, religious, and political conflicts of the seventeenth century were "the men of property," and during the superficially static, dignified eighteenth century they were able to establish ideals of manners and education not only to their own satisfaction, but for the emulation of the respectful, successful burghers of the nineteenth century. Until about 1870, the industrial worker or the tradesman, like the agricultural laborer, was simply not included in the oligarchical cultural design and it was only at the beginning of the twentieth century that he began hammering at the gates.

While it is perhaps characteristic of England that the masses were given a political initiation before institutions of higher learning were really opened to them, it is as well also to remember as a general consideration that political democracy was until very recent times less important in England than the liberty of the subject and even now competes with it on something like equal terms for public esteem. In the eighteenth century the small privileged class was united in curbing the pretensions of the state toward property and individual freedom, and the common law reflected the same desires. In the nineteenth century, while political democ-

[1] The standard book of reference is *The Year Book of Education*, London, Evans Brothers, Ltd., 1932-34, of which Lord Eustace Percy is editor-in-chief. For critical current surveys of various parts of the educational system the annual *Educational Yearbook of the International Institute of Teachers College, Columbia University*, edited by I. L. Kandel, New York, 1924-34, will be found useful. In preparing this essay and the essay on "Education in Canada" for publication, I have profited greatly from discussions with Professor F. Clarke of McGill University.

racy came very slowly, policemen were never allowed to forget that they were servants of the public. Even today, when circumstances have converted England into a strongly socialized political democracy, more warmth is likely to be reflected in letters to the newspapers over civil servants who have forgotten their true rôle than over irregularities in the franchise or deficiencies in primary education.

In fact, it is difficult to say just what democracy amounts to in England. Even in politics, where there is now universal suffrage, class and special interest are frankly recognized. In society, gradations are not only admitted but cherished. Perhaps one would not be far wrong to speak of English society, with its admitted divisions, as being organic and functional in an almost medieval sense, so that in many matters democratic standards simply do not apply. In place of general democratic values there is a vaguely defined but very strong sense of community which perhaps overflows Great Britain to explain in part the sentiment which unites Great Britain and the autonomous Dominions. The individual may be strongly individualistic, he may or may not believe in democratic standards for his national institutions, but he is likely, consciously or unconsciously, to have his spiritual anchorage in a sense of "belonging" to his group and his nation, to which he gives character and from which he derives it. That he and his tribe may conflict seems almost to give him a sense of being alive. He is in a perpetual ebb and flow of asserting his independence and of finding himself among his kind.

It is too much to expect that, in general, education will not, consciously and unconsciously, conserve the most valued elements of the national tradition, and in England events have allowed tradition to sink deep. Her insular position is so well-known that the effects of it are in danger of being lost in familiarity. No hostile invasion of her shores has taken place since the thirteenth century, if we except "Dutch William's" arrival in 1688 and the two romantic lost causes of the Stuarts in the eighteenth century. Continental movements and influences have, of course, bridged the Channel, but in doing so they have had to weaken the ties to their origins. The Englishman has for centuries been accustomed to discriminate

and to choose what he willed from these importations. He has
Anglicized them sometimes out of recognition. He has seldom felt
indebted to his outer world. There is more than a joke in the English newspaper bulletin "Gale Sweeps Channel, Continent Isolated."

An extraordinary continuity has existed in English culture and
its custodians. It is tempting, therefore, to go back to Anglo-Saxon
and Norman-French origins to find the matrix of the tradition. Unquestionably the Middle Ages do provide many a clue. A William
of Wykeham who (in 1382) provided his Winchester College with
the motto "Manners makyth man" certainly gave expression to a
vital aspiration in English culture. The fact, also, that when England had her own deep Renaissance and Reformation in the seventeenth century her ruling classes were but slightly touched by Puritanism, makes the continuous heritage from the Middle Ages seem
more impressive. It is folly to expect Puritanism in a Chesterfield
or a Walpole. That form of Protestantism made its way upwards
from the despised sects, not downwards from the country houses.
It only began to storm the citadels at the beginning of the nineteenth century, when a social amalgam of burgher wealth and territorial aristocracy admitted Methodism, the Evangelical movement,
and humanitarianism in small doses to a society which still produced such eighteenth-century rakes as "Old Q."

Yet closer examination makes it appear that the civil, religious,
and political settlements of the seventeenth century and the prosperity and the domestic tranquillity of the eighteenth stamped England with the mould which only the events of the last fifty years
have cracked and broken. Walpole's *"quieta non movere"* typified
the extraordinary respect for property, and for the property rights
of control in church and state and local administration, which gave
the landed aristocracy and gentry the chance to set up their ideals
and standards so firmly that a subsequent century of burgher power
only faintly altered them.

1. *The Eighteenth-Century Ruling Class*

Any attempt to generalize about the character and aspirations
of the ruling class of the eighteenth century and the modifications
which those qualities have since undergone is bound to involve

some partial truths, but the risk must be taken in order to approximate the setting for English educational ideas. It has been said, for instance, that a similarity exists between the English provincial universities and those of the British Dominions and the United States, but that Oxford and Cambridge still conserve a sufficient fraction of the eighteenth century to set them apart. Oxford and Cambridge are still "the universities." What was this eighteenth-century mould?

The answer to begin with is that the dominant society had its firm foundation in the land. "County" society in England can even yet look down on "Court" society and be fairly oblivious to the existence of any society at all among the residents of London and the other urban boroughs. Such Olympianism must have deep roots in the past. In spite of the laws and customs of primogeniture which ejected the younger sons of the nobility from the formal rank and family property of their class, and in spite of a continuous infiltration into the landed aristocracy by marriage with the burgher class, the "county" basis of social exclusiveness was still fighting a stout rear-guard action in 1914. Its privilege began, of course, in feudal times, when land was the only convenient payment for military and other services, but feudalism's passing happened to coincide with Protestantism's coming, and when the confiscated estates of the old church were sold and given away, the new owners did their best to become indistinguishable from their feudal predecessors as quickly as possible. In the same way, the merchant adventurers of the seventeenth century, the Indian "nabobs" of the eighteenth, and the industrial magnates of the nineteenth, when they or their families had social or political ambitions, bought country estates, painstakingly acquired the rural accomplishments of the "county" class, and began a slow social siege with the humble conviction that if they could not pass the pale their children or grandchildren might.

The core of society, then, was a physically robust, assured, and assimilative group of landlords and land managers, to whom their own social position and, to some degree, noble rank were more important than mere wealth. Their oddly unconscious class consciousness has puzzled observers from Chaucer to Gissing and Santayana.

If it was hypocrisy, it was often unconscious hypocrisy. At its worst it meant the abominable and insolent treatment of outsiders of any sort which one finds in Fielding's novels. At its best it meant the benevolent paternalism and *noblesse oblige* which Disraeli (in his novels and his politics) tried to transmute into a still broader sense of social responsibility in the changed England of the nineteenth century.

In the second place, the dominant oligarchy was Anglican. Once the Civil War and the Cromwellian period were over, the "men of property" fought ruthlessly to maintain the privileged position of the very elastic state church, which provided, after all, an important portion of their estates. They defeated the attempts of three successive sovereigns to admit dissenters to full citizenship, and the thirty years from 1660 to 1690 sealed their ownership of a non-Puritan, highly rationalistic ecclesiastical system. They owned its livings, their nominees chose its hierarchy, and the sovereign Parliament which they controlled and from which dissenters were excluded forced the whole population to contribute to its support. Membership in the Anglican communion was the necessary passport to a political career, to civil or military office, or for admission to the universities and almost all good schools.

Finally, the social oligarchs were also the governors of England. They had turned their kings into constitutional conveniences, and they stubbornly thwarted both the Stuart and the Hanoverian attempts to circumvent that fate. Parliament, not the king or the people, ruled England in the eighteenth century. Landed peers and Anglican bishops controlled the House of Lords. Cadets and nominees of the territorial princes controlled the House of Commons through an anachronistic but conveniently manipulable constituency system. As Mr. L. B. Namier has recently shown, commercial wealth, metropolitan finance, and colonial interest had a powerful voice in government, but only through a binding bargain which the "Country Party" by its numbers could always revoke. The business men were usually allowed to work out financial, foreign, and colonial policies, but, in return, local government (which *was* government to most men in an agricultural England) by Lord Lieutenant of the county, and by justices of the peace and churchwardens in the parish, was almost the monopoly of the Anglican landed aristocracy and gentry.

The notable cultural product of this triple monopoly was the English gentleman who can be seen in suggestive caricature in the "milord anglais" of the more romantic nineteenth-century French novels. Temperamentally, of course, individuals of the class varied as individuals do, but because there indubitably was a class, its members externally conformed to a code of manners. Indeed, one of the most profound social paradoxes in England is that of a remarkable respect and toleration for extreme individuality or even for eccentricity combined with an abrupt certainty over what is and is not "done." The determinant is impossible to define, save that eccentricity must enrich, not impoverish or contradict, the sense of community to which reference has been made. Toward the end of the eighteenth century the gentleman was either the arrogant, if paternal, squire whose rural tyranny was as yet not seriously threatened, or the "Town" dandy whose London elegance owed more to Paris than occurred to him during his complacent acceptance of the admiration of things English so forcibly declared by MM. Montesquieu and Voltaire. It was politically expedient to encourage the masses in their contempt for "Mounseer," but the enlightened kept up their visits to, and correspondence with, France in spite of the many interruptions of wars.

2. The Rise of the Burghers

The first great onslaught on this oligarchy began to be felt shortly after the middle of the eighteenth century, but before its weight could be made effective, any kind of change had been made rank heresy by the excesses which were associated with change in the French Revolution. For a year or two the Revolution seemed by its constitutional experiments to be paying tribute to the divine rectitude of British institutions, but the Terror converted every English critic into a Jacobin to the ruling class, and when Napoleon commandeered the Revolution for his own grand designs, the exigencies of a fight for British survival pushed at least the recognition of change into the background. Between 1760 and 1820 England changed profoundly, but it was not until after 1820 that the bulk of institutional adjustments to the changes could be made.

The new forces which could not be denied recognition were the antitheses of Land, the eighteenth-century Anglican Church and a semi-feudal Parliament. Capitalistic commerce had laid its expansive demands on industry and an explosive response in techniques of production raised the burghers to an economic eminence which commanded attention and promised a further even more rapid rise. The Land's first reply was agrarian reform and a greedy agricultural capitalism, but even before the wars with Napoleon were over, English agriculture had failed to hold its own in world competition and had sought refuge behind a subsidy system which Parliament maintained until the Irish famine in 1846 made its anomalies too obvious to maintain. Then the supposed economic foundation of the landed aristocracy was exposed to forces which by 1880 destroyed it, and the landlords sought coal and iron on their estates or rushed to capitalize their titles on the boards of directors of the new commercial, industrial, financial, and transportation enterprises. The burghers secured a regularization of the parliamentary system and a share in its operation in 1832.

In their rise, the burghers brought up with them a large cluster of habitual ideas, many of which such scholars as Mr. R. H. Tawney have been able to group convincingly around their religion. Calvin may have dealt with the taking of interest "as the apothecarie doth with poyson," that is, by the use of small doses, but Calvinists made its legitimacy the chief foundation stone of their economic structure. They added the idea of "calling" and developed it until for them prosperity tended to be synonymous with divine approval. In their own way they were as assured within their own territory of finance, business, and industry as the landed aristocracy had been for all England. Their philosophy was so matured and certain that it could absorb and unthinkingly pervert to individualistic aims even the social utilitarianism of Jeremy Bentham. When it was reinforced by the "natural laws" of economics which were propounded by Malthus and Ricardo, the total result was the convenient, if logical, structure which we know as *laissez faire*. In economic and social matters, free play was insisted upon for the individual and the cardinal crime was governmental regulation.

If sense and sensibility could have been kept apart during the nineteenth century, England would unquestionably have had a revolution or a series of revolutions like the rest of Europe, but they could not. Perhaps it is true that sentimentalism has never really been absent from England, no matter how masked by the ardours of the Renaissance or the studied moderation of the eighteenth century. At any rate, the roots of the "feeling" which Rousseau systematized as romanticism can be found in Thomson's poetry, the landscapes of Old Crome and Constable, and the fervors of eighteenth century Methodism. Not only the burghers, but a section of the aristocracy as well, carried over into the nineteenth century a humanitarianism and an evangelical piety which were to contradict Anglican rationalism and social *laissez faire* so violently that compromises had to be found.

The process of reconciliation was too complex an affair for complete description here, but its effect on society and culture should not be misunderstood. As commerce grew and factories sprang up, the landlords and burghers of England saw a small industrial working class expand into a third estate which threatened to swamp the nation by sheer numbers. Its sudden growth strained a society and a civilization ill-adapted to receive it, and its growing-pains therefore took the form of a series of abominations in living and working conditions. Economics and sociology were still supposedly subject to "iron" laws of nature which seemed to exclude any fundamental reforms. Nature must take her course of starvation, disease and poverty until the balance was restored. It was in these circumstances that humanitarianism began to find expression in many experiments.

Gradually English humane impulses came to flow chiefly in three channels. The first was an unexampled proliferation of charitable societies, many of which have served as models for the rest of the world and have continued to find work to do under modern state socialism. The "Personal" column of the London *Times* with its long list of appeals has for a century been a monument to their variety. The second channel was a broadening of eighteenth-century aristocratic paternalism into what might be called the Conservative or Tory program of specific rather than general social reform to be effected by legislative action. This benevolent reform of abuses from above ranged from the criminal law to factory conditions and dignified the record of the old aristocracy and their new adherents to a degree which has not always been admitted. The third channel was the Whig or Liberal policy of political reform to the end that all classes might unite in using the political machinery to better society. There was a blight of caution on that policy which coincided with the deepest period of *laissez faire* about the middle of the century and a parliamentary situation developed whereby it was the Conservatives who made the first real step towards democracy in 1867. By then, however, Darwin and Huxley and Spencer had committed the Liberals to the idea of progress, and political democracy became almost a reality in 1884 and 1885.

Before turning to the effects of admitting practically the whole population to the vote, it should be noticed that the burghers in the nineteenth century did about as much to perpetuate the idea of the English gentleman as to change it. The process during the first half of the century is consciously and unconsciously revealed in Thackeray's *Vanity Fair*. At bottom is the "sound" burgher's idea of decency, moderation, and safety in business. Superimposed on it are the manifold devices of the City folk to secure acceptance from high society. It is true that County does not play as conspicuous a part as in Fielding, but there are few signs as yet of a change in the mould which County cast for gentlemen. The clamorous new note is the crass materialism which infects every one. It had been one of the canons of gentility never to talk about money. On the whole, it had never been very necessary for the gentle to do so. Consequently the old attitude towards money was one of the sturdiest barriers for the burgher to surmount.

On the one hand, then, was the burgher obsession with conformity to the model set up for him by those who "belonged." On the other were the pervasive influences of his own standards when he himself arrived. He struggled and plotted to get into the right houses, clubs, regiments, schools, universities, and even church congregations.

When he got there his blunt decency could not fail to have its effects on some of the careless indecencies which had not before been much exposed to criticism. Moreover, the prevalent romanticism was a mighty aid. Scott and his followers brought up from the past medieval ideas of chivalry and piety which may have been extravagantly pure, but which could influence a humanitarian reformer like William Cobbett. The English gentleman was in process of becoming, ideally at least, a humane Christian who blended appropriately the qualities of the medieval knight and the cultivated man of the Renaissance. He was forgetting the relation of landlord and peasant, but he was finding it difficult to evolve a fruitful sense of solidarity in such a relation as that of a shareholder to the industrial workers.

It was a canny idea of the Liberals to stick to political reform, for that was gradual in its effects. It took the proletariat over two generations to learn that it might get further by creating its own representatives than by choosing between those of the two older upper-class groups. Of course its votes and other support had not gone for nothing. Conservatives and Liberals had found it expedient to win support by a variety of concessions, but, in general, the old aristocracy and the new burghers had spent the nineteenth century in reaching a tacit agreement in outlook which, although not unanimous in all respects, was still paternal towards, rather than coöperative with, the proletariat. England was still, socially and in a cultural way, aristocratic. Initiative was in the hands of the few rather than of the many. Only in the twentieth century did the direction appear to begin to change.

3. The Thrust of the Proletariat

It is the thrust and drive of the working population to get what they want which is a more serious threat to the old mould of English culture than the burghers' rise to power. The distance between classes is greater and the consciousness of it more marked than when landlords faced burghers. The instruments which reflect the workers' power were wrested from the Liberals as the price of political support against the Conservatives. The state socialism which was set up by the Liberals between 1906 and 1914 and the removal of the veto power of the House of Lords barely antedated the war period, during which England became accustomed to state monopolies, controls, nationalization of necessary services, and the like. Since the war England has had two Labour governments whose minority position prevented them from embarking on Labour's full national design. Yet the only device which has succeeded in temporarily eliminating Labour's political influence has been the use of panic such as was developed around the Zinovieff letter or the passing of the gold standard in 1931. And meanwhile England has become a socialized state so confirmed by twenty years of responsibility for the aged, the sick, employed and unemployed workers, and education, that no political party dares to repudiate what are now held to be necessary state services.

IV

THE EVOLUTION OF ENGLISH EDUCATION

Against the above organic, if arbitrary, generalizations about the evolution of English society it may be possible to describe the educational situation in a more summary way. England has at present one of the least systematic educational structures in existence among the leading countries of the world. Perhaps the most serious part of the price which she is paying for the late war is the denial of the financial support necessary to set up in its completeness the national educational system which was envisaged and planned between 1911 and 1921. Today England has an uneven educational apparatus which is labouring towards integration (but not towards uniformity) under heavy handicaps, most of them financial, but a substantial part of which derive from inability to reconcile the points of view which can be related to the most vital aspirations of the eighteenth, nineteenth, and twentieth centuries.

1. *The English Educational Structure*

In the case of English education it is necessary to differentiate between variety of institutions and unevenness among them or failure to integrate them in a useful structure. Variety is warmly cherished as an evidence of health and serviceableness. There is an inherent distrust of whatever threatens to regiment the youth of the nation and an almost passionate desire to conserve even oddities which have been serviceable in the past, even if only in an imponderable way. This concern over richness and tradition in the educational fabric is sometimes directly responsible for weaknesses in the total system and for strong emotional differences which prove destructive. Yet it has had an invigorating effect in the modern evolution of a national system of education, by insistence that it must provide many paths to many different educational ends. The national educational authorities can be depended upon to balance English love of variety with the bureaucrat's love of system.

The English educational structure is in many ways analogous to one of those English country residences whose foundation is a medieval abbey, confiscated for lay purposes in the reign of Henry VIII, remodelled on Tudor lines, twisted into an external compromise with Palladian symmetry during the seventeenth and eighteenth centuries, equipped with drains and adorned with some romantic Gothic additions in the nineteenth, and brought up to date by bathrooms and electric light in the twentieth. The final product ought to be, and sometimes is, an offensive, meaningless medley, unlovely and inefficient to boot. Yet sometimes in its whimsical eccentricity it is charming and humane. In these cases, mere antiquity and tradition have played a part, but there has also been some odd harmony between builders and dwellers and between both and the countryside they occupy.

Perhaps the analogy might be stretched a little further. The visitor to the variegated mansion will find many evidences of patching. The floors are at different levels and odd numbers of steps are necessary here and there to connect them. A window opens on a corridor instead of on the outer wall. A chimney intrudes to give a room an irregular shape. Roofs do strange things to ceilings. So it is in education, where medieval schools and colleges and modern technical institutes, Anglican and non-Anglican ideas of religion in education, the classics and applied science, the life of contemplation and the life of action, the ideal of self-cultivation and the ideal of social service, and aristocratic, burgher, and proletarian aspirations, are all pulled together in an effort to make an integral system which shall afford full opportunity for any chosen path to education. Somehow mere Englishry holds the structure together, and strong empiricism and practicality make it work, but deep anomalies, some of which are objectionable, continue because deep contradictions continue to exist.

Comparatively few Englishmen would be offended at being taken for Etonians or Oxonians or their nearest equivalents. That statement is not synonymous with saying that most Englishmen are snobs. Nor should it be forgotten that there has always been a substantial number of the Englishmen able to choose their educational paths who have avoided the formal institutions. Faraday, J. S. Mill, and Ruskin were privately educated, and many another leader educated himself for distinction after he had left school or college. Yet Winchester and Eton, Cambridge and Oxford, have conserved a valued tradition and because they have done so successfully they confer an English distinction on their members.

For these and other reasons it is convenient to look at English education from the top down,[2] at least until our own generation, when pressure from below has been stronger. At the top in terms of prestige are three institutions of medieval foundation: the old universities or groups of colleges, the ancient public schools, and the local foundations or priests' schools which became grammar schools in the sixteenth century. All of them began with the idea of corporate groups composed of rich and poor and devoted to a life of scholarship and service to the universal church. All of them that survived the confiscations became Anglican during the Reformation. All of them paid at least lip service to the Renaissance ideal of sound mind in sound body. Most of them suffered badly from the conservative complacency of the eighteenth century and the black reaction of 1793 to 1820. In spite of their antiquity and their cherished tradition, it is in general true that they acquired their present blend of predominant characteristics in the nineteenth century, when burgher practicality was brought to bear on what had become eighteenth-century privileged lethargy. New life and purpose were injected into the Oxford that scandalized Gibbon and Bentham, Arnold re-made Rugby and by his success compelled the other public schools to follow suit, and King Edward's School at Birmingham became much more than an interesting survival from the past. It is that Victorian compromise between the ideals of aristocracy and middle class which is now being adjusted to the needs of a socialized England. It should be said at once that the universities have proved more adaptable than the schools.

[2] For convenience and brevity this study will not deal separately with the education of women and girls. Except for a time lag which postponed the serious beginnings until after the middle of the nineteenth century, women's education has developed along lines remarkably imitative of that of men.

2. *Nineteenth-Century Ideals*

Continuing for the moment to look at English education from the top down, it is possible to establish some outlines of the educational ideals which found expression in the nineteenth-century public school and university. Because of their prestige at the top of the ladder, they were earnestly imitated and their practices could be found in interesting, if sometimes pathetic and ill-judged, dilutions in lowlier institutions. Perhaps the central tenets of the *credo* were dependence on study of the classics to provide intellectual discipline and fibre, on man-to-man team games to provide physical courage, self-control and endurance, and on corporate organizations of all sorts to establish gradually acceptance of the responsibilities of command and obedience inherent in a pyramidal system of authority. Interested observers have been surprised to discover in this aristocratic education for governance surprisingly little conscious nationalism and a late, weak consciousness of imperial destiny. If it is remembered that public school and university men were the elect of a domestic social hierarchy and chiefly concerned with it, the situation is not so surprising. Except for a few great proconsuls of empire, the British Empire was made and governed chiefly by self-reliant younger sons without great domestic inheritance. They also officered army, navy, and civil services, while eldest sons prepared for and assumed the honours and duties at home which they had inherited from feudal times.

Defence of the Greek and Latin languages and their literatures as the core of education has been made so often that it need not be repeated in detail here. Stripped of all the pros and cons which have been built up around logical structure, notable content, value as models for expository or aesthetic emulation, and historical utility, the most vital argument seems to be that next to knowledge of, and mastery over, one's own language, the most useful second educational acquisition is almost equal control of another. It serves as a criterion for clarity and precision, it naturally enriches vocabulary, and it forces attention to fine modulations of meaning. The complementary relation between articulateness and clear thinking is sufficiently obvious, and rigor in the exact use of language (usually English and Latin) was a popular ideal not only in school or university but in home and press and public life. The mental discipline involved in mastery of Greek and Latin was given preëminence over mathematics, and the social as well as intellectual distinction arising from such mastery flattered the aspiring middle classes. They gave new life to a tradition which ran back to the *trivium* and *quadrivium* of the Middle Ages. The voices which questioned the utility of ancient as compared with modern languages had little effect before the end of the nineteenth century, except in the appointment as masters and tutors of harassed foreigners whose efforts were almost fruitless and who could not understand the careless scorn of the response. The boy who could make correct and graceful verses in Greek or Latin often could not extract the savour from the French models of his own literature, let alone speak another modern language. One can balance the Walpole who was the intimate of Mme. du Deffand with the English traveller of the nineteenth century who could not get along without the services of Thomas Cook and Son.

The nineteenth-century emphasis on competitive games as a necessary part of education was not such a pure response to the Renaissance idea of "l'uomo universale" as has sometimes been represented. A cursory examination of the old Oxford cautionary statutes which antiquarian piety still places in the hands of newly matriculated students will serve as a reminder that boys and young men have always found vent for their energies in violent games as well as in bouts of fighting and drinking. The English aristocracy of the sixteenth, seventeenth, and eighteenth centuries built up almost a monopoly for itself of the hunting rights which medieval kings had only grudgingly shared with their forefathers. They varied these pursuits in the summer by playing cricket. Their sons at school and university naturally practiced the same diversions. Yet what we know of the eighteenth century at the universities and at some public schools perhaps explains why a substantial portion of aristocratic youth avoided them. There was unquestionably a rather sodden brutality about faculty and student life which found expression in cockfighting, dog-fighting, rat-killing, fist-fighting, and heavy drinking rather more than in cricket and football, or the endurance of riding to hounds, or following the beagles. The records of modern team sports and of competition between schools and between universities belong to the nineteenth century.

It is tempting, therefore, to associate modern educational athletics with middle-class influence, but to do so remembering that "amateur" in England meant "gentleman." The Stewards of the Royal Henley Regatta, when confronted by application from oarsmen of the Dominions and foreign countries, must nowadays close their eyes to their own regulations which confine competitors to those who have not earned their livings by their hands. The artisan, whose occupation made him muscular, was not thought an appropriate opponent for one to whom exercise was an avocation. In older times the aristocrat who stepped out of his class to fight with an artisan might heighten his condescension by making him a gift of money when it was over. The competitive games of the nobility and gentry were regulated by a tacit punctilio which can be traced back through Castiglione's *Book of the Courtier* to generous gestures at medieval tournaments. It was presumed that the lower classes would not understand its odd combination of fierce competition and what we now call sportsmanlike behavior. When the Corinthians used to play against professional association football teams or the Gentlemen met the Players at cricket there was felt to be an educational element involved.

England undoubtedly gave to the world her own athletic version of chivalry and the ideas which a large part of the world attaches to the words "sportsman," "amateur," and "gentleman." The code which those words represent was an integral part of nineteenth-century education. It may have flattered its supporters somewhat. For instance, school and university rugby in England today deliberately avoids certain fairly obvious tactics which are not provided against in the rules, but there is compensation in the feeling of superiority towards the teams of the Northern Union which have exploited all opportunities to the limit. Yet this should not be allowed to weigh down the balance against the educational contribution of games as they evolved in England. They served to promote physical fitness, to produce valuable skills, courage and endurance, and to develop self-control. Because many more persons play games than can be outstanding at them, there is still a genuine amateurism which resents world championships and Olympic Games. Another revealing characteristic is the preference for team games over individual. In many ways the eight-oared crew, which must be the essence of skilled coöperation with a single pace-setter, is even more typical of English athletics than the adroitly distributed cricket team or the thrust and grind of bodies in a rugby "scrum."

The corporate idea of the team is one expression of the third great characteristic of nineteenth-century education. It can be found in the early colleges of Oxford and Cambridge or in the original statutes of Winchester. To use a political analogy, each corporation was a self-governing republic, usually with a diluted internal democracy. The fellows and scholars of a college or the masters of a public school accepted the laws and regulations of their community in order to preserve its integrity. They also knew that they might share in making new laws for it or perhaps some day serve as its head. The same conception in a lesser order regulated the lives of schoolboys and students. The boys governed themselves through prefects and school or house captains. They had their aristocracy and accepted leaders. The university students were less formally organized, but their colleges corresponded to school houses and their universities to whole schools. Both groups were more democratic socially than the outside world, for benefactions opened educational opportunity to the gifted man even if he were poor or of low birth. This whole apparatus of the exercise of authority and the acceptance of it was an ever-present part of English education and a preparation for the hierarchies of merit, privilege and seniority in the outside world.

On the face of it, this education seems aristocratic and in general it was so. Only a tiny percentage of the youth of the nation came under it and they were educated to be governors and privileged above the rest. The saving graces were a sense of *noblesse oblige* which deepened almost into a religion in the humanitarian nineteenth century, and a rapid extension of the socially democratic idea that intelligence, wherever found, deserved the opportunity for development. It was not until 1871, however, that the old universities abolished the upholding of the Thirty-Nine Articles of the Anglican faith as a test for admission.

Before turning to the impact of political democracy and the sense of comprehensive social responsibility on English education, there are two peculiarities which should be added to the broad outlines given above. Horace Walpole wrote in 1740 to Richard West: "There are no people so obviously mad as the English. . . . In England, tempers vary so excessively, that almost every one's faults are peculiar to himself." He there hit upon an element of Englishry that is very near the core of the old outlook. Cultivated English society cherishes a respect for individuality which can come close to being a cult of eccentricity so long as it is not dangerously destructive of society as it is organized. It may seem improbable when placed beside the Spartan regimentation of the public schools, but it is there none the less and it emerges more clearly in the universities. The eighteenth-century aristocrats enjoyed an extraordinary degree of freedom to become what they wished and they handed on the tradition. Education, in these circumstances, tended in the long run to be a quest for a personal philosophy, for an individual critical position and for the cultivation of private taste. Intellectual independence was, and is still, very highly esteemed and oddities of behaviour are tolerantly regarded so long as they do not outrage accepted social canons too deeply. This circumstance seems to explain English diffidence about dogmatic teaching after pupils have outgrown the schoolboy stage. Respect for individuality and an instinctive desire to see it grow make college dons shun any appearance of indoctrination. Textbooks and the lectures of teachers who organize their materials arbitrarily are both frowned upon.

These remarks apply, of course, only to what must be called "amateur" education. Technical and professional education were until recent times the monopolies of craft organizations and of such close corporations as the Church, the Bar, and the Royal Colleges of Physicians and Surgeons. Not that any disrepute attached to narrow expert knowledge of a non-vocational sort. In cultivated English circles knowledge was ultimately esteemed above opinion and what was often a false modesty or diffidence about general knowledge was frequently combined with great assurance in a particular field.

Perhaps the use of the classics and mathematics as apparatuses for mental training will provide the clue to a second generalization which is a necessary modification of the general character here attributed to the public schools and universities. Again and again one finds it implied and occasionally stated of English education that its formal structure provides merely an introduction to education and that its service cannot be more than to reveal the opportunities and methods of real self-education. Moreover, the careers of many Englishmen have shown this to be true. It would be too much to expect that a large percentage of schoolboys and students should think of their formal education as preparatory to genuine self-education, but there has always been a substantial minority which has discovered the fact. It is perhaps needless to say that the second group has been the principal reservoir from which college and university teachers have been drawn. For many Englishmen school and college exist chiefly to instruct the young in ways to acquire knowledge, to think, and ultimately to educate themselves.

It is clear that the educational ideals which have thus far been described are those of a privileged class, somewhat leavened by middle-class decency and nineteenth century humanitarianism and by the rise of the most talented from the lower classes, but linked to a society and economy and polity strongly individualistic and tending towards a philosophy of *laissez faire*. It remains to see how the mere weight of the new industrial working class, the gradual decline from English economic preëminence in the world and the disaster of the recent war have altered the picture.

3. *Steps toward Integration*

In so far as education was concerned, Englishmen spent the nineteenth century in altering everything but the foundations, and the habit of tinkering and fitting grew so deep that it pretty thoroughly devitalized the first comprehensive scheme of the twentieth century, leaving to a debt-ridden postwar generation the unenviable task of starting again from the bottom. It was not so much that leading statesmen and thinkers were opposed to extension and change in education as that it was impossible to achieve a majority of support from among Anglicans and Nonconformists, aristocracy and burghers, paternalists and proletarian democrats. The examples of Prussia and France in introducing universal education at the end of the eighteenth century had been powerful goads to action. George III wanted every child to be able to read the Bible, and such different persons as Samuel Whitbread, Southey, Robert Owen, Wordsworth, Coleridge, and Henry Brougham believed in universal education. In 1802 factory owners were legally compelled to train their child workers in the rudiments of knowledge.

Moreover, the nineteenth century brought with it powerful forces to aid in the extension of education. The Evangelical Movement sought to dignify the lowly who had been moved by the Spirit. Sunday schools had already begun to make their feeble contribution towards leavening the lump of lower-class ignorance. Romanticism, particularly when coupled with belief in the perfectibility of man, was another strong influence. When Cobbett affirmed that England should be merry yet, he doubtless anticipated additions to the number of those who could read and enjoy his *Political Register*. There was even among the English aristocracy an uneasy sense of compunction which had been produced by the sad fate of their French cousins during the Revolution. If privilege had been destroyed in France it might be wise to conciliate its potential destroyers in England. This expedient sense, mixed with humanitarianism, met the omens of coming democracy with the phrase "We must educate our masters" and later those of coming socialism with the assertion "We are all socialists now."

The persistent blight on a national scheme of education in the nineteenth century was sectarian propaganda. The often notable Dissenters' schools of the eighteenth century suffered severely after 1792, and, at the beginning of the nineteenth century, Anglicanism, although by no means either universal or uniform, set out to monopolize primary education. A rivalry among the sects sprang up from which English boys and girls in the long run profited. By 1831, for instance, the Church of England controlled 13,000 endowed schools with 400,000 pupils. It was apparent, however, that sectarian differences would block any comprehensive national scheme for a long time to come, and for two generations progress was made only at the cost of wasteful competition. The pity was that the achievements for

Dissent were to a considerable degree confined to the small field of higher education. Non-sectarian University College (1827) in London joined Anglican King's (1829-31) in 1836 to form the new University of London. It in turn systematized non-sectarian higher education for the lower middle class all over England until Victoria University, Manchester, in 1880, and half a dozen other provincial universities in the twentieth century really began to break the monopoly which Oxford and Cambridge had implemented with Anglican tests until 1871. Special Dissenters' schools had meanwhile anticipated the "provided" schools founded and maintained by the State, but increase in numbers was slow and the Anglicans kept their advantage. Mechanics' Institutes grew out of George Birkbeck's Glasgow lectures in 1800. Oxford provided a measuring-stick for achievement in the schools by giving local examinations after 1857. The Oxford and Cambridge Joint Locals and University Extension began in 1873. Royal Commissions examined the old universities in 1850-52 and 1872-74 and recommended changes which should check college particularism and create universities to serve the whole nation.

It was apparent, however, that education in England still looked towards the top whose concepts and standards it emulated and accepted. Meanwhile primary and secondary education, which were almost the only educational services available to the working masses, continued for long to be inadequate and propagandistic. Only in the seventies did a scheme for universal state education emerge to follow the beginning of political democracy in 1867. It did not become compulsory until 1880 or free until 1891, and it was forced to retain as the main part of its structure a great medley of old institutions weakened by sectarian rivalry, inadequacy of teachers and absence of even-handed control. In 1902 it came under the direction of the county councils and began to acquire some evenness of quality and standards, but primary and secondary educational institutions, public and private, still made a curious and dispiriting mosaic by their incompatibility. The London County Council, because of its wealth and vigour, distinctly outstripped the rest of the country, but in so doing aggravated the disparities. The universities and the technical institutes which public and private enterprise had provided in the nineteenth century made a somewhat better showing, but they too were disunited by conflicting ideas of what education should be. In 1914, England, as compared with France or Germany, was getting along with an amazingly haphazard educational apparatus, and there were not lacking those whose passion either for the maintenance of privilege or for free scope for some kinds of individuality made them content that it should be so. The believers in variety and in the conservation of what had been cherished in the past could present a strong case. No one denied the efficacy of some parts of the apparatus. Some institutions were still unique and even internationally supreme. Yet the whole fabric was being strained by the absence of an appropriate national design and by the push and pull of ill-coördinated objectives.

The war of 1914-18, which signalized the passing of the economic leadership which had been challenged by Germany and the United States for fifty years, and which temporarily converted England from a democracy to a dictatorship, made the old ways unprofitable to maintain. The political Labour Party had served a thirty-year apprenticeship, had even before the war forced the Liberals to do part of its will and had learned the lessons of state tyranny during the war. Old group loyalties had weakened, and increasing numbers regarded the state as a paramount association entitled to obedience. This tended to be particularly true of the poor, who were being given a new group-consciousness by their education by the state and their dependence upon it for aid in economic emergencies. The English as a whole had become socialists by habit to a degree of which not all of them were aware. The postwar educational situation, accentuated as it has been by social and economic crises, demonstrates very well the deep contradictions which still exist and which are slowly being resolved in spite of the pendulum swings of party politics.

It might be said that education in England is now committed to integration and that rapid progress has been made towards it. The most powerful agency in the process is the dependence of the majority of institutions, from Oxford and Cambridge down, upon public funds. The Board of Education, which supervises these grants, has preserved to an astonishing degree the traditional policy of avoiding even the appearance of dictating educational policy, but inevitably beneficiaries have listened to the counsels of the benefactor. Year after year very competent committees drawn from several circles of English society have submitted reports and recommendations which have irresistibly made over the national scheme and have gradually altered sectional attitudes. If public support and the taxpayer's resources continue to be available even to the extent determined by the economies of 1931, within less than a generation England ought to have an adequate, admirable educational structure. It will not be uniform, for variety is genuinely esteemed. Old foundations of distinct sectarian or social complexion will survive, but all the parts will be so adjustable to a large variable design that many paths to education will be provided. It will not be based on belief in the equality of men. It will, however, exist to provide careers for the talented, however poor, and it will endeavour to give training for a great variety of careers.

4. *Professionalization and Preparation for Self-Education*

This is not the place for a description of the many kinds of institutions—free nursery schools, endowed independent schools, workers' tutorial classes, and so forth, rural and urban—which now exist, nor of the extraordinarily complicated ways by which they cohere. Yet it should be less surprising than it is to find that England, in spite of the strength of her traditional ways, is wrestling with exactly the same technical and administrative problems as the rest of Western Europe and North America. The ages for compulsory school attendance are from five or six to fourteen or sixteen, depending on certain local options, and most "provided" schools have been organized on those terms. Moreover in England the corporate idea is still strong enough to make the individual school, rather than a grade or a division across all similar schools, the natural unit. Yet now there are unmistakable, substantial conformities to the belief that age groups from two to seven should be consolidated into a natural unit, although of varying kind, everywhere. Another obvious tendency is to regard age groups from eleven to fourteen as naturally falling within secondary education. In the United States the junior high school, and in some Teutonic European countries the "middle school" is evidence of the same problem. Elementary education is breaking up.

In another sense, professionalization and vocational training are reaching down further towards childhood to win their recruits. This impact is having its effects on secondary education and the emergent design for the future appears to be that of a central group of secondary schools with a potential lower age limit of eleven, which lead their best and most privileged students naturally to the universities. These will be paralleled by all sorts of vocational schools (commercial, technical, trade, art, and so forth) which deliver most of their pupils to commerce and industry, there if they like to continue their education on a part-time basis. Their excelling minority goes to the technical colleges which parallel the universities. Secondary schools and teachers' colleges (now adjuncts to universities) in sequence provide a broader, shallower channel for intending school teachers. Superficially this design is not novel and it conforms roughly to contemporary western ideas of national education. Its operation, however, still involves fundamental clashes with older ways.

It is convenient to repeat that although contemporary national policy is characteristically being concentrated on elementary and to a lesser degree on secondary education and emphasis is being given to the provision of technical education, none the less most English educational criteria are still drawn from the old universities. Oxford and Cambridge and the older public schools form a natural alliance of great prestige and ancient tradition, although the universities have proved to be much more responsive to change than the public schools. They and their students are unaccustomed to questioning of their rule and they are almost impregnably autonomous. They are not very aware of the parallel institutions of a technical or local character and can be easily amused or condescending when they find them imitative of their own more obvious characteristics.

The importance of this situation, however, derives from the school examinations given by Oxford and Cambridge and London to all secondary pupils who want to take them. These were originally intended to prevent specialization and unevenness in secondary schools and to provide convenient standards to measure achievement. By this very popular agency the pupils of one set of institutions, the majority of which do not belong within the charmed circle of public school and university, shape their training and ambitions in what must be somewhat alien terms. Moreover, the modern habit of the universities of accepting the First Schools Examination (taken at sixteen) as matriculation makes for undesirable cramming at an early age, and the acceptance of the Second Schools Examination (taken at eighteen) as equivalent to the intermediate university degree examination means that many begin reading for a degree while still in school. They tend to stick to familiar subjects in order to excel. They carry over a reliance on textbooks and a preference for indoctrination over free inquiry. In other words, the junior college or the senior high school of the United States has its equivalent in secondary education in England. If its effect on university education is bad, then the universities and their acolytes, the public schools, must bestir themselves. They must admit that they have made themselves an important qualitative part in a structure whereof they are a tiny minority. If they treasure for themselves certain qualities which they feel are now threatened by popular pressure, they must hasten to assist in substituting a variety of examinations as channels to higher education, in order to divert to other kinds of colleges and universities those students to whose demands they do not wish to accommodate themselves. It should be added that in recent years the examinations have become increasingly varied and there are now substantial examining bodies which are independent of Oxford and Cambridge.

In several senses the oldest and most distinctively English ideas of education are at the present moment almost in the position of a besieged garrison. The obvious contemporary tendencies of the state, of society, and of education are operating in England as elsewhere. The vastly increased field of factual knowledge is an irresistible temptation to specialization at an early stage. Urgent economic pressure makes for demands that education be "practical" from its beginnings. Time seems such an important element that many, from necessity or preference, insist on being instructed instead of reflecting and learning how to learn. Even in the fields of sport and other relaxation the unmistakable tendency is towards watching professionals or being thrilled by mechanical devices. Democracy and socialism are impatient of individual differences, privileges and ways of living. The parliamentarians who emerge from the Union Societies of Oxford and Cambridge are less and less the governing class of England and more and more the true delegates of the masses of the people. The tasks now piled on the ever more powerful state make bureaucracy swamp responsible parliamentary government. *Noblesse oblige,* like "the liberty of the subject," sounds a faintly archaic note.

In these circumstances, it is very important to draw out of the old education the elements which have best withstood changing circumstances and which by their persistent essential appeal commend themselves to systematic perpetuation. It can probably be assumed that for most Englishmen, as for the masses everywhere, education will continue to be indoctrination and training. It would appear that a highly varied, but suitably integrated, educational apparatus will be available in England to sort them out in terms of preference, ability, and national needs. Yet there will also be a small aristocracy of the intellect, accompanied by the sons of wealth or privilege (even Soviet Russia has the Kremlin School for the children of the ruling statesmen), and it seems natural that these will continue to be the students at the public schools and at Oxford and Cambridge. Their aristocracy in those aristocratic institutions will continue to give them a weight far beyond their numbers, and their standards will affect the most sensitive fractions of the whole educational design. In England change has usually been made by compromise between past and present. She has been Fabian, not Leninist or Fascist, in her adaptation to the changing world. Certain traditional elements of the older education seem likely to persist during England's acceptance of what modern states call education and may thereby earn the attention of the outside world.

In the matter of total attitude, the odd combination of strong corporate sense and almost as strong libertarianism is still vigorous. The now almost paradoxical principles of Mill's essay "On Liberty" still strike a responsive chord. The college as a community and the college's pride in its own eccentrics are not incompatible. There is also the combination of aristocracy with tolerant assimilation of brains or wealth, even when these have lowly social recommendation. Granted a sense of internal station and of progression in local authority, a fine democracy exists within the chosen group. For a large part of behaviour, a code of manners is considered incumbent. Its superficials may be a sort of traditional posturing, but its core is the surviving sense of *noblesse oblige.* In general the highest tribute is reserved, not for the outstanding specialist in knowledge, but for the richest personality. It is here that physical fitness and sportsmanlike playing of games come into the design. The man among men, Cecil Rhodes's seldom attained ideal for his Oxford scholars, is the desired product of this education. It is tacitly assumed that he will be the active director of affairs and will call upon the specialists for assistance when he needs it. His trust in them will be great, but in turn they will accept as natural his use and disposition of their knowledge.

Such concepts throw a good deal of light upon general method in education. To begin with, a sharp break has been made between boyish and manly education, hitherto at about eighteen, but now working down toward sixteen, as it used to be before the nineteenth century. Boyish education means predominantly the acquisition of tools, manly education their use. The old almost exclusive emphasis on the classics is rapidly altering and a new grouping of subjects is taking their place. The basic tool is mastery of the English language, next to it the ability to *use* one foreign language (classical or modern), and, following, elementary knowledge of mathematics, history, geography, economics, physics, and chemistry. There is a similarity here (but in the schools) to the orientation and training courses which inadequate high-school training has forced American colleges to provide for their freshmen. Incidentally, it is felt that the break between this and manly education can be emphasized by not accepting the Second Schools Examination as equivalent to any examination towards the university degree.

The provision of abundant opportunities for the playing of games in both boyish and manly education is an underlying assumption. On the purely intellectual side, manly education, for most of those who seek it, means more than anything else the development of an agile and acquisitive mind. No one presumes to define what a "general education" should embrace, but there is enthusiastic belief that almost any broad field of study which is kept humane rather than allowed to be utilitarian can be used as a mental gymnasium. Lectures and textbooks are distrusted, but the give-and-take of tutorial discussion and the reading of special monographs are confidently maintained. The phrase "to read for" a school or tripos, that is, prepare for a final comprehensive examination and the first degree, is most appropriate, and "reading parties" during vacations mean the transportation of many books to a quiet country spot where discussion by members of the group of what they have read can take place. The underlying principle is of education as being the revelation of the desirability of self-education and the two methods are learning how to learn and how to defend judgments.

This general scheme for manly education is considered to be a wise, almost a necessary, preliminary for specialists, whether professional, as university teachers, doctors, lawyers, engineers, or the pioneers of further knowledge, as researchers in the humanities and natural sciences. After receiving the first degree, professional specialists should go to their own guilds, to teachers' colleges, medical and surgical colleges, Inns of Court, and colleges of engineering. The other specialists should remain within the university, assisted when necessary by scholarships until some time convenient to record their achievement by the granting of a graduate degree. From their ranks are normally recruited the tutors of the colleges, with a considerable exchange among the universities.

The actual content of work, mastery of which would secure the first university degree, is determined by a number of habitual divisions of knowledge and human curiosity. Breadth, however, is insisted upon and is achieved by subject divisions within the larger divisions which are in turn emphasized in the final comprehensive examinations. Yet the rare person, who even at this stage in his education has satisfied some deeper curiosities than are ordinary, can use the generous options open to him in the examinations to display his erudition or even confidently take considerable liberties with the formal apparatus. The examiners' emphasis is on thought about matter rather than merely on matter and the questions they ask quickly separate the merely acquisitive from the intellectually distinguished.

Broadly speaking, this education contains almost none of the instruction which generations of American students have described as "cultural." Few men except specialists study English literature, and no others are encouraged to. There are no degree courses in fine arts or in the appreciation of music. The reason lies in assumptions appropriate enough to the privileged young men who were at the universities before the war, but which have always meant an additional handicap to the poor student or the one who came from a meagre intellectual or aesthetical home background. It has been assumed that the university student would already have read the great books and would have learned of his own intellectual heritage well enough to let his own taste guide him after passing out of boyhood. It has also been assumed that if his tastes ran to painting or sculpture or music he would already have begun to cultivate in himself the appropriate knowledge and discrimination. Temperament and taste have been so unanimously regarded as being the sacred concern of the individual that the most which diffident university communities have been able to bring themselves to do is to assist voluntary self-cultivation by the provision of libraries, galleries, choral societies and music halls. With these facilities students may cultivate themselves for their own satisfaction.

The persistent traditional elements which have been generalized and arbitrarily woven into a design above have never materialized and may never do so in anything like the purity and simplicity which has been given to them. Yet they do form an ideological core for the universities in the present time of stress and change, and within the terms of that ideology compromise will be made and compromise whose influence will continue to be felt in secondary and even in primary education. The English university idea seems to many to be the survival of an aristocracy which is anomalous in days of democracy and socialism. It is aristocratic, but it perpetually purges itself of the dominance of mere birth and property and it has been alert towards social and economic change. What remains to be seen is whether it has now really become anomalous or whether it might not be an almost necessary and significant coping-stone for the new society now in the building. The world's new societies, fascist, communist, state socialist, or democratic parliamentarian, do not customarily make much of the existence or the usefulness of aristocracies, yet all of them have them in one guise or another. It may be that Fabian England can quietly go on maintaining an aristocracy, using it for her political and social designs and welding it firmly to her educational structure. This would at least be not alien to her own tradition.

EDUCATION IN FRANCE: ITS THEORY, PRACTICE AND WORTH

BY
JACQUES BARZUN AND ROBERT VALEUR

V

A DESCRIPTION OF FRENCH EDUCATION

To understand the educational system of France it is necessary not only to be familiar with its internal and governmental organization but also to appreciate the spirit and purpose which animate it. The present brief survey, therefore, is divided into three parts: descriptive, critical, and comparative.

1. *Introduction*

The basic principle of the French educational system is that of centralization under state control. Historically, it is but one aspect of the reforms undertaken by the Revolutionary assemblies and completed by Napoleon for the purpose of putting an end to local particularism in France. The former provinces were abolished together with their privileges and recast in the new mold of the departments, administered by prefects dependent upon the central administration. Each department was likewise divided into *arrondissements* under subprefects, themselves dependent upon the prefect and through him upon the government. Each *arrondissement* in this scheme was in turn divided into *cantons,* comprising a given number of *communes*. Fiscal centralization replaced the traditional distinction between the *pays d'état* and *pays d'élection*. Uniform codes henceforth applied to regions both of written and of customary law. Lastly, a University of France was created under the headship of a Grand Master, taking rank as minister of state, who, through a complex hierarchy, paralleling the several hierarchies—administrative, judicial, military, and financial—was enabled to exercise his control of French education to the very outermost *commune* of France.

In its present form, the University of France has at its head the Minister of Public Instruction in place of the Grand Master of the Imperial University. He is a member of the cabinet, on the same footing as the other ministers, and is like them responsible to the chambers. French education is thus an integral part of the governmental machinery, so that a cabinet may be overthrown after a pedagogical debate, as well as upon any other more obviously political question. The Minister of Public Instruction is assisted by a deliberative council—the *Conseil supérieur de l'instruction publique,* created in 1880, and comprising *ex-officio* members as well as elected representatives of the several educational units mentioned below. The council advise the minister on all projects relating to curricula, administrative and disciplinary regulations, standards of study, examinations, and requirements for degrees.[1] The minister is also assisted by bureaus, divided into three groups, headed by directors of higher, secondary, and primary education, respectively.

Just as France is divided into departments for administrative purposes, so for education it is divided into sixteen "academies."[2] Each of these academies extends over a territory covering from four to six departments. At the head of each is a rector, directly subordinate to the Minister of Public Instruction in Paris. Unlike the latter, however, he is not a politician, but a regular professor in the field of higher education, appointed by the government to preside over an academy district.[3] The rector has general administrative powers over all public educational establishments within his academy—primary, secondary, technical, and vocational.[4] Since there is one university in each academy, located at the chief town (*chef-lieu*), making sixteen universities in France, the rector is president of the university council. As such, however, he wields much less power over the university than an American university president. He is assisted in his task by as many academy inspectors as there are departments

[1] We should also mention the three advisory committees—on higher, secondary, and primary education—which give advice relating to appointments, transfers, and promotions within the teaching personnel.

[2] Seventeen, if the Academy of Alger is included. The academies of continental France are: Paris, Aix-Marseille, Besançon, Bordeaux, Caen, Clermont-Ferrand, Dijon, Grenoble, Lille, Lyon, Montpellier, Nancy, Poitiers, Rennes, Strasbourg, and Toulouse.

[3] It happens, nevertheless, that such a professor becomes a rector after having been for a time deputy or senator; but he cannot hold both the political and the educational post.

[4] He is assisted by an academic council, chiefly concerned with disciplinary action over the personnel of private institutions and secondary public schools.

under his rule.[5] In other words, there is in the chief town of each department, an academy inspector, directly under the rector, which inspector is in charge of all secondary educational institutions of the department. This inspector is assisted in turn by inspectors of primary education, whose task, as is indicated by their name, is to inspect the primary schools of the department.[6]

It is thus apparent that the University of France forms a logically elaborated hierarchy. When, for example, a professor at the *Collège d'Autun* wishes to be transferred or promoted, he must address his request to the head of his institution, namely, the principal of the collège. The latter will transmit it, with comments, to the academy inspector of the department, at Mâcon; it will then be forwarded with additional comment to the rector of the academy, at Lyons, who will submit it to the Minister of Public Instruction, in Paris. The minister will have the petitioner's record and the opinions of the intermediary heads examined by the bureaus in charge of secondary education, and will then take action. The final decision will reach the professor of the *Collège d'Autun* only after having passed once more through the rector of the Lyons Academy, the academy inspector of Mâcon, and the principal of the collège at Autun. The process may be a trifle slow, but it is at the price of this slowness, one may truthfully say, that nothing occurs in the entire French educational system that escapes the notice of the minister, or at least of his bureaus. It is at this price, again, that centralized education has been established and assured in France.[7]

At the same time, it does not follow that in France the state enjoys a monopoly of education. There are numerous private schools

[5] Paris constitutes an exception in having several such inspectors, as have also the departments of *Nord* and *Alger*.

[6] There is also in each department a departmental council for primary instruction, presided over by the prefect, with the academy inspector as vice-president, the function of which is to enforce the regulations and programs issued by the higher authorities.

[7] This is not altogether true of primary education, which, as will be seen below, enjoys a certain amount of local independence within each department. Also outside the centralized hierarchy are seventeen inspectors general of secondary education, and twelve inspectors of primary education.

(*écoles libres*) for primary, secondary, and higher education. The majority are Catholic schools, and the parents can comply with the legal requirement of compulsory education for children between the ages of six and thirteen by sending them to the *écoles libres* rather than to public schools.[8] But the state has retained the right to require that professors in these "free" schools be holders of certain university diplomas, conferred by examination juries composed exclusively of professors from state institutions. The private schools are, moreover, subject to periodic inspection by public authorities. On the other hand, whereas the primary public schools are open to all without fees, that is not the case with the "free" schools, which depend for their maintenance upon payment of tuition by the students.[9] The result is that parents who send their children to private schools pay not only for the upkeep of these schools but also contribute like every one else in the form of taxes to the maintenance of public schools. It is not astonishing, therefore, that the number of students attending private schools has fallen from one-third of the total of children in primary schools in 1886 to one-fifth in 1925.

As regards public secondary schools (which are not free, though the principle of free tuition is being gradually applied to them also) , they still retain the advantage of being less costly than the private ones, because they receive state aid. In general, they have also the benefit of a better trained teaching personnel, especially in the sciences and modern languages.

Similarly, the institutions of higher education that are private, such as the Catholic Institute in Paris,[10] suffer the same financial disadvantages as the private secondary schools. Furthermore, the diplomas they award have a merely honorary value: they do not confer upon the holders the same precise advantages, determined by state laws and decrees, as those bearing the state seal. Thus, an

---

[8] The law of 1901 prohibiting the existence of church associations, and the laws of 1905-7 enforcing the separation of Church and State, have not interfered with the existence of Catholic schools. At first, the members of religious orders had to give up either teaching or monastic life; later, and particularly since the war, widespread toleration of their activities in both capacities has been the fact.

[9] In 1929-30 there were 11,787 "free" schools giving instruction to 844,000 children.

[10] Private institutions of higher learning may not style themselves "universities."

LL.B. from a French state law school is required for admission to the Bar, for the entrance examination to the Bench, and for other important positions; which means that in practice a student who prepares at a private law school in France must take his examinations at the end of each year at the neighboring state law school. He is tested there by a board upon which his own instructors are not represented; and he thereby suffers a serious disadvantage as compared with his fellows in the state school. To summarize, it may be said that if the French government does not exercise a legal monopoly over education, it does not control it the less thoroughly and effectively in practice.

2. *Primary Education*

As we have seen, public instruction in France is divided into three orders or categories—primary, secondary, and higher education. There are, however, certain institutions which by their nature belong to none of these classes, but which are connected with them in fact and in law, and will be briefly enumerated later.

At the bottom of the edifice are the primary schools.[11] Although they are the ultimate units in the centralized university scheme of France, and therefore under the control of the Ministry of Public Instruction, they are in reality administered more departmentally than nationally. The primary-school teachers of both sexes are in effect recruited from each department, prepared for their life work in a departmental teachers' normal school situated in the chief town of each department, and after graduation they remain until their retirement in that same department. They are appointed, promoted, and transferred by the prefect, the highest administrative authority in the department—with the advice of the academy inspector, the highest university authority in the department. But the educational autonomy of the department stops at this point. As regards all programs and teaching methods, supreme authority rests with the minister, so that there is almost complete uniformity throughout France.

Since the Guizot Law of 1833, there is at least one primary school in each commune; but it is only in the least populated communes that there is only one school for both boys and girls. Everywhere

[11] An important adjunct to the system below the primary schools is the system of "dame schools" (écoles maternelles) of which there were 3,146 in 1929-30.

else, the two sexes are segregated, and this principle is also applied in secondary schools. The higher institutions form the only exception to the rule.

To return to primary education, it was not until the eighties, that the Ferry Laws (1881-86) made primary education compulsory for all children between the ages of six and thirteen. These laws have been enforced with sufficient rigor to decrease the proportion of illiterate conscripts from 16.12 percent in 1881 to 9.42 percent in 1891; to 5.63 percent in 1901; 4.26 percent in 1911; and 3.51 percent in 1922.[12]

The course of primary instruction is divided into four sections: preparatory, elementary, intermediate, and advanced. Each of the last three requires two years of study, which, with the first, makes a total of seven years, reducible to six for the better students. The subject matters include: moral training, reading, writing, French grammar, French history and geography, arithmetic, general science, drawing, music, physical education, and manual training.

The teachers in the primary schools are themselves the products of this branch of the French system. After seven years in a primary school, they spend three years in post-primary schools (*écoles primaires supérieures*), where they usually follow the "general course," which corresponds roughly to the three years of junior high school in the United States. The prospective teachers must then take competitive examinations to enter the departmental teachers' normal school, and if successful, they study for three years, not only to add to their general culture, but also to learn correct teaching methods.

These methods have often been criticized in France itself, where the name "primary" is sometimes used to designate a limited mind. Possibly the methods may be too severely narrow. They may rely too much on memory and not enough on intelligence; but we shall be better able to discuss in Chapter VI the relation of these methods to the caliber of the students for whom they are intended.

The more intelligent and the wealthier of the primary-school pupils pursue their studies in the post-primary schools, which afford

[12] In 1929, for various causes, among them the war, the percentage had retrogressed to 9.16, but the absolute increase in illiterates represented by this percentage was only 2,000.

an additional three-year course. The last two years offer a choice of a general course, and agricultural course, a manual arts course, a commercial course, and a home economics course for girls. Aside from the general course, these post-primary schools have a distinctly vocational purpose, although general culture is not neglected, and the learning of a foreign language is required of all. These schools, like the primary schools described above, are open to all without fees.

In 1929-30, there were 3,515,000 pupils in the primary schools and 79,600 in the post-primary.

It must be clearly kept in mind in this connection that the pupils in primary schools who wish to further their studies as far as the *baccalauréat* or the university do not enter the post-primary schools after their seven years of elementary training. They go direct to a lycée or a collège. Those who enter the post-primary schools intend only to complete their study of the essentials previously learned, and to acquire the rudiments of a trade. After three years, the majority of these will begin to earn their living. The rest will enter a normal school to become teachers, or else a technical school. In this last category, manual trades, watch-making, textile, tanning, and hotel management are but a few of the subjects available to post-primary school graduates.

3. *Secondary Education*

The scheme of secondary education is perhaps the most remarkable feature of the entire French education system. While primary education is intended for the mass of the people, the lycées and collèges are attended by a relatively restricted élite,[13] which comprises two distinct groups: first, the children of the lower social classes who have shown special ability during their primary studies and who have passed an examination in their respective departments to obtain scholarships enabling them to pursue their education at state expense as far as the *baccalauréat;* second, the children of families sufficiently well off to pay the tuition fees—which are, incidentally, extremely low and which are gradually being abolished—and the expenses of maintenance to the age of seventeen or eighteen—the

[13] Lycées and collèges in France and Algeria were attended by 128,300 boys and 54,600 girls in 1929-30.

normal age for attaining the *baccalauréat*. The boys and girls in this second group have not usually pursued their primary studies in the free public schools attended by the masses, but rather in elementary classes given in the secondary schools themselves as a specific preparation, more direct than that of the primary schools, for the cycle of secondary education properly so called. These elementary classes are given by teachers graduated for the large part from the primary schools but taught along broader lines, better adapted to less numerous classes with a higher intelligence level.[14] Another difference between the two groups of pupils is that those of the first group are somewhat older than those of the second when they enter the sixth grade:[15] the latter are generally 12-13 years old as against 10-11 in the first.

Secondary schools in France are divided into lycées and collèges. Theoretically, there is one lycée for each sex in each department— usually at the chief town; and one collège for each sex in each arrondissement. This rule, however, is subject to numerous exceptions: in the important departments and the large cities there may be several lycées.[16]

From the educational point of view there are no differences between the lycées and the collèges, no more than between the establishments for boys and those for girls. The lycées differ from the collèges only in that the former are national whereas the latter are communal undertakings. The lycées are financed by the state with the aid of tuition fees; the collèges are maintained by the commune in which they are situated. In fact, however, the state grants important subsidies to all communal collèges. In the collèges, the state determines by means of decennial agreements the nature of curricula and the number of instructors; and also appoints the members of the teaching staff with the principal at their head.

The methods of teaching and the subject matter taught in both lycées and collèges are identical. The same programs, established for

[14] In 1930 there were 75,800 pupils in these elementary courses.

[15] The numbering of grades in France follows the reverse order from that used in the United States. The French child begins his school career in the lycée by entering the twelfth grade and graduates by completing the first.

[16] In the Department of the Seine (Paris) there are fourteen lycées and one collège for boys, and seven lycées for girls. In all of France there are 359 lycées and collèges for boys; 169 for girls.

all France by the minister, obtain; and the staffs of both kinds of institution are required to have state diplomas. The only difference may reside in the fact that the quality of the teaching personnel is usually superior in the lycées, the professors in the latter institutions being required to pass a competition called *agrégation*, to test pedagogical aptitude, whereas, to give instruction in a college,[17] it is sufficient to hold a teaching license from a university.

The curricula in the lycées and collèges, not only in France but in the colonies[18] try to reconcile as far as possible the old French notion that it is important to give young men and women a substantial liberal education, and the requirements of modern economic life.

Whereas, in the nineteenth century, French secondary education was almost entirely a "classical" one, intended to endow students with a general culture based upon the study of Latin and Greek, the decrees of 1902 attempted to organize side by side, in the same secondary schools, parallel courses imbued with a common spirit, but organized so as to prepare young men for very diverse careers. On entering the sixth grade (the first year of secondary school) the students were divided into two groups, according to their inclination or that of their families. In Group A, the compulsory study of Latin and the optional study of Greek were combined with a thorough study of French, one modern language and literature, elementary mathematics, general science, history, geography, and freehand drawing. In Group B, still according to the law of 1902, neither Latin nor Greek was studied, but a greater amount of time was devoted to French, the sciences (including mathematics), and modern languages and literatures. At the end of four years, the differentiation between the two groups grew sharper. In the second and first grades, accordingly, students were divided into four instead of two groups.

[17] In 1929-30 there were 121,000 students in the lycées as against 61,900 in the collèges.

[18] French India has two collèges; Indo-China, one collège and one lycée; French West Africa, one lycée; Madagascar, two lycées; the island of Réunion, one lycée; Guadeloupe and Martinique, one lycée each; and New Caledonia and French Guiana, one collège each. French North Africa has even better advantages: Algeria, constituting one academy, comprises six lycées and nine collèges; Tunis has two lycées and one collège; and Morocco, six lycées and two collèges.

Students in the four groups followed the same courses in French, history, and geography. All studied, also, one modern language and literature. Students in Groups A, B, and C had nearly the same programs in Latin. Students in Group D studied no Latin, but an additional modern language in its stead. Only students in Group A had Greek. For students in Group B, a second modern language was substituted for Greek. Groups A and B were the only ones to study ancient history. Group C replaced Greek and ancient history with advanced mathematics and physics and chemistry; the scientific courses for C being identical with those for Group D.

To summarize in tabular form, subjects were distributed among the four groups as follows:

TABLE III

FRENCH SECONDARY EDUCATION, FIFTH AND SIXTH YEARS, 1902-23

SUBJECTS	GROUP A	GROUP B	GROUP C	GROUP D
French	x	x	x	x
Latin	x	x	x	o
Greek	x	o	o	o
Modern Languages	one	two	one	two
Free-hand Drawing	elective	elective	x	x
Mechanical Drawing	o	o	x	x
Modern History	x	x	x	x
Ancient History	x	x	o	o
Geography	x	x	x	x
Elementary Mathematics	x	x	o	o
Advanced Mathematics	o	o	x	x
Physics	o	o	x	x
Chemistry	o	o	x	x

After the first (i.e., last) grade, students attended secondary school for one additional year, devoted either to philosophy or to mathematics according to the purpose of their preparation. Groups A and B were in fact fitted only for philosophy; C and D being alone in a position to choose between philosophy and mathematics.

But

the multiplicity of educational choices which the Law of 1902 had introduced into our lycées necessarily resulted in a retrogression of the liberal arts before the encroachment of special disciplines. A principally literary training was given to the students of Groups A and B who thus lacked the corrective of scientific precision in their habits of thought. Those in Group D received a purely scientific education and thus were deprived of the flexibility that an application to letters develops in the mind. As for students in Group C, for whom semi-literary and semi-scientific curricula had been designed, they were unable to assimilate the divergent disciplines. Forced to make a choice, they usually stressed the sciences with a view to their future career, which reacted to the detriment of their literary capacities. Throughout the system, in short, specialized training meant an incomplete culture. . . .[19]

The government therefore resolved to simplify the scheme of secondary education and to increase the requirements in those disciplines most likely to contribute to the formation of the mind and judgment of the students. But the conflict was sharp between the partisans of the classical studies and the great number of those who did not want to see the lycée abandon the preparation of French youth for modern economic life. At the beginning, the champions of classical studies triumphed with the principle that a liberal education can suffice for all occasions, and that the principal task of secondary education is to form young men and women who, whatever their ultimate specialization, will be characterized by the ability to find an interest in the diverse creations of the mind. Why not, urged the classical-minded, send to post-primary schools or to technical and vocational schools those desirous of obtaining a purely utilitarian training?

It was in answer to this query that Léon Bérard, Minister of Public Instruction in 1923, decided upon a radical reform which was applied in part during the school year 1923-24.[20] Instead of dividing the students into two groups, A and B, they were all to follow during the first four years of secondary school identical courses, including compulsory Latin and Greek. Beginning with the second grade (the fifth year), the students could choose between a classical group implying compulsory Latin and optional Greek and a modern group involving the advanced study of French, building upon the Graeco-Latin culture of the first cycle of four years, and including in addition the study of a second modern language. As for the scientific

---

[19] "Le plan d'études secondaires de 1925, Préface des instructions relatives à son application," *Journal Officiel,* 3 septembre 1925.

[20] *Décret du 3 mai 1923* and *Arrêté du 3 décembre 1923.*

program, it remained identical for all students during the first six years. Only in the seventh year was specialization possible through option as in the past between the mathematics and philosophy sections.

This reform aroused lively opposition. The compulsory study of Latin carried with it the danger of discouraging many students and of denying them access to higher education through failure at the *baccalauréat*. The study of Latin in France has traditionally been pursued according to extremely ruthless methods which eliminate students devoid of literary instinct. However desirable in itself, Graeco-Latin culture was not considered by the majority to be essential to a scientific, professional, commercial, or military career. Further, it was thought undesirable by many to have to rely altogether on the products of the primary schools to fill these positions. The lycées and collèges should graduate men and women destined to fill equally the ranks of the educated élite in the ordinary pursuits of economic life and of the smaller group of those devoted entirely to letters and the arts.

These are some of the reasons which led, under the leadership of Herriot, to the reinstatement as early as the opening of classes in the fall of 1924 of the groups Sixth B and Fifth B.[21] The next year the program of studies[22] provided for the application, now complete, of a plan of "modern" secondary education for France, parallel throughout to the classical studies. The present scheme specifically avoids the creation of impassable barriers between the two courses and tries to afford as far as possible a unified training for students through the use of identical methods and corresponding curricula.

In the course of the first six years of study (from the sixth grade through the first) the students of the classical group (Group A) take two-thirds of their work in common with those of the modern group (Group B). These courses deal with the French language and literature, history, geography, one modern language, and freehand drawing. Both groups likewise follow—and this is the principal characteristic of the new system—the same courses in mathematics

---

[21] *Décret du 9 août* and *Arrêté du 11 août 1924.*
[22] *Journal Officiel*, 3 septembre 1925.

and the natural and physical sciences.[23] Students in Group A necessarily take Latin; they begin Greek in the fourth grade (third year), but can drop it in the second grade (fifth year), substituting, if they wish, the study of a foreign literature and civilization. Students in Group B take correspondingly greater amounts of French; they do further intensive work in history and geography, modern languages and the natural sciences; they begin in the fourth grade (third year) an additional modern language and in the second grade (fifth year) the study of a foreign literature and civilization. This system seeks to avoid the dangers of a too hasty specialization.

It is only after six years of secondary school that the students must choose between the two sections—mathematics and philosophy—that complete the edifice. Students in the mathematics section usually go into scientific careers—research in science, medicine, engineering, business administration, or military life. Students in the philosophy section generally plan to become professional men—lawyers, economists, diplomats, writers, and artists. Even within these two branching groups, the study of history and geography, modern languages, natural science, logic, and ethics remains common to both. Other subjects studied by the two groups are divided as indicated in the following table:

TABLE IV

FRENCH SECONDARY EDUCATION, SEVENTH YEAR, SINCE 1902

PHILOSOPHY SECTION	MATHEMATICS SECTION
Mathematics (1½ hrs. weekly)	Mathematics (9 hrs. weekly)
Physics and Chemistry (4 hrs. weekly)	Physics and Chemistry (5 hrs. weekly)
Psychology	
Metaphysics	
Literary Criticism	

These studies lead to the degree of bachelor, a state diploma conferred after examinations taking place at the end of the two last years of study, and enabling the holder to enter the university and occupy certain positions in the civil service. The examining board

[23] It will be remembered that the 1902 provisions offered no physical sciences during the first four years in the case of Group A, and the last two of A and B; see above.

includes professors from the nearest university and professors from
a lycée other than that of the candidate.[24]

Professors for the lycées and collèges are recruited in the following manner. Professors in the collèges must be holders of a teaching
license granted by a state university; the best among collège professors may be appointed to a lycée, but this is an exception to the rule
that professors in the lycée must have passed the competitive *agrégation,* held each year in Paris and open to the above-mentioned li-
cense-holders. The competition consists of written examinations
lasting seven hours and the delivery of prepared lectures one hour in
length, designed to test the aptitude of the candidate for teaching.
The number admitted is very small.

4. *Higher Education*

We must now revert to the above-mentioned principle adopted
by the French government of not retaining to itself the monopoly
of education. Any Frenchman or naturalized foreigner over twenty-
five years of age, or any association legally organized within the
country which has filed a declaration either with the rector or with
the inspector of an academy, has the right to give courses or open
institutions of higher learning. No one, however, is permitted to
teach medicine and pharmacy if he has not complied with the requirements for practicing these professions. At the same time, private
establishments of higher education are closely supervised and limited
in their activities by the academic control of the state. They must
communicate both the list of instructors and the programs of studies
to the state authorities. They are periodically inspected by delegates
from the Ministry of Public Instruction, whose powers, however, are
limited to insuring that private teaching is not contrary to good
morals, the constitution, and the laws.

We have seen, in addition, that the granting of university degrees
such as the *baccalauréat, licence, doctorat,* is reserved to the state
universities. This assures the latter so considerable an advantage over
private institutions of higher education that no serious competition

---

[24] Professors in the collèges do not sit upon these boards, before which both
lycée and collège candidates must appear.

between the two is possible. We shall therefore limit ourselves in this survey to the description of the state institutions.

In its details, the present scheme of university organization in France is of recent date. In Revolutionary and post-Revolutionary times, higher education in France was vested in schools—heirs to the royal schools, themselves often descended from the medieval universities—independent one from another though all subordinated to the central government. Since 1896[25] these schools or faculties have been grouped into universities, properly so called—autonomous bodies situated in the chief town of each academy.[26]

Each university comprises theoretically all the public institutions of higher learning to be found within the academy district. Other establishments of the same order, and scientific institutes depending upon other ministries of state than education, or from local bodies such as the department, the commune, the chamber of commerce, or special foundations, can be associated with the several faculties on the basis of special agreements.[27] A university can also in certain cases create an annex in some other academy district and organize institutes in foreign countries.

A large measure of autonomy from the state has been granted the French universities. Each has its own budget and is administered by a council presided over by the rector of the academy. The university council includes representatives from each faculty or school, and persons outside the university chosen by the council itself. Students elected by their fellows sit on the council when it deliberates on disciplinary matters. Each university includes—with the exception of certain lesser universities which lack faculties of law and medicine—four faculties which are, in hierarchical order, the faculties of law, medicine,[28] science, and letters.

The outstanding characteristic of these faculties is that they are essentially academic and not professional schools. Their courses do

[25] *Loi du 10 juillet.*

[26] There are in France itself sixteen universities, plus one in Algeria and one in Indo-China.

[27] Cf. in the United States the understandings subsisting between universities and city museums, state libraries, and so forth.

[28] The most important universities have a fifth faculty, that of pharmacy; the rest have a joint faculty of medicine and pharmacy.

not in fact prepare students for the exercise of a profession. They do not aim at the formation of engineers, architects, or librarians. They seek to impart to the students a body of theoretic knowledge which they will be able to use with profit later in the exercise of their calling.

It does not follow, however, that the universities take no thought of professional teaching. The universities organize, frequently with the coöperation and financial aid of local bodies, a variety of schools and institutes more or less directly connected with such and such of the university faculties. University professors give their services, together with the appropriate technicians and practitioners. If we take as an example the University of Lyons, we find that the faculty of law has organized an institute of applied law, an institute of comparative law, and a school for notaries.[29] The faculty of medicine and pharmacy has institutes of bacteriology, of hygiene, forensic medicine, an institute of hydrology and medical climatology; the faculty of science has organized a school of industrial chemistry, a school for tanning and allied arts, an agronomic institute, an observatory, and a maritime station for biology; the faculty of letters has an institute of pedagogy, an institute for the history of art, an institute of geography, and one of oriental studies.

Outside the University of Lyons, but in the city itself and making use of the university facilities, are to be found a business high school, an engineering school, a school of textile manufactures, and a school of dentistry.[30]

Certain large cities in France, notably Paris, boast, in addition, schools of fine arts, conservatories of music, and engineering and military schools, which are not attached to any university but which give courses included in the term "higher education." Above and outside the centralized hierarchy of the French universities stands the *Collège de France*. Organized in 1530 by Francis I, this institution has ever since given an opportunity to the most eminent authorities in all fields, whether they hold university degrees or not,

[29] The French notaries are not mere recording clerks but fulfill some of the functions of the English solicitors.

[30] The list of similar institutions connected with the University of Paris would of course be considerably more extensive.

to present their researches to all interested students without payment of fees.

Professors in the field of higher education are variously selected by the several faculties. In letters and science, the faculty itself elects incumbents to the vacant chairs. The only limit to their choice is that the candidate must hold a doctor's degree. The faculties of law and medicine require not only the doctorate but in fact, though not in law, that the candidate have successfully passed the particularly rigorous competitive examination known as the *agrégation*.[31] Professors are not removable at least until the statutory retiring age of seventy.[32]

In general, only holders of the *baccalauréat* can enter the universities.[33] At the university, students are not subject to frequent "quizzing"; they undergo semi-annual examinations in the faculties of letters and science, and annual ones in the faculties of law and medicine.

Most usually, it requires three years to obtain a license in law, letters, or science. Again usually, the degree of doctor is granted chiefly on the basis of one or two theses, which naturally require an indeterminate amount of time to prepare. In medicine the doctorate takes six years to complete; while in the other schools of the state, not connected with the universities as explained above, the stipulations vary with the given training and diploma.

[31] This *agrégation* must not be confused with that required of professors in the lycées. They differ in degree of rigor though not in kind.

[32] The limit for members of the Institute of France is 75. The Institute, which is the collective name for the five academies, is an honorary self-perpetuating body not integrated with the educational system.

[33] Between 1890 and 1930 the number of students enrolled in the state universities has grown from 16,587 to 73,601. Of the latter total, 16,254 are foreigners.

VI

A CRITICAL ANALYSIS OF FRENCH EDUCATION

1. *Primary Education*

The principal criticism which may be leveled against the French system of primary education is that it does not sufficiently prepare the student for practical life. Especially in the country districts, it would be far more important to teach future farmers the uses of chemical fertilizers and modern methods of agriculture than to impart in detail the genealogy of Clovis and Brunhilde.

The post-primary schools fill this need of vocational and practical training much more adequately, but only a very slight proportion of the total primary-school pupils pursue their studies for the additional three years.[34] At this point, certainly, there is room for great improvement in both the theory and the practice of French education; for we have already referred to the fact that in France itself the methods of primary-school teaching have been severely criticized, usually on the ground that they depend too much on memorizing and lead to mechanical habits of thought. The absorption of countless rules of grammar and arithmetic or fragmentary passages of literature results frequently in a very imperfect understanding of the substance. Still, it must be realized on the other hand that the majority of primary-school children come from working-class and peasant families and usually show no taste for the play of the mind upon subject matter. They seem to need sheer discipline in order to acquire the elements of literacy in such a way as to retain them in field or factory; at the same time, it must not be forgotten that this same discipline often reveals in these same children outstanding capacities, which intelligent schoolmasters are not slow to encourage. Enabled by these talents to enter the secondary-school system, working-class children not seldom outmatch in scholastic ability the sons of the

[34] Roughly 2.5 percent for the years 1920-30.

business and professional classes, in spite of the latter's advantages of
heredity and environment as well as of schooling in the special elementary classes of lycée and collège.

As a healthful sign of the inquiring and experimental spirit in
French education today, the latest development sponsored by the
Ministry of Public Instruction—the Labbé system—must be briefly described here. It bears the name of a bureau head in the ministry,
who, as director of primary education, felt the lack of coördination
between the theoretical and practical branches of teaching criticized
above, especially for children who do not plan to enter professional
life. M. Labbé's system, which he terms the "technical humanities,"
consists in adapting the traditional practice of *explication* to the requirements of modern life for the masses. Let us suppose a class in
a primary or vocational school in which the children are destined
to become artisans. The teacher, instead of teaching his pupils
French, history, geography, and technical terminology in separate
water-tight compartments, does so simultaneously by discussions he
has previously prepared, which unite these branches at their common points. To translate an example into English terms, let us
imagine that in spelling or French the word "drill" arises. The
teacher first explains, if need be, the meaning of the word; its derivation, gender, and so forth; and its cognate significations—military
drill, the cloth of that name, and the various kinds of implements
so called. In connection with military drill, he may indicate that it
was Louvois who first introduced marching in step into the French
army, and refer to other innovations in military formation from the
time of Caesar to that of Napoleon. In dealing with the textile, he
can, if properly equipped, briefly describe the various manufactur-
ing operations, state where in France or Europe the stuff is made,
and thus teach both economics and geography; finally, in dealing
with the numerous kinds of drills—hand, mechanical, and electric—
he has a vast subject matter limited only by his own knowledge.

At first it may seem as if the Labbé system were an artificial and
somewhat far-fetched pedagogical method, but a moment's reflection
will suggest that one's own best teachers in early youth did that very
thing in those interesting asides which always remain clearest in

one's memory. The *explication de textes*[35] is nothing more than a limited use of this method, which, psychologically, is the universal one of association. By association, the skillful teacher will impart spelling, French grammar and usage, history, geography, economics, the principles of mechanics, and as much science as he will deem suited to the age of his pupils. To be sure, trained and skillful teachers will be needed to apply the principle, as they are needed to apply every other principle. The "associations" must not be allowed to fatigue the child and must not wander too far afield, but as a direct path to the child's imagination, as an integration of words, thoughts, and living facts, the Labbé method seems an improvement upon the arbitrary division into "subjects"; especially in vocational teaching, where the pupils themselves are not decided about their future trade and therefore must not be taught exhaustively any one skill at the expense of other attractive choices.[36]

2. Secondary Education

Since the Herriot reform of 1925, secondary-school curricula are not so exclusively classical in content as they previously were. The largest share of time, however, is still given to the study of French, Latin, and mathematics. The teaching of science, history, geography and the modern languages undeniably comes second. As for the social sciences, apart from some rudiments of ethics and sociology during the very last year of study, they are entirely overlooked. The existence of such a subject as economics, for instance, is not even taken cognizance of.

Consistent with this lack of practical purpose is the way in which subjects like history and geography are taught. The object of their inclusion in the curriculum is not to acquaint the student with a mass of facts or a body of knowledge, but rather to furnish him with materials upon which he can learn to exercise his mind—to reflect and to reason. As an illustration we may cite here the final examination question in geography given to one of the co-authors of this chapter when he was but seventeen years of age: "Compare, in the light of their geographic positions, the part played by England in Europe

---

[35] See below under secondary education.

[36] For a full and more precise exposition of M. Labbé's scheme, see *Revue universitaire* for January, 1928.

and by Japan in Asia." It is obvious that to write a dissertation of two hours on such a subject requires something more than a good memory. The possession of factual knowledge is not on that account despised in French secondary schools, since it is impossible to think *in abstracto,* without supporting conclusions with data. The point here made is simply that of the two elements without which no thinking is possible, the French system definitely emphasizes, cultivates, requires the ability to think.

In the application of this rule, the French secondary school is thoroughgoing. In the teaching of modern languages, the aim of the instructor is not so much to enable the student to speak a foreign tongue fluently as to have him decipher correctly and translate felicitously literary texts in the given foreign language. The student may be completely at a loss when it comes to ordering a meal in Breslau or London,[37] but he is usually able to produce a very fair French equivalent of a passage in Shakespeare or Goethe. His knowledge of the foreign nation's literary history is likewise remarkably adequate.

Naturally, it is from the principal subject matters that the formation of the mind aimed at by the French system is to be expected. The study of the French language, therefore, primarily seeks to inculcate the correct, and even literary use of the student's mother tongue. In this respect, professors in the lycées and collèges display a kind of fierce implacability worthy of a greater reward. Both writers can recall in their own school days the professorial practice of tearing up any composition containing a single misspelling, with a consequent zero for the day's work. The question of spelling, however, in spite of this fact, is of secondary importance in the teaching of French. The main devices for disciplining the mind are text criticism (*explication de textes*) and composition.

Text criticism consists in subjecting a difficult passage from a

[37] But cf. the report of an American exchange instructor in a French small-town lycée: "The students understood English quite well. They were eager to learn how to improve their speaking knowledge of it, too. I think I can safely say that they speak English better than American students of the same age speak French. However, it must not be forgotten that all have had from 2 to 6 years of English." Herbert S. Shapiro, *Report to the Institute of International Education,* Le Puy, France, January 10, 1931.

French author—twenty lines of prose or verse—to the most complete
and varied examination. Style, grammatical features or difficulties,
terminology, figures of speech, ideas and their relation to the author
and his times—all these are painstakingly threshed out for the purpose of developing the students' critical sense, literary judgment, and
discrimination in the use of language.[38]

The composition is really an essay requiring several hours of work
—three is the usual minimum—and occurring in a variety of forms:
description, narration, letter, oration, leading up in order of difficulty to the most elaborate of all, the literary dissertation. Particular
attention is paid to the presentation of original ideas in logical order,
beyond the mechanical requirements of correctness, nicety of vocabulary, and so forth. Certain instructors even go so far as to require
the composition to be divided into numbered paragraphs, each summarized in the margin in a single sentence, the body of the work to
be preceded by an introduction and followed by a conclusion.

One such composition a week is required during the first six years
of secondary school, and the only change in the seventh consists in
substituting philosophical subjects for literary ones. It may be super-
fluous to add that a French student, from the age of twelve on, never
contemplates the possibility of writing a composition offhand. A
rough draft, worked and re-worked, is the basis of his finished product, for which he will esteem himself lucky to receive the mark of
14/20.

The study of Latin, which takes up so many semester hours, has a
twofold function. In the first place, the French language being derived from the Latin, a knowledge of the latter facilitates a correct
understanding of the former. In the second place, Latin is, in the
eyes of French educators, admirably suited to sharpening both the
mental processes and the literary instincts. The logical thinking
found in most Latin authors and the precision of their speech make
the task of translating them (version latine) a strenuous but beneficial exercise. A rather short passage—again twenty lines of prose or
verse—is assigned to the students, who have three hours to produce
a French version that is both as literal and as clear as possible. The

[38] For this technique see G. Rudler, L'Explication française, principes et applications, Paris, 1902.

two qualities are not always reconcilable, but in the difficulty lies the profit of the performance. In addition to this weekly task, the student takes part in numerous *explications* of Latin texts during class hours.

The only exceptions to this general method of teaching and testing occur in the science and history classes, where the instructors and students more nearly resemble their American counterparts in the use of lectures and recitations as pedagogical devices. But in all subjects, the type of examination invariably tests the capacities developed by the teaching of Latin and French, namely, analytic skill and powers of synthetic expression.

Examinations, consequently, are of the essay or subjective type and bear usually upon a single topic which the student has the privilege of selecting from a list of three. The question is phrased so as to make the student think and produce a complete treatment within a limited time. The time allotted depends upon the age of the student and the nature of the subject tested, the average being three hours; less during the first four years and more during the last year (philosophy and mathematics sections). The basis of judgment of the papers is, as usual, organization of knowledge rather than knowledge itself. The preparation of a first draft laboriously improved is here also a current practice. One such examination is given in each course every three months; and at the end of the two last years in the lycée comprehensive examinations, both oral and written, are given by a board of professors outside the lycée. Upon satisfying these examiners by his previous work and his present answers, the student is awarded the *baccalauréat* or bachelor's degree.

The philosophy of the entire system of secondary education in France might be summed up as the inculcation of thinking techniques—literary, historical, linguistic, geographical, and scientific. From the student's point of view it is not enough that he has worked hard: he must be clear about what he has learned; after seven years of training he must prove that he knows how to think about some new and unexpected angle of his subject matter. He is as responsible as an adult for what he says and writes, and he cannot hastily commit himself in speech or writing in the hope that a few disconnected facts will suffice or that he will be credited with good intentions.

The remark of a chemistry examiner is typical, that it is useless to remember the molecular weight of chlorine when tables can be consulted; but essential to know the chemical significance of molecular weights.

Whatever the intrinsic value of this philosophy, it is clear that its practical value depends altogether on the teaching body. It is unfortunately difficult to judge objectively the qualities and faults of secondary-school teachers in France. Certain remarks are nevertheless relevant here.

Governmental centralization throughout the scheme brings about well-nigh complete uniformity in the recruiting of teaching staffs, which in turn guarantees that every professor in the lycée or collège has undergone a long and arduous training. Taken together with the uniformity in curricula, this standardization results in the possession of a common cultural background by French youth of both sexes. National homogeneity, at least for the élite, is thus made possible.

On the other hand, the control by distant state bureaus of lycées and collèges and the very fact of centralization leave the teachers largely independent of the particular lycée or collège in which they teach. As state employees, they are guaranteed immunity from the possible arbitrary acts of their immediate superiors. This freedom from intellectual or actual restraint is of course necessary for all scholarly pursuits. But it is unfortunately subject to abuses. Lazy and unconscientious teachers continue in their posts, to the detriment of their students. The price paid for complete liberty brings returns, however, in the intellectual honesty that prevails in a teaching personnel whose convictions are not subject to censure and who can, further, devote themselves to entirely disinterested research in their field.

As regards the students, it can truthfully be said that the intelligence level is remarkably high, in spite of relative youth. Quickness, precision, and subtlety are their distinguishing features, though it must be categorically asserted that the discipline to which the best students subject themselves frequently robs them of spontaneity and health. French lycée and collège students live a semi-military, semi-monastic life which savors of medievalism. It must be remembered that the French lycées were organized by Napoleon on the monastic basis of the Jesuit collèges and in the spirit of the imperial barracks. These facts serve to explain the origin of the uniform worn by the boarders in the lycées, the marching in ranks inside the school, and the use of the drum for signals during the day's routine.

Students are divided into four groups: boarders (*internes*), semi-boarders (*demi-pensionnaires*), supervised day students (*externes surveillés*), and ordinary day students (*externes simples*). The boarders live in the lycée; the semi-boarders eat and study in the lycée but sleep outside; the supervised day students stay after classes to do their home work under the guidance of assistants, together with the boarders and the semi-boarders. The schedule of a boarder in a French lycée will give some idea of what is meant by physical discipline in that institution:

Waking drum at 6:00 A.M. every day including Sunday. Daily: 6:00-6:30, toilet; 6:30-7:00, study period; 7:00-7:15, breakfast; 7:15-7:30, recess; 7:30-8:00, study period; 8-11, classes of one or two hours; 11-12, study period; 12-12:30, lunch; 12:30-1:30, recess; 1:30-2:00 study period; 2-4, classes; 4-5, recess; 5-8, study period; 8-8:30, dinner; 8:30, bedtime.

The boarders sleep in common dormitories numbering from ten to twenty beds, supervised by an assistant; they take their meals, still supervised, at large tables seating from eight to ten boys. The recesses allow them to play in the graveled courts between the buildings. Where no provisions are made for organized games, tennis and football thrive in very rudimentary form; the older students prefer to pace back and forth arguing and conversing. Physical education, for which greater appropriations have been made of recent years,[39] is ordinarily optional for all but the youngest secondary-school students.

The daily routine sketched above obtains six days a week. On Thursday afternoons, however, there are no classes, and boarders are taken for walks in groups of twenty-five or thirty, led by a master and marching in ranks. On Sundays, the boys who are fortunate

[39] A total of 19,138,935 francs was budgeted in 1931-32 for physical education throughout all French public schools.

enough to have friends in the town may be called for at the lycée, which, incidentally, requires from the callers written permission from the parents. The others, less fortunate, are taken for another walk during the afternoon.

3. *Higher Education*

The French universities, as we have seen above, are not professional schools. They limit themselves to the dissemination of purely theoretical knowledge to students who will find this knowledge useful and profitable after they have learned their profession. Even the application of theory forms no part of the university program. Just as in the secondary school the student's mind was habituated to techniques of general thinking, so in the university he is accustomed to the special mental techniques of the four great branches of learning —law, medicine, science, and letters. It is expected that if the theory of one of these fields has been thoroughly assimilated, the practice will be acquired all the more rapidly and intelligently. The French faculties of law do not attempt to make lawyers; they try to develop the juristic sense of the student. He is therefore exposed to a more varied subject matter than his American friend. Roman law, the history of legal institutions, legal philosophy, comparative law, and, above all, political economy in all its branches, are his materials for the entire course of three years. Thereafter the student has ample opportunities to learn the practice of law, since he is required to serve an apprenticeship of three years—*le stage*. Likewise, the faculties of medicine give courses entirely separate from the required clinical work to be taken at a hospital. The university does not feel an obligation to teach the student how to operate; it does feel an obligation to inculcate those notions of anatomy, histology, physiology, and so forth, without which the modern physician would be little better than the dextrous barber of the eighteenth century. In the same way, the faculties of science do not graduate engineers, nor the faculties of letters journalists.

A second principle underlying the French university system is the guarantee of freedom of thought to the teaching personnel. The professor is in reality possessor of his chair (*professeur titulaire*) from the day of his appointment to the retiring age of seventy. He can be removed only for an infringement of the criminal law. No one, not even the Minister of Public Instruction, has power over him. Promotion is automatic and by seniority. Transfer to a more important university depends solely upon the vote of that faculty. This arrangement corresponds admirably to the desire of the French for security and is, in addition, an incentive to independent scholarly work. Be he royalist or socialist, in lycée or university, the French professor is responsible to no higher authority for his personal opinions. Similarly, the French university student is considered to be an adult and independent person. In sharp contrast, therefore, to his secondary-school days, the university student in France finds himself set entirely at liberty with regard to his private life, hours of work, class attendance, and political or religious opinions. The university exercises no control of any sort over its student body; its function is to pass upon their accomplishments and grant or withhold the sought-for degrees. The consequences of this liberty, as well as other social and intellectual considerations arising from this critical account of French education will be set forth in the next section.

VII

A COMPARATIVE SURVEY OF FRENCH EDUCATION

From the comparison of any two educational systems material for volumes could easily be gathered, since the theory and practice of education inevitably reflect and condition the social ideals and the social life of the countries involved. For brevity and convenience' sake, therefore, the present items of comparison between the American and French systems will be distributed under five general headings: curricula; freedom for teachers and students; teaching theory vs. teaching professional techniques; democracy; social thinking and social reform.

1. *Curricula*

The characteristics of French curricula are without doubt thoroughness and continuity. Latin, as we have seen, is taught on the average of five hours a week during the first six years of secondary school; whereas the same number of hours for only four years, and without equivalent home work, is, in the United States, the usual elective maximum possible in high school for those possessing an inclination towards letters. Most colleges require only two years of Latin for entrance, supplemented, it is true, by two years of a foreign language; but others waive the Latin requirement altogether when additional units of modern language are offered.

Nothing less than steady application to the classics, it seems, will give worth-while results. The compromise between the French method[40] and the American, represented by English training, has long been disavowed by its very products. To cite only one, that sagacious philosopher, Samuel Butler, says: "How skin-deep that classical training penetrates on which we waste so many years, and how completely we drop it as soon as we are left to ourselves."[41]

An even more striking example of the thoroughness and continu-

[40] Based ultimately on plan, *Ratio ac institutio studiorum,* 1599, of the sixteenth-century Jesuit general, Acquaviva.

[41] Samuel Butler, *Alps and Sanctuaries,* pp. 204-5; see also *Erewhon,* passim.

ity afforded by French education is the inclusion of geography in
the curriculum from the bottom to the top of the school system.
Started in primary school (or in elementary classes) it may become the subject of a doctorate. In secondary schools it is the necessary adjunct of history, modern languages, literature, and other
disciplines. To a French instructor who comes to teach in an American college, the lack of geographical knowledge, and, more, of
geography teaching, is perhaps the most striking deficiency of the
American curriculum. It is not in our province here to indicate that
geography is a subject as susceptible of advanced treatment as English or ancient history.

But apart from the intensiveness of study in given subjects, the
chief advantages of the restricted French curriculum lie in the avoid-
ance of scattered efforts. Options are offered the student, as in the
American schools, but they are options of *groups* of coördinated
courses. The same applies in the French universities in sharp contrast to college practice in the United States, where the wide range
of individual choices often leads to what one educator called "four
years of Freshman work."[42] From the intellectual point of view, the
lack of coherence resulting from course-option rather than group-
option tends to stultify the student's interest, and nullify the profit
derived from each separate study.

Whether state control of curricula in the French schools fosters
the indoctrination of nationalism is a difficult question to answer.
There is a widespread opinion that the highly nationalist character
of the subject matter in the curricula, and the overemphasis on
French history and geography, on the French language and literature, tend to imbue every French boy and girl with the idea that
his country is foremost in literary, artistic, and scientific as well as
military achievements.

Professor C. J. H. Hayes, who has made a thorough study of
this problem[43] remarks, however, that

in the higher primary schools as well as in the *lycées* and *collèges*
foreign languages and literature are taught; that in the secondary education of *lycée* and *collège* much general history—ancient, medieval,

[42] Herbert E. Hawkes, *New York Times* for April 26, 1929. See H. J. Carman, "An
Experiment in Higher Education," *The Historical Outlook*, April, 1930, p. 161.
[43] C. J. H. Hayes, *France, A Nation of Patriots*.

and modern—is given, and major attention is devoted to foreign languages and natural science, philosophy and mathematics, rather than to French national subjects.[44]

The point deserves even more emphasis. If we consider geography, which is regarded in France as a highly important subject, we find that only two years out of the seven in the lycée and collège geography sequence are devoted to the study of France and her colonies. During the remaining five years, students of the ages of thirteen to eighteen study physical and ethnic geography and the geography of the rest of the world, with particular emphasis on the chief economic world powers. If we consider history, we find the first two years of the lycée course given over to the study of the ancient eastern powers and the history of Greece and Rome. The remaining five years cover the study of world history with special attention to European history and more particularly French history. It is interesting and relevant to examine here the history course preparing for the *baccalauréat,* and based on Malet's standard work which was used during the war, in the classes of *première* and *philosophie.*[45] This required textbook contains in effect 989 pages on French history proper for the period 1715-1914 as against 1,138 pages on the history of other nations during the same period. The foreign nations studied are: the British Empire, Russia, Prussia, Austria-Hungary, Germany, Spain, Belgium, Switzerland, the United States, Canada, Latin America, Japan, and China. Full chapters, moreover, are devoted to such subjects as "Colonial Rivalry in the Eighteenth Century," "European Imperialism in Africa and Asia in the Nineteenth Century," and "The Near East Question." To be sure, there is more emphasis on French history in the thousand pages in which it is treated than there is on any of the other countries included in the eleven hundred remaining pages; but it cannot be said that France is presented as the foremost of the nations treated, either politically or culturally. The uninspired clarity and orderliness of the volume in itself prevents any "thesis," nationalist or other.

In point of quantity, the liberal parliamentary reforms of 1925, which we sketched above, provided for an even greater proportion

[44] Hayes, *op. cit.,* p. 48.
[45] For these terms, see above, pp. 102-3.

of world history. These reforms led also to the inclusion of fine arts in the secondary-school curriculum. Three years are devoted to the subject, which must be treated, according to ministerial instructions, neither historically not technically, but aesthetically, through the direct study of the most expressive works of great artists. Greater attention is paid to foreign artists than to French in the first year of the course (Renaissance), following the relative importance of the schools; equal attention in the second year (seventeenth and eighteenth centuries); and only in the third year (nineteenth century) does the French School receive predominant treatment, as indeed it does wherever art is studied, from the very nature of its contribution.

To the study of foreign literatures described above, the decrees of 1925 further added the study of a foreign civilization to complete the student's previous language specialization.

Now, it is true that only a small percentage of all French boys and girls enter the lycée or collège, and the tendency of the system must not be judged exclusively on the basis of the training for this élite. But with the *baccalauréat* as the gateway to responsible positions in public and private life, it is evident that the character of lycée education is more likely than that of the primary schools to have influence on at least the shaping of public opinion in the country.

The primary schools, producing as they do the masses whose opinions are necessarily shaped, nevertheless require our attention in respect to nationalist propaganda. It is undeniable that in these schools which train children between the ages of six and thirteen, very little attention is paid to the study of "foreign" subjects. We must keep in mind, however, just what the purpose of these schools is: namely, and in brief, to make the working-class children literate. To teach them a language other than French when they do not know the latter adequately would be foolish. The same principle applies to the teaching of history and geography. We have ourselves criticized the overstressing of Merovingian dynastic history in these elementary grades, but the evil lies in the specific details of the history taught, not in the general subject of French history. It might even be wiser to give the children of rural populations a thorough knowledge of the economic and political history of their own region before attempting that of France, since all good teaching proceeds from the known and familiar to the unknown and unfamiliar; and to teach the history or the geography of Denmark and Siam to infants ignorant of the location of Bordeaux or the origin of the departmental division of France, would be to reverse the practice of successful pedagogy.

Apart from abstract notions of what should be done, the amount of nationalism in the primary-school curricula must be estimated, *first,* comparatively, in terms of other nations' practice[46]—not that the propaganda in one country excuses or balances that in another, but that the elementary curricula of all modern nations contain almost exclusively and necessarily "national subjects" in varying amounts which, by themselves, mean little—and *second,* in terms of the prevailing opinions[47] among elementary-school teachers. It is notorious that in France, these men—for men are in the majority and not in the minority as in the United States[48]—are of liberal and radical tendencies, belong to the radical-socialist, socialist, and communist parties, and have of recent years evinced marked internationalist and pacifist leanings in their professional organizations, in textbooks, and by inference, in their classroom teaching. These opinions obviously do not imply any lack of appreciation for France and her culture, but they certainly temper, when they do not forbid, that uncritical admiration and that exalting of national doings which characterize the chauvinist of any country.

2. *Freedom for Teachers and Students*

Two factors determine the freedom of restraint upon French professors in the universities: titularization and light teaching schedules.[49] In considering the practice of titularizing university professors and thus making them irremovable owners of their teaching positions, the additional circumstance must be mentioned that

[46] For a criticism of French schools by the Germans in the nineteenth century, see Ludwig Hahn, *Das Unterrichts-Wesen in Frankreich,* Breslau, 1848; and Dr. Rommel, *Au Pays de la revanche,* Genève, 1886.

[47] For such a treatment see J. F. Scott, *The Menace of Nationalism in Education.*

[48] See H. E. Buchholz, *Fads and Fallacies in Present-Day Education,* Ch. vii and *passim.*

[49] We saw above the condition of teachers and students in the lycées.

their compulsory teaching schedule never exceeds three hours. The abuses of privilege that we noted as possible in the lycée apply here: the indolent can practically "retire" on their state salary. As a proof that monetary incentives and the fear of dismissal are not the only urgings to industry, however, it must be said that it is the exception rather than the rule when professors fail to devote themselves to scholarly or scientific research.

To the same extent as in the United States—and this is perhaps the only exact parallel between the two systems—university professors in France are largely independent of control in the internal organization of their courses (subject matter, readings, emphases, and so forth). It should be remembered on the other hand that French professors have practically no administrative duties.

As regards the French student a very critical change occurs in his life when he is suddenly freed from the barrack existence of the lycée and left utterly to his own devices in the university town. A number of *lycéens* find the adjustment extremely difficult, as do indeed to a very much lesser extent the high-school graduates in America when they enter college. Although it is true that many French students badly misuse this *Lernfreiheit,* yet the élite find it useful to develop the quality of originality so essential to workers in the professional and social fields.

In another place we shall see that viewed from the strictly American angle French education does not appear democratic. Another phase of university life in France open to the same charge is the lack of official contacts between professors and students. The system merely leaves the opportunity to certain professors of devoting a large part of their time to their best students, who frequently become genuine disciples, guided by a master hand in their first essays and inspired by friendly intimacy with an outstanding personality.

Taken all in all, however, higher education in France does not present so sharp a contrast with foreign methods as does French secondary education. Whatever advantages or superiority French university students may show over their fellows in other lands are due less to the French universities themselves than to the exacting mental training which they have learned in the lycée and collège.

3. Teaching Theory vs. Teaching Professional Techniques

The emphasis on theory rather than practice was found in the chapter just preceding to be a consistent feature of the French educational system from the lycée or collège onwards. The idea is so divergent from that underlying most American educational theory[50] that it deserves the comparative treatment which alone can bring out the pros and cons of the issue.

The value of possessing theory in any field probably consists in complete awareness. As President Nicholas Murray Butler has neatly expressed it, the man who disclaims theory, "knows neither what he is doing nor why he is doing it." Not only, then, as affording intellectual satisfaction, but also as creating self-confidence and the ability to deal with the unexpected, the French faculties of law, medicine, science, and letters deem it their function to impart the theory of the respective professions to which they lead. The apparent waste of time that results is thought to be negligible in proportion to the benefits derivable from the mastery of theory, since it is a matter of experience that a man who knows what to expect will be more adept, let us say, at removing an appendix, than one who proceeds largely empirically. There are few cases, in fact, where even American professional schools do not anticipate practice with some amount of theory. The startling fact, to the French critic of American education, consists in the very sudden jump taken by the student when passing from two or three years of "college" to the typical law school or college of physicians and surgeons. Especially since the introduction of the case system in law and the great increase in laboratory work in medical and engineering schools, the American student seems to the foreign observer to dig over his head into specialization without previous survey of the field. This remark applies equally well to the branches of study which in France would be included under letters, and in the United States under graduate academic studies.

The other side of the picture, however, is not hard to see. For the question may pertinently be asked of French educators, "Why

[50] See A. J. Nock, *The Theory of Education in the United States,* for the similar distinction he makes between "training" and "education."

spend precious time delving into the history and philosophy of a given profession when the exigencies of economic life make quite different demands on the graduate? Is not the relevance of much of the theory the mere survival of a dead tradition?" And when it is answered that theory is the key to intelligent practice, it may still be asked, "Why not combine the two, as the greatest of French educational philosophers, Rousseau, himself suggested at a time when veneration for theory was petrifying the mind and bringing any practice whatever to a standstill?"

The answer to the latter question lies perhaps not so much in the *theory* of French education as in the *practice* of French teachers; and the value of the latter may best be judged in the secondary schools. In the lycées and collèges there can be little question of practice. The *baccalauréat* opens the door to numerous civil service positions but prepares specifically for none; and yet the practical sense of the lycée and collège graduates when they fill these positions does not seem to be in any way inferior to that of their colleagues in other countries who receive a different training. It is, in fact, very likely that a thorough study of a passage of Tacitus— let us say *Historiae,* I, xxi—concerning governmental corruption, is as good an introduction to practical life—*if Tacitus is understood*— as a general course on municipal government. Granting that this is so, the principle arising out of it is obviously thoroughness, around which, as we have shown, the whole scholastic edifice in France is built.[51] Now, when it is considered that the French schoolboy's working day is at least twice as long as the American boy's[52]—not to speak of intensity of application within that time—the problem is, how could a more varied curriculum serving the same purposes be introduced into the lycées, without losing thoroughness or adding intolerably to the student's burden? It is in the face of this dilemma

[51] At this point, the critiques of such distinguished French writers as Renan, *Questions contemporaines,* 1868, and Lavisse, *Souvenirs d'une éducation manquée,* 1903, must not be overlooked, but must be read in the light of the reforms brought about in the system since the latter date.

[52] See above the schedule of a French *lycéen* totaling ten and a half hours of work daily. The American high-school student of corresponding age usually attends classes from 9 A.M. to 3 P.M. with an hour off for lunch, that is to say, five hours in all.

that even the most convinced champions of a wide practical offering in secondary schools must pause.

But the limited thoroughness achieved in the schools of France has certain implications which must be discussed. These implications may be summed up in a word as the premature aging—mental, moral, and physical—of the French youth. Interest in problems beyond his years, an acquired and precocious cynicism in his relations with his fellows, and a perpetually fatigued mind and body are the direct consequences of the Spartan ideal. A signal example of what this means can be found by the reader in any trustworthy account of the life of Arthur Rimbaud.

When comparing the relative maturity of French and American students, then, two factors are to be kept in mind. First, the length of time devoted to the specific subject, daily and weekly; second, the age at which corresponding kinds of work are customarily accomplished. For instance, the French *bachelier* is usually seventeen or eighteen years old, which is the usual age for entrance to college in the United States; but the French doctor is often older by four or five years than the American Ph.D., and the difference in the temper of their theses can thus be accounted for in part. The other element which creates contrasts between their respective dissertations is undoubtedly due to different traditions. In France, the principal criteria of judgment are correct style, originality of thought, breadth of culture, depth of information, and mastery of scholarly technique (footnotes and bibliography) in descending order of importance; whereas in the United States some have gone so far as to say that by and large that order is exactly reversed.[53]

4. *Democracy*

A frequent criticism of French education in general is that it is not democratic, and especially when the French system is compared to the American does the allegation come into play as one of the chief differentiating factors. The striking fact is that out of a total of 3,840,000 pupils in French public schools during the years 1928-30, only 57,347 were in institutions of higher learning. On these

[53] Cf. O. W. Mosher, and G. Quesnel, "The Teaching of History in French Universities," *Historical Outlook*, October, 1931. French dissertations in law and medicine, for various reasons, are generally inferior to those in other subjects.

statistics, together with the figure of 1,470 scholarship holders in the universities,[54] for the same period, must rest any purely objective estimate of the extent to which democracy obtains in French education, taking the term democracy in its loose sense of "the many."

In dealing with the question, however, it is necessary first to gain a clearer understanding of what democracy in education really means. If it means that every child, regardless of sex, social rank, and wealth shall be given at state expense an education carried to the most advanced grade that he can reach, then is it true that French education is undemocratic? It is a matter of recorded fact that scholarships (*bourses*) are available to primary school children who have not the means to continue in school but who have the aptitude to do so.[55] The scholarships are indeed granted only after highly competitive examinations; but the latter are characteristic of the entire system and apply at any point to *all* students, rich or poor, male or female. With regard to the scholarships, one valid objection might be made, that they support the recipient during his schooling, but that they do not fill the lack in the family budget which the student's earnings would supply if he were gainfully employed: in other words, there is no opportunity in France as there is in the United States for gainful employment during the adolescent school years. As against this fact we must consider another, namely that college scholarships in the United States seldom pay more than the student's tuition—which is much higher than in France[56]—and that consequently student self-support on this side of the Atlantic seldom goes to eke out the family budget. In short, balancing these dissimilar but equivalent factors, it can be concluded that *financially*, the French and American systems are equally democratic.

Intellectually, the similarity or difference between the two systems

[54] To these must be added all those students, French or foreign, who are exempt from the payment of fees under various dispensations, and whose higher education costs them only their maintenance. See Université de Paris, *Livret de l'étudiant*, 1930, p. 17.

[55] In the primary school itself, the children of poor parents are given food and clothing paid for out of local funds (*caisse cantonale*).

[56] For the year 1929-30 the fees normally charged by the University of Paris amounted to 160 francs a year, or less than $7.00.

is not so easily evaluated. As we have seen above, the successive examinations at all stages of the student's progress are ruthlessly competitive. If forty percent of a given class receive the *baccalauréat* it is a subject of wonder and congratulations. For fellowships, for entrance to the *École normale supérieure,* and for the *agrégation,* only the first few in the ranking are chosen. These are the facts which, compared with the great American trek into the colleges, strongly suggest that French education is undemocratic. Though we shall not attempt to settle the issue, we can at least indicate another way of looking at it. If democracy, to repeat our basic definition, implies in theory equal opportunities, then the competitive examination system used in France is not undemocratic. Democracy means, then, not education for all, but education for all who can keep up with it. In this view of the matter, it is the American system that would seem undemocratic.[57] By lowering the requirements to admit a larger mass of the population, the American college system creates a privileged class in the middle—the privilege of mediocrity. This injustice at the expense of superior brains works its utmost mischief in the secondary schools and colleges, where the efforts of certain American educators to sustain the flagging interest of mediocre students leave the élite untaught to shift for itself.

From the French point of view the consequences of this misapplication of the democratic ideal are many and dangerous. First in order, is the production of an "intellectualized" working class dissatisfied with its lot and unable to better it; second—and this is of special importance when the notion of "planning" is being urged as an effective social remedy—so-called democratic college education creates far too many "qualified" applicants for a limited number of available positions. Granted that education is "good" in itself—so are bread and steel, and yet we know that an oversupply of these in our unplanned economic world is worse than dearth. Third of these consequences, the admission of a majority of students to the seats of learning has the demoralizing tendency of making relative ignorance the social norm: "highbrow" would not be a term of

[57] In modern practice, at any rate. We should not forget that Thomas Jefferson's plan for public education in Virginia provided that "twenty of the best geniuses shall be raked from the rubbish annually."

reproach applied to a minority if the "lowbrows" were not in the majority. Fourth and last, the ensuing degradation of the various diplomas tends to substitute for their significance a kind of indefinite social prestige, which is in turn extinguished under the great mass of those participating in it.[58]

Such are, in the eyes of French observers, the evils that would result from spreading higher education to all those that want it, regardless of motive or capacity. To correct the picture, it must be said that the elimination by the French system of many second-class talents is at once wasteful and unjust. Especially when the subjective and limited nature of the examinations is considered, the competitive system appears barbarous. The ability to discern his own aptitudes is required of the French student much too early, and his theoretic specialization is thereafter so narrow as often to preclude the possibility of change. Whatever the subject, the concentration of effort on the passing of a single *concours* is frequently harmful to health and spirits; when it is not actually destructive of both. In this connection, two features of the system that are necessary adjuncts to the inhuman notion of unmitigated competition must be treated separately; first the results of life in the lycée, and second the type of examinations.

Lycée life and discipline is without question unbalanced and harmful to young men between the ages of eleven and eighteen. To be submitted to an unceasing surveillance, to be forbidden to smoke, to read newspapers, to go out alone, might seem intolerable in a country where individual liberty has a large share. And yet there are few in France to find fault with college life. In many cases it is only an exact replica of what family life would be for the same child if he were not a boarder at school. Stronger spirits among boys tend to rebel, but there is always the threat of expulsion to act as a deterrent, not so much by the disgrace attendant upon it as by the consequent impossibility of entering another lycée or collège. Naturally enough, most lycée students retain roseate memories of their school days, but these can be ascribed either to the sentimental rationalizing which goes on unconsciously in all of us

[58] Cf. A. J. Nock, *The Theory of Education in the United States*, p. 12.

to smooth over the unpleasant past, or to genuine gratitude for the gift of dearly bought but fruitful intellectual habits.

The French system of examinations may also seem unfair to those who believe in democratic education, and feel that "a chance"—of a nature unspecified—must be given to everybody. Still, it cannot be denied that all minds are not equally able, and the very purpose of college, as understood in France, is to select the best minds and train them to become the leaders of society.[59] If it is urged that this is aristocracy and not democracy, it can be answered that it is to a large extent an aristocracy of brains, grounded in nature, and not necessarily detrimental to political democracy. Certainly intelligence and culture have seldom sharpened the anti-social impulses of men, and most aristocratic societies have collapsed not when the aristocracy was vigorous and intelligent, but when it was indolent or incapable of recruiting its ranks from below. Since the lycée aims at selection,[60] the *baccalauréat* must not be, and in fact is not, merely a certificate of attendance and regular work, but a certificate of intellectual capacity, that is, capacity for pursuing studies in a specialized field—medicine, engineering, or law; capacity for filling certain public offices; capacity for teaching. In the United States, on the contrary, it seems as if the bachelor's degree is too liberally given.[61] The result is that many expect that their college education will enable them to fill a higher position than they can get. Certain business men have even stated that they preferred non-college men as

[59] Even Renan, cited above as a severe critic of French education, upholds this principle as the very basis of civilized society, and contrasts it with the mistaken notion of popular education current in the United States. E. Renan, *Questions contemporaines*, Paris, 1868, p. vii.

[60] An indication of the degree of selectivity in French examinations may be gathered from the following figures and estimates: For the *baccalauréat*, 10 out of a possible 20 is the passing grade, and 60 percent of the candidates never get that average for all their subjects; the mark of 12 enables the student to graduate with the mention *assez bien* (fair), but 25 percent at most of those who graduate, or about 10 percent of all candidates, get it; 14 carries with it the mention *bien* (good), obtained by 5 percent of the graduates; 16 is necessary to reach *très bien*, which almost never happens.

[61] President F. A. P. Barnard as early as 1879 complained that there were "too many colleges and not too few" with consequent lowering of standards. *First Commencement Address at the University of the State of New York*, Albany, July 10, 1879.

clerks in their offices or factories, at a time when the number of those entering college was increasing and at a time when economic conditions were becoming far less indulgent to the individual than the college instructor.

For the purpose of selecting their élite the French have developed the system of examinations previously depicted, which presents many points of contrast with the American practice. All examinations are of the essay type, but we shall use here the term dissertation in preference to the word essay. For it appears that the deficiency of the essay type of examination as used in the United States is that it is not sufficiently different from the so-called objective type of test.[62] Short essays to be written in twenty-five minutes or at most in fifty minutes; and worst of all, short questions to be answered in five minutes or less, do not constitute anything but a way to check the student's factual knowledge. These "essays" are written in great haste with the obvious purpose of impressing the instructor with range of knowledge rather than with ability to use this knowledge to reach original conclusions. It would never occur to students taking this type of test—and they would not have the time to do so if it did occur to them—to make an outline before beginning to write. In the great number of papers written by American students there is no plan, no style, no division of the subject into sections, no transition between ideas or paragraphs, and, too often, no conclusions. The inculcation of such sound intellectual habits therefore makes it easier for a bright student to pass the French *baccalauréat* than to get the American A.B.; but many a mediocre student who finally obtains the American A.B. would never reach the *baccalauréat*.

In rebuttal of these criticisms it might be said that the object of higher education is not to produce accomplished littérateurs, but business men or lawyers well grounded in facts. Indeed, this is the answer made by most students when confronted with their lack of constructive ability. Conceding the truth of the rebuttal, it is none the less irrelevant; for facts alone do not constitute the ultimate reality of any situation—be it legal or economic. Facts in coördination, facts interpreted, are the only approaches that language can

[62] Cf. A. C. Krey and E. B. Wesley, in *Historical Outlook*, January, 1932.

make to reality, and the inability of the student to realize his mistake when he has stated an undeniable fact in a wrong context is the basic fault of all ineffectual thinking anywhere and at any time.[63]

5. *Social Thinking and Social Reform*

With central control of education, with uniform programs, and with the exclusive application of the latter, it is to be expected that the French school products will be remarkably standardized. More than that, they will in many cases be utterly ignorant of certain aspects of life which their very assiduity has not permitted them to examine. Such is the result, to a certain extent, of any form of training, but it is very much accentuated in France, as can be inferred from the fact that many of the basic principles of French education are seldom questioned by the majority of Frenchmen themselves. It is difficult, therefore, to determine whether the boasted individualism of the French or their national and acquired capacity for collective action is the dominant trait inculcated by a uniform schooling.

It seems to be equally true that some of the most powerful and original French geniuses, such as Bonaparte, Balzac, and Berlioz, fought or escaped school regimentation; and that others, no less original, such as Stendhal and Delacroix, excelled in the same discipline. Certain it is that the pressure and restraint of school life, when they do not stunt, produce strong individuals by reaction; and that the common cultural background corrects the individualism. France has produced fully as many social thinkers as any other nation not so unified educationally. But if we compare the antecedents of Voltaire and those of Proudhon, we discover the first to have been educated at a very strict Jesuit college and the second to have been mainly self-educated. As far as leaders are concerned, then, it is impossible to determine the effect of the educational system, except that it does not unfit them for political life—the chief defect of American education in the eyes of President Butler of Columbia University.[64] With regard to the mass, it is impossible to determine whether its realistic conservatism results directly from a

[63] Cf. the article by Professor John Erskine in the *New York Herald Tribune* for May 28, 1932.
[64] *The Meaning of Education*, p. 112.

given system of education or indirectly from an agrarian civilization. In any case, the unwillingness of the bulk of the French people to change their routines is a fact that finds plentiful illustration in everything from farming to literary art.

On the part of the leaders, a more serious impediment to untrammeled social thinking is the bent given by "tradition" to their studies. *Abeunt studia in mores.* It is a matter to reflect on, for example, that the radical-socialist prime minister, Édouard Herriot, should escape, in his literary work, to the boudoir of Mme. Récamier and her friends; that the brilliant minds of *Normaliens* like Painlevé and Borel should abstract themselves in mathematics; and that even the liberal-minded in politics should find it difficult to overcome an unreasoned worship of Louis XIV's administration.[65] It would be difficult in France to conceive of a parallel to the English Fabian Society, with its members straddling social reform movements and academic distinctions.

Indeed, it was perhaps in France that the word "academic" first came to mean pedantic and unprogressive. The whole weight of organized intellectual life exerts its pressure in the direction of conservatism and orthodoxy. No field of endeavor is free from this incubus. The academies and the faculties wield in fact a kind of legislative power over everything from language to scientific research, with a kind of judicial power to enforce it through the withholding of official recognition. We need only recall the fact that Balzac was never a member of the French Academy; that Pasteur had to fight his way to fame in the teeth of opposition by the Academy of Medicine; that Ravel never obtained the Rome prize in music; that Foch was assailed for his military heresies before becoming a national hero. And the list of those whose capacities did not survive official neglect or opposition cannot, in the nature of the case be drawn up.

In conclusion, we must notice the allegation of some that for those destined to remain in the narrow circle of French provincial life the

---

[65] As early as 1909, the late Aristide Briand, who, incidentally, was hardly a typical product of the French schools, declared in the Chamber, "the time is not far distant when this country will have to be rejuvenated in its administration." *Journal Officiel, Débats de la Chambre* October 29, November 24, etc., pp. 2426.

austere and rigid discipline of French education is an excellent preparation, which does not exclude the genuine satisfactions of inner intellectual life. It may be questioned, however, whether a different school training might not improve the social milieu, instead of perpetuating its limitations.

6. *Conclusion*

It may be useful, in concluding, to summarize the results yielded by our comparative survey fo French education. In evaluating the "most centralized educational system in the world" the defects must not be glossed over. Administrative red tape, the consequent opportunity given to laziness and lack of conscientiousness among teachers, the narrowness of outlook engendered by functionarism, and the inescapable uniformity of state programs of study tend in part to detract from the originality and inspiration of the teaching body. The parallel regimentation of student life, the absence of physical exercise as an outlet for youthful spirits and the denial of legitimate satisfactions, coupled with inhuman burdens of study are, in modern France, unjustified survivals that have aroused criticism among Frenchmen themselves.[66] We have shown, moreover, that the sudden freedom granted to the university student can lead to complete demoralization. Further, the curriculum content of primary education has hitherto been in a large part irrelevant to the life work of the graduates, although the new Labbé system is a courageous experiment in the right direction undertaken in the face of conservative opposition.[67] In the secondary schools of France the study of Latin, French, and mathematics is still preponderant to an extent justified by its intrinsic results, but not necessarily adapted to a changing economic and international world. The framework and purposes may be excellent, but the practice must be of necessity broader in scope if timely social reforms are to be guided by the élite formed in the lycées and collèges.

On the credit side of the balance sheet, we find opposite the serious liabilities enumerated above certain assets derived from the same type of organization. Centralization and uniformity, as we nave shown, permit of intellectual freedom for professors and for stu-

[66] See *New York Times* editorial, November 8, 1931.
[67] See article by Pierre Gaxotte in *Candide* for December 3, 1931.

dents when they have reached the university. A common background of "general culture" is in addition one of the social charms of the French élite which makes it, as it were, intellectually self-supporting. For those who can withstand the lycée discipline, there results an ability acquired for life to concentrate mind and body for long periods on arduous problems. Again, the intelligent inculcation of the classics can, and in many cases does, form the mind to see life in terms of theories and principles, rather than as a series of unrelated facts; to understand rather than to know. It is only a question of desire and opportunity for such an intellect to contribute his best talents to the solution of increasingly complex social problems. In fine, the French educational system offers the machinery and the tradition wherewith to keep the leaders of the nation enlightened. The faults, grave as they are, are not inherent in the scheme and can be removed without destroying it as soon as the nation or its leaders make up their minds to do so, that is to say, as soon as the products of the system itself, utilizing the chief advantage of centralization, desire the change and make it into law.[68]

Bibliography

This list of books and articles makes no pretense at exhaustiveness and is included merely to refer the reader to fuller treatments of the points specifically raised in the foregoing report.

Arnold, Matthew, The Popular Education of France, London, 1861.
—— Schools and Universities on the Continent, London, 1868.
Barzun, H. M., L'Action intellectuelle, Paris, 1907.
Buchholz, H. E., Fads and Fallacies in Present-Day Education, New York, 1931.
Bureau de la statistique générale, Annuaire statistique de la France, 1930.
Butler, N. M., The Meaning of Education, New York, 1915.
—— Education: New and Old, New York, 1927.
Butler, Samuel, Alps and Sanctuaries, London, 1931.
Carman, H. J., "An Experiment in Higher Education," *Historical Outlook*, April, 1930.
Dewey, John, Democracy and Education, New York, 1921.
—— and Evelyn Dewey, Schools of Tomorrow, New York, 1915.
Erskine, John, The Moral Obligation to Be Intelligent, New York, 1915.

[68] Note the facility of change in programs, at least, visible in the Plans of 1902, 1923, 1925, above.

Erskine, John, "What's the Matter with the United States?" *New York Herald Tribune,* May 28, 1932.

Flottes, Pierre, La Révolution de l'école unique, Paris, 1930.

Gromaire, G., Démocratie et éducation, Paris, 1914.

Hayes, C. J. H., France, a Nation of Patriots, New York, 1930.

Krey, A. C., and E. B. Wesley, "Does the New-Type Test Measure the Results of Instruction?" *Historical Outlook,* Philadelphia, January, 1932.

Lavisse, Ernest, G. Lanson, *et al.,* L'Éducation de la démocratie, Paris, 1903.

Leonard, R. J., An Outlook on Education, New York, 1930.

Martin, Everett Dean, "Education" in *Whither Mankind,* edited by C. A. Beard, New York, 1928.

Monroe, Paul, Essays in Comparative Education, "Studies of the International Institute of Teachers College," New York, 1927.

Mosher, O. W., and G. Quesnel, "The Teaching of History in French Lycées and Collèges," *Historical Outlook,* October 1, 1930.

—— "The Teaching of History in French Universities," *Historical Outlook,* October, 1931.

Nock, Albert Jay, The Theory of Education in the United States, New York, 1932.

Plan d'études et programmes de l'enseignement secondaire, Paris, 1931.

Pottier, Edmond, "La Vie d'un lycéen sous l'Empire," *Revue des Deux Mondes,* October 15, 1932.

Renan, E., L'Avenir de la science: pensées de 1848, 2d ed., Paris, 1890.

—— "L'Instruction supérieure en France," and "L'Instruction publique en France jugée par les Allemands," in Questions contemporaines, Paris, 1868.

—— "Lettre sur la liberté de l'enseignement supérieur," in Mélanges d'histoire et de voyages, Paris, 1898.

République française, *Journal Officiel.*

Richard, C., L'Enseignement en France, Paris, 1925.

Rudler, G., L'Explication française: principes et applications, Paris, 1902.

Scott, Jonathan, The Menace of Nationalism in Education, New York, 1926.

Shapiro, H. S., Reports to the Institute of International Education, January 10 and July 7, 1931.

Temperley, H., I. Strayer, and R. McMurray, "History Teaching in Other Lands," *Historical Outlook,* 1931-32, passim.

Valeur, R., L'Enseignement du droit en France et aux États-Unis, Paris, 1928.

Veblen, T., Higher Learning in America, New York, 1918.

SOCIAL OBJECTIVES IN SOVIET EDUCATION

BY

BORIS SCHOENFELDT

VIII

PHILOSOPHY AND HISTORY OF SOVIET EDUCATION

1. *The Soviet Philosophy of Education*

The Soviet Union fascinates the world. Now and then other big issues may eclipse it, but none holds so steady or so partisan an interest. Extremists at one end deny the very existence in the USSR of elements constituting a modern state, and see there nothing but a continuous violation by these modern Tamerlanes of all principles of civilization. At the opposite pole are those who almost worship this fairyland where, as they believe, the most cherished daydreams of mankind are becoming realities. More significantly, a great and ever increasing number of people are in the process of a cautious retreat from both extremes, and are critically reëvaluating what they now tentatively call an "experiment."

But if the term "experiment" has any meaning for the social sciences, it must signify either the endless panorama of all human history, or a certain social experiment conceived as such by its authors. *Tertium non datur.* Christianity, from the broader standpoint, is an experiment which has been going on for almost two thousand years; even now it embraces only about one-third of mankind and is still so far from realization in terms of the original teachings of Christ that it presents a striking example of the futility of altruism when confronted by an "immutable" human nature. Doctor Faust stands humiliated, and Mephistopheles triumphantly exclaims: "Satan rules the world!"

The way out of this apparent impasse seems to lie in the adoption of a less seductive but more scientific method of reasoning. The history of the USSR must be regarded as a social process in a changing world—with inevitable contradictions and struggles, successes and failures, ups and downs; a dramatic race between the rational and the irrational; a new step in man's long (perhaps endless) way toward mastery and wisdom. No one can understand this mighty struggle without studying the educational institutions of the Soviet Union, which embody the general philosophy and the policy of Bolshevism.

The Soviet Union is waging a war upon idealism with all the fanatical fervor that communists can generate. Every boy and girl is brought up with the conviction that idealism, like religion, is a devilish invention of the bourgeoisie, a temptation to the faithful, an instrument of spiritual intoxication for the oppressed. It is feared and hated by communists as the greatest of heresies. A Party member suspected of idealism is faced with merciless expulsion; even a non-partisan professor denounced as an idealist is boycotted and sooner or later deprived of his job. The very manner in which the word "idealism" is pronounced in official circles reveals a contempt which is intentionally stressed, and which all citizens sense. Father and son, husband and wife, the closest friends, are likely to be irretrievably separated if one of them should fall into this "error." Interestingly enough, the communist shows a much greater intolerance than his opponent, and feels himself separated from a disclosed idealist by a bottomless gulf. This quality of the communist mind is manifesting itself more and more frequently among the great masses of people in the USSR.

The crusade against idealism usually causes great alarm in the outside world. It is condemned in pulpit and forum as the harbinger of Antichrist, and as a menace not only to our material civilization, but also to the very foundations of Christian culture and our most cherished spiritual values. Yet a closer study indicates that idealism in its moral sense, as a principle of social behavior, has never been denied by Marxism. To be sure, communism does not recognize a universal code of morals in a class society. But class society, according to Marx, is not an eternal institution; being a product of specific historical conditions, it is doomed to disappear in compliance with the dialectic law of development. The dictatorship of the proletariat is merely the threshold to a classless society, and its mission will be accomplished with the eradication of the last remnants of the capitalist order. Not until then will "universal solidarity" attain its real power, and such solidarity can imply only a universal idealism manifested in life as well as in thoughts and aspirations. This is the dialectic of the historic development to come. In the meantime, class idealism (or class solidarity) is actually an operating principle required of and assumed by every conscious warrior for the coming "kingdom." Thus idealism as a universal principle of behavior of *homo sapiens* is not denied by communism but rather postponed. All that is denied is idealism regarded as a philosophical conception embodying a certain *Weltanschauung* which must be *displaced by dialectic materialism*.

The question arises whether idealism is deeply rooted in human nature. All that we know of civilized mankind speaks eloquently. Man's actual behavior shows a flexible correlation between selfishness and selflessness. Wherever solidarity is not forced upon him by law or custom, he consents to it only to the extent to which it coincides with his personal interest. The Kantian conception of a human being as an end in himself (*Selbstzweck*) rather than an instrument for others' welfare is a respectable tenet found in books and orations. One of the most discouraging of occupations would be an analysis of the elements of Christ's original teachings which have failed to become embodied in the daily activities of men. On the other hand, research in anthropology has weakened the Paulian concept of the inherent depravity of man. Every religious system proclaims the antinomy of good and evil. Ormuzd and Ariman, Ra and Osiris, City of God and City of Satan, angels and demons— all of these concepts seem to reflect the contradictory elements or motives within humanity. Human relations are the battlefield for these vigorously competing motives, and concrete human conduct reflects transitory victory or defeat.

Education involves the transmission of knowledge as well as wisdom. As a matter of fact, the acquisition of the former is aimed at in the Baconian sense of equipment for success in the struggles of life, rather than in the Socratic sense of its worth as the road to virtue. Ever since Socrates sealed with his life the harmony between his aspirations and conduct, the western world has been visited by numerous teachers of morality and apostles of education. Their precepts have been stored in the hinterland of our memories and on the dusty shelves of our libraries. Indeed, Descartes was quite correct in his startling pronouncement that our convictions and beliefs are not revealed in our discussions, nor even in our thoughts, but in our ordinary actions. Does sad historical experience force us to a conception of the immutability of our moral nature? If we incline that way, we may be warned by the manner in which those who attempted to depict original human nature have disagreed. To mention one instance, Thomas Hobbes described original human nature as entirely corrupt, and Rousseau portrayed it as fundamentally good. Furthermore, both of these men admitted the feasibility of considerable change, and the noble Helvetius extended his belief in Locke's *tabula rasa* so far as to proclaim the somewhat naïve and vague formula that man is purely the product of his education, and that improving the science of education is the shortest and safest way to insure individual perfection and social harmony.

Today we are more apt to avoid all hollow *a priori* judgments, and to depend on obvious facts. Such a technique compels us to accept the flexibility of human nature. While bodily changes occur within comparatively narrow limits drawn by the biologic factors of heredity, the elements of mind seem to possess a wider range of variation. The belief that *plus ça change, plus ça reste la même chose* has been shaken. Experimentation with conditioned reflexes discloses the possibility of modifying human behavior. Conscious use of some habits and disuse of others create new responses and new correlations. The attempt to separate and counterbalance the so-called egoistic and altruistic elements of human conduct, when their constant interaction is fully recognized, can be no more than an abstraction similar to many others which are useful in various fields of science. Social institutions are embodiments of prevalent habits and thoughts and possess tremendous inertia.

What then is the driving power behind moral and institutional changes? The idealistic formula of the eighteenth century (*ce sont les opinions qui gouvernent le monde*) has lost its prestige. And the more elaborate Hegelian notion of the self-developing and self-manifesting "Absolute Spirit" has given ground to the more prosaic concept of environment.

Mr. J. B. Watson appreciates this. Nevertheless, in a kind of behavioristic fervor, he has said: "Some day we shall have hospitals de-

voted to helping us change our personality, because we can change
the personality as easily as we can change the shape of the nose, only
it takes more time." He simplifies the problem even further:

I am not asking for revolution. . . . I am trying to dangle a stimulus
in front of you, a verbal stimulus which, if acted upon, will gradually change this universe. For the universe will change if you bring
up your children, not in the freedom of the libertine, but in behavioristic freedom—a freedom which we cannot even picture in words,
so little do we know of it. Will not these children, with their better
ways of living and thinking replace us as society and in turn bring
up their children in a still more scientific way, until the world finally
becomes a place fit for human habitation?[1]

Mr. Watson does not define his concept of environment, and he appears to confuse individual changes with changes in social habits and
thoughts. In the Marxian conception, the economic environment
furnishes the influence which is all-important in shaping the character of human habits, thoughts, and institutions, including those
which are educational. True, social life is never absolutely uniform;
it always maintains a museum of obsolete habits of thought, as well
as a nursery of newborn ideological offspring. But the main line of
social behavior is that which results from ruling institutions. Thus,
while elements of altruistic thoughts and behavior are to be found in
family life, in philanthropy, and in deeds of self-denying patriotism,
they do not characterize everyday life in our society. Noble pedagogic
theories and experiments are of short duration and slight effect. Like
rare springs in a vast desert, they are not able to water it.

Social and economic conditions exercise an educative influence of
decisive importance. For in shaping the hard struggle of earning a
livelihood, these conditions breed corresponding habits, thoughts and
forms of conduct, which first become dominant, and which finally
come to rest with almost complete inertia. Schooling as a formal
relationship between teacher and pupil is of small educative influence except in so far as it is consistent with the requirements of the
struggle for life. While it is true that the institutions which constitute
environment have no conscious educational purpose, they are all-
important in molding behavior. Before entering school, youth ac-
quires definite distinctions between good and evil, which are im-

[1] J. B. Watson, *Behaviorism*, pp. 302-4.

planted by the family, street life, and many other factors. As soon as school is finished, the imperative requirements of a competitive environment erase the transitory idealism of schooling. And even during schooling itself, the teacher—the soul of a school—is bound to be the exponent of the ideas of his environment, since school must prepare men for life. Comenius, the famous pedagogue of the seventeenth century, expressed in a naïve manner the contradictory tasks of education. He advised teachers to bring up their children in a way "worthy of heavenly blessing," and to do this by setting the pattern of an angelic life. He added also:

Since the teachers have to do with children, whom they are not to lead to heaven, but to prepare them first of all for a pious life among men, they ought to inculcate in the children ordinary knowledge and faithful obedience toward the laws of human society.

This compromise is typical of modern education. Schools must produce the approved type of human being, whose habits, thoughts and behavior give promise of securing an easy adjustment to social and economic life. As the school displaces gradually the old system of home instruction, it becomes easier for education to imprint this unified pattern upon the newer generation.

From the Marxian standpoint, the modern school is merely a servant of the ruling class, which class identifies its aspirations with the interests of the whole nation (or even of all mankind), and claims to live and to think in compliance with the unchangeable laws of human nature. The Bolshevist theory of education rests upon the general philosophy of Marxism. In the main it is not consciousness which determines existence, but, on the contrary, social existence which determines consciousness. However, while this viewpoint has been vulgarized by some followers of Marx, neither he nor Lenin denied the importance of consciousness, ideologies, or human will as mechanisms for realizing the objectives of historic development. For the manifestation of the dialectic law in modern society is the class struggle, and the ruling class in its fight for self-preservation uses ideologic factors as well as economic pressure. Among these factors are the institutions of schooling and education. Competition instead of coöperation, selfishness rather than altruism are cultivated by the capitalistic order. Therefore, an effective education for social behavior is conceivable only when the existing economic system has been abolished and the transition to communism completed. The Soviet state embodies the dominance of the once oppressed proletariat; it naturally accepts the dictatorship which promises transition to communism; and it includes education among the instruments for this purpose.

2. The History of Education under the USSR

The Russian Slavophiles repeated ecstatically: "Russia is beyond ordinary understanding; she cannot be measured with a common yardstick; she has her own peculiar destiny." Alexander III endorsed this Messianic creed when he commented on a report of his minister of education with the words: "All evil comes from the fact that the peasants are sending their children to school." On another occasion he remarked that education simply ought to be prohibited. On the other hand, the Bolsheviks, no less than other intellectuals in prewar Russia, regard as axiomatic the necessity of universal education. Until his death, Lenin did not cease repeating, "What we shall need first of all for the reconstruction of our state apparatus is study, study, and study." One of his first suggestions after the October Revolution was the introduction, within ten years, of universal instruction. The Party supported him in this. But the old régime was so despised, the enthusiasm for destruction among the rank and file of the Party so intense, that they were willing to repudiate the whole cultural inheritance—to throw out the baby with the bath. Lenin had to exert all his authority to convince them of the values contained in the scientific and artistic creations of the bourgeoisie in the previous ages in Russia and abroad. He always insisted that one of the causes of the failure of previous revolutions was the fact that their leaders did not realize the inadequacy of violence and coercion alone.

Against the old school system, however, Lenin fought with a Catonian energy. On this point, he admitted no compromise, no reconciliation. "We must destroy it" was his slogan. And this, of course, was consistent with the Marxian thesis that, in the capitalistic society,

the school is made an instrument of the class rule of the bourgeoisie; the claim of its neutral or non-political character is but an hypocrisy and deception of the masses.

Interestingly enough, some leading Bolshevist pedagogues were inclined to proceed to a conclusion amounting to a gradual abolition of the school system itself in a society moving toward communism. Their logic was: if the school is an agent of the ruling classes, it becomes unnecessary with the disappearance of class society, and therefore it is wasteful to establish and extend a school system under the temporary and preparatory régime of the proletarian dictatorship in the Soviet Union. But the official organ of the Commissariat of Education of the RSFSR contains the following "bold" statement: "In any society, even in a communistic one, the education of the younger generation is necessary. Children will not be born communists, they will have to be educated."[2] This controversy indicates the leaders' confusion regarding education.

The founders of Marxism have not produced a comprehensive work on socialistic education. Its principles had to be drawn from their general sociological conceptions, and from a very few incidental remarks by Marx and Engels. These remarks, however, show a great depth of thought. In the resolution written by Marx and adopted at the first Congress of the First International in 1866, he suggested for children of all ages a liaison between instruction and productive labor. This principle became the corner stone of the Soviet school system under the name of "polytechnization." Education is divided by Marx into mental, physical, and technological (or polytechnical), the last seeking to acquaint children with "the general principles of all productive processes," and giving them "practical knowledge and habits of using the simplest (basic) tools of all forms of production."

The founders of Marxism were against the exercise of any educative influence by the state and the church in a capitalistic society, and insisted that these agencies confine themselves to the transmission of "information." But the proletarian dictatorship must accept the polytechnized school and use it for political education to "raise the working class to a much higher level than that of the existing middle and higher classes." The only recognized forerunner of the Soviet régime, the Paris commune of 1871, tried under the "plenipotentiary of education," Vaillant, to put into effect the educational principles of the First International, but during its short existence of seventy-two days

[2] *Kommunistitsheskoe Prosvestshenie*, No. 20, 1931, p. 36.

accomplished very little. It proclaimed the principles of free universal polytechnic and secular instruction and education, and organized school workshops and political festivals for children. With no more than this for precedent, and with no more guidance than the general principles of Marxism, the Soviet leaders had to create a positive system of education that would be at once socialistic and efficient. Lenin wisely warned his impatient followers that "the cultural problems cannot be solved as rapidly as political or military problems."

The first reform of education was proclaimed by the Provisional Government as early as April, 1917. But its realization was handicapped during the eight months of the Kerensky régime because of the incessant struggle for power which absorbed every energy. Four days after the Bolshevist capture of Leningrad, the newborn Soviet government published its first declaration concerning education, signed by Lunatsharsky. The declaration might have been issued by any radical school reformer in Western Europe, and contained very little typical Bolshevism. This was due to the unpreparedness of the government for victory, and to sabotage on the part of the great majority of the intelligentsia (the teachers included). The declaration tried to compromise with the demand for reform that should be radical but not at all Bolshevistic. The statute of the unified labor school was not published until a year later. In fact, the first five years of the Soviet régime, years of civil war and military communism, were devoted by the educational leaders to the gathering of scattered forces and the working out of tentative programs and methods. In addition, financial support was neglected in favor of more pressing needs; the percentage of educational expenditure in the budget of the RSFSR fell in 1922 to three and a half percent.[3]

The year 1922 marks a turning point. The tenth All-Russian Soviet Congress proclaimed in martial language: "further retreat on the front of enlightenment must be blocked." Lenin demanded vigorously "a shifting of the entire state budget in order to satisfy first of all the needs of primary instruction."[4] From then on support for the

[3] In discussing the Soviet educational system, the material will concern mainly Russia proper—the RSFSR. It differs slightly in the other parts of the Soviet Union without, however, affecting the fundamental principles.

[4] *Pedagogicheskaia Enziklopedia*, Moskva, 1929, I, 1047.

educational system was constantly enlarged. Content and method show many hesitations and changes during the last decade, and reflect to a certain extent the flexible policy by which the Soviets have sought to face reality without sacrificing basic principles. In the year 1926, Lenin's widow, Kroupskaya, published a book on education, under the significant title *In the Search for New Ways*. Groping did extend to "new ways" and new methods, but never to new aims. Literacy and communism remained ever the primary objectives.

Every school and reading room in the Soviet Union has on its walls a colored poster with Lenin's aphorism: "Communism cannot be built in an illiterate country." He dreamt of the day when every kitchen-maid would have learned how to rule the state. The class nature of Soviet education is thoroughgoing. It manifests itself in privileges for the workers, in the selection of teachers, and in the methods and courses of study. Lenin wrote: "Some people blame us for the organization of a class system of schooling, but schooling always was permeated with class interests." And Zinoviev, once president of the Communist International, pointed out: "The bourgeoisie conceals the class character of its school system, but we do not consider it necessary to conceal the fact that . . . education in the communistic spirit constitutes the core of our school work."[5] It is contemplated that this attitude will remain dominant until the enemies of the proletariat have disappeared *as a class*. Only thereafter, in a classless society, will education become merely human.

The basic document relating to education under the Soviet régime is the program which was approved during the eighth congress of the Russian Communist party in 1919. It requires "the transformation of the school into an instrument for the communistic regeneration of society." Furthermore, the school must become "an agency of ideological, organizatory, educational influence of the proletariat upon the half-proletarian and non-proletarian groups of the toiling masses, with the purpose of bringing up a generation which will be capable of a final establishment of communism." Stalin, the highest Party authority after Lenin's death, declares that dictatorship of the proletariat means not only violence, but also reëducation: "The

[5] *Ibid.*, p. 1062.

Party fights with rifle in hand for physical power, but the struggle for souls goes on during the whole period of dictatorship!"[6] "The method of persuasion must be the chief method employed by the Party in its leadership of the Class."[7] The concrete measures of the Party program provide for "free and compulsory, general and poly-technic instruction for all children up to the age of seventeen; for a full realization of the principles of unified labor school in the native tongues of pupils, with coeducation, absolutely secular."

This goal of Soviet education is to be accomplished according to the principle of rational planning which permeates the whole Soviet system. Side by side with economic there are cultural *piatilietkas* (Five-Year Plans) based on material premises and potentialities and coördinated with the universal social-economic plan. The current planning is viewed as a subdivision of a farsighted perspective planning and is being corrected constantly according to the hard checks of actual experience. The planning organ of each commissariat of education prepares the details of future planning for a state planning commission of the USSR—headquarters of the whole planning undertaking. This planning organ is, at the same time, the chief mechanism supervising the realization of the general plan in the field of education.[8]

Notwithstanding the fact that the educational principles of the party have been worded in a rather unequivocal manner, the last ten years have shown a great variety of views, interpretations, and practical methods of realization. Roughly speaking, the central controversy concerns the proper proportion between the general instruction of children and the rôle of manual labor in education. The close connection between theory and practice constitutes a fundamental principle of Marxian thought. Truth is concrete and checked by action. Action is senseless and may become fatal if it lacks clear orientation. "The philosophers before us," said Marx, "attempted to interpret the world, yet the dialectic materialism is destined to remake it." Stalin insists that "theory becomes objectless unless it is tied up with revo-

[6] Joseph Stalin, *Leninism*, p. 38.
[7] *Ibid.*, p. 45.
[8] See *Report* of the delegation from the USSR to the World Social-Economic Congress, Amsterdam, August 23-29, 1931.

lutionary practice, and practice becomes blind unless its road is illuminated by the light of revolutionary theory." In compliance with this principle Lenin demanded that "youth should be occupied every day, in every village, in every town, with the solution of some practical problem, be it the smallest and the simplest." At the same time, he preached constantly that

our school ought to give youth the foundation of sciences, the ability to work out communistic views. It must make of them educated men. One can become a communist only if and when he has enriched his mind with the knowledge of all the spiritual wealth of mankind.

These and other formulas led to conflicting attitudes among the pedagogues. One group stressed labor at the expense of general knowledge;[9] another favored the improvement of more traditional general instruction. This fundamental disagreement, accompanied by experimenting with all possible methods, resulted in the greatest confusion among teachers, and caused such harm to actual educational work that the central committee of the Party devoted a part of its session in 1931 to this crucial problem. A resolution emerged which is considered, after the program of the Party, the most important expression of the aims and methods of the Soviet school.

This resolution contains less than the usual amount of revolutionary phraseology and much more than is customary in the line of concrete suggestions. It is permeated with pedagogic realism. It insists that the school must be primarily a *school*, rather than an annex to a factory, or an experimental station for trying out various methods, or a forum for discussion—such as it had tended to become during the early years of the Soviet system.

It is the opinion of the Committee of the Party[10] [the resolution declares] that the Soviet school is far from meeting the tremendous demands imposed upon it by socialistic construction. One of our fundamental criticisms is that the school fails to provide a sufficient body of general knowledge, which is indispensable for entrance to the "technicums" and higher schools. Graduates of elementary and

[9] A member of the Commissariat of Education, Schoolgin, thus expressed his contempt for "verbalism." "It is," he said, "important to accomplish the five year plan, and if as a result children remain illiterate, why should we worry?" (*Sa Politechnitsheskuiu Shkolu*, No. 10, 1931, p. 46.)

[10] The citations from the resolution which are given here are from the text as published in *Pravda*, September 5, 1931.

secondary schools are not well enough grounded in such fundamental subjects as physics, chemistry, mathematics, native language, and geography. In a number of instances, polytechnization assumes a purely formal character, thus violating our basic principle of preparing educated builders of socialism able to integrate theory with practice and possessing a mastery of technique. . . . Any attempt [the resolution continues] to introduce polytechnization into the school at the expense of a systematic and thorough grounding in the fundamental sciences, particularly physics, chemistry and mathematics, is a glaring distortion of the idea of polytechnization of our schools. The teaching of the fundamental subjects must conform with carefully elaborated teaching plans and courses of study.

The foundation of communistic education is polytechnical training, which aims to equip the pupils with the "elements of science," acquaint them "in theory and practice with the main branches of production," make them see the "intimate relation between theory and practice." The resolution pays special attention to the frequently confused relation between labor and acquiring knowledge in schools: "the merging of theory with productive labor must be so conducted, that the entire socially productive work of the pupils will be subservient to the academic work of the school." To secure the productive work of the pupils "every necessary aid should be extended to the commissariats of public education and instruction by the factories, Soviet farms, machine tractor stations, and collective farms."

In regard to experimentation with novel methods detrimental to educational efficiency, the committee advises

avoiding employment on a large scale of methods which have not been tested. An unfortunate example is the wide use of the so-called "project method." The recent anti-Lenin attempts to base all school work on the project method has actually led to the disorganization of our schools.

At the same time the committee advises the organization

in every region and in all cities of a network of model polytechnical schools, to facilitate the understanding of their character among the teaching staff and the population. The education research institutions are to concentrate their work in the school, and particularly that part of the work which deals with the polytechnization.

A special institute of experienced instructors "is to render permanent practical assistance to the teacher in his every day work in school."

In accordance with the new tendency of the Party to favor personal instead of collective authority and responsibility and to foster successful leadership, the committee points out that

the improvement of the quality of school work is impossible unless the quality of the leadership is considerably raised. This entails due recognition of meritorious leadership, and of political position, as well as of the geographic location of a given region. . . . The "equalizing" approach in distributing forces and funds should be entirely eliminated. . . . The Commissariats of the republics must increase the responsibility of teachers for the quality of school work, rewarding and encouraging conscientious teachers who know their work.

The resolution prescribes the increase of salaries for elementary and secondary-school teachers, as well as differentiated salaries based upon zones, types of training, and quality of work. At the same time, teachers are to be supplied with provisions and merchandise at the same rates and under conditions similar to those enjoyed by industrial workers (a very important privilege, in view of the shortage of commodities in the USSR). Special attention is given to school buildings and to teaching equipment. Gosplan is ordered to work out a five-year scheme of new school building construction, and the local Party and Soviet authorities are asked "to vacate all former school buildings now used for other purposes, and to turn buildings confiscated from the kulaks into school houses."

It is interesting to note that a special provision tries to limit the rights of the pupils' organizations, stating that "children's self-government in the schools is to be directed primarily towards the quality of school work and raising school discipline." This restrictive definition of the school children's competence became imperative in view of their predominance in the school organization at the expense of the teachers' authority and efficiency.

The resolution contains also the usual appeal for the inculcation of communistic principles:

During the period of socialistic construction, while the proletariat is gradually effecting an eradication of all class distinctions and a consequent acute class struggle, it is particularly imperative to stress communistic training which will tend to counteract any attempt to inculcate anti-proletarian ideology in the minds of the Soviet school children.

This resolution will not, of course, produce miracles overnight; but it is likely to become a milestone in the development of the

Soviet school. By special decrees of the government of the RSFSR, teachers' salaries have been raised, polytechnical equipment has been improved, and courses of study, as well as methods of instruction, have been subject to a radical uniform revision. Numerous decrees and instructions issued during the years 1932-34 showed a consistent adherence to the new principles of educational policy embodied in the above-quoted resolution. The problem of efficiency has been prevailing, and displacing haphazard "leftist" experiments.

IX

THE EDUCATIONAL SYSTEM AND ITS OPERATION

1. *The Soviet School System*

The USSR presents a striking example of a state in which politics has become conscious pedagogy. Education has been made a special form of politics; it is treated as an instrument of dictatorship. But, since dictatorship is merely a means of socialistic construction, education in the last analysis is not a servant of the state, but one of the roads to the realization of communism. Education is thus in full harmony with the pulse of Soviet life, and every manifestation of this life is permeated with the same dominating spirit. Education is strictly centralized and constitutes a link in the chain of socialist institutions in a country where labor is "a matter of honor, a matter of glory, a matter of valor and heroism."[11] The educational system claims to be the most progressive in the world; it defies all prejudices of the past and takes over the latest achievements of other countries in order to apply them with appropriate communistic corrections. It claims also to be the most democratic system, since the working classes enjoy all of its privileges. It claims to be an institution of revolutionary internationalism, national in form, socialistic in substance. It claims to be a secular, godless institution substituting science and human progress for all the creeds of a six-thousand-year-old society. Finally, it claims to be a factor in the spiritual triumph of the proletariat, and its weapons are materialism, collectivism, and activism.

The following chart impresses one primarily with the thorough centralization of all the possible channels of instruction and education. Private educational institutions are prohibited.

The chart shows a design for a smooth transition from one school grade to another, serving always the purposes of the state, particularly that of urgent industrialization. No charge is made for school instruction, with temporary exceptions in regard to the remnants of the bourgeoisie. The two main divisions of the schools are those

[11] Stalin.

CHART 3

SCHEME OF PUBLIC EDUCATION IN THE RSFSR

INSTITUTIONS

General

Research Institutions

Vocational

Vus

Industrial Agricultural Pedagogical Medical Art Socio-economic

Technicums

Industrial Agricultural Pedagogical Medical Art Socio-economic

Trade school Factory school School of peasant youth

Primary School

Preschool Institutions

Kindergarten Playground Playrooms Children's homes

Nursery

AGE
Above 22

Second cycle of
Secondary school

15-17

First cycle of
Secondary school

17-22

12-15

8-12

3- 8

Under 3

devoted to child education and those devoted to adult education. The former division is subdivided into general (social) education and special (vocational) education. The latter division extends its direct propagandistic energy to all the interests and activities of the population.

The general (social) system of education provides for children until the age of seventeen. Its subdivisions are: 1) pre-preschool education of babies until the age of three years, which is intended to furnish them with a healthy environment and to relieve working mothers of double duties; 2) preschool education (third to eighth year), represented by kindergartens, children's homes, playgrounds, children's rooms in the workmen's clubs, and so forth;[12] 3) polytechnic labor school education (eighth to seventeenth year). This last type of school consists of two grades: *a*) four-year primary school (eighth to twelfth year); and *b*) five-year secondary school (twelfth to seventeenth year) which is in turn subdivided into two cycles; first, twelfth to fifteenth year, and, second, sixteenth to seventeenth year. The first cycle of the secondary school together with the primary school forms the so-called "semilietka"—a seven-year school which is expected to become universal and compulsory. The introduction of a compulsory nine-year school (eighth to seventeenth year) is postponed until financial conditions, equipment, and staff make it practicable. The "seven-year" school prepares students for the next general grade. It also prepares them for life through the various vocational bifurcations which correspond to the practical needs of the country: thus there are the trade schools or FSU (industrial schools attached to mills and factories), the SKM (schools of peasant youth), and some others. The same principle applies to the second cycle of the secondary school which opens the way either to the *Vus* (universities and similar institutions) or to vocational life. Parallel to the general second cycle of the secondary schools, there exists a widespread net of *Technicums* (middle grade of vocational education). Attendance at the general schools or at the technicums is a prerequisite to admittance to the *Vus*. The purpose of the *Vus* is

[12] In view of the insufficient number of preschool institutions which exist at present, there is often a "zero" class, receiving children of about seven years of age, attached to the primary schools.

to prepare specialists of the highest qualification as well as those aspiring to scientific or professorial careers. There are six varieties of technicums, and six corresponding faculties of *Vus,* each variety providing training for a particular specialized occupation. This co-ordination is designed to provide continuity of training along technical lines.

In order to expedite the creation of a "proletarian intelligentsia" and to make entrance into the *Vus* possible for adult workmen and peasants who have had no chance to secure the full ordinary general education, the *Rabfak* or "worker's faculties" have been organized as an important additional institution with a four-year course. The special research institutes afford training for various types of specialists, including those who will become teachers in the *Vus.*

A large group of institutions is devoted specifically to the political education of the adult population. It begins in a wide net of "liquidation points" or schools for adults and spreads over all forms of interest and activity. The "party schools" have to prepare functionaires for the party or government institutions. There are even *Comvus* or special communist universities for the training of future political leaders.

The monopoly of the party-state is shown in the administrative concentration of almost all branches of education in the commissariats of education of the several republics (there is no commissariat for the Union). The typical organization of the commissariat is as follows:[18] at the head is the commissar, who has wide authority, and is supported by a council. Besides the administrative department the commissariat includes: 1) the *Gus* which supervises the preparation of courses of study, the methods of education, and the appointment of professors and teachers in the *Vus,* and directs the preparation of scholars; 2) the *Glavsozvos,* which supervises the system of general (social) education; 3) the *Glavprofobr,* which directs vocational education; 4) the *Glavnauka,* which supervises scientific work in academies and other scientific institutions, scientific museums and libraries, and so forth; 5) the *Glavlit,* which supervises and censors the press, literature, theatrical productions, printing offices, libraries, bookshops, publishing offices, and so forth; 6) the *Sovnazmen,* which

[18] We take as a pattern the commissariat of the RSFSR.

supervises the education and enlightenment of all non-Russian nationalities in the RSFSR; and 7) the *Glavpolitprosviet,* which supervises and directs the propaganda of communism through all channels outside the general school system, which symbolizes the inseparable ties between education and politics, between the Party and the State, and which permeates all the pores of the intellectual life.

In considering the courses of study in the system of general education, it is necessary to begin with a negative observation. Some traditional subjects like Latin, Greek, and religion have been abolished. Religion, however, does play an important part, as a target for incessant attacks, in schools of all grades. Further, the emphasis given to various subjects in the courses of study has undergone a substantial change. For example, in the Czarist *gymnasium* (high school), about sixteen percent of class time was devoted to mathematics, physics, chemistry, and natural sciences, while in the Soviet school of the same grade, these subjects occupy about forty percent of class time. The study of different crafts as special subjects has emerged and takes about ten percent of class time. Physical culture, neglected in old Russia, is a regular subject occupying five to ten percent of the time, and replacing in addition, the prayer which formerly was held each morning before the school day commenced. The social sciences are a special and most important subject in Soviet schools.

A characteristic of the general schooling is the complex investigatory method of instruction. The whole curriculum centers around three chief elements: 1) *nature* (physics, chemistry, zoölogy, biology, and so forth) ; 2) *labor,* as the decisive factor in exploitation and in the control of nature and its resources (agriculture, technology, industry in its various forms, including "anarchic" and "planned" systems of organization) ; and 3) *society* (family, school, social classes, capitalism, parties, Soviet régime, Five-Year Plan, Komintern, trade unions, current problems, and so forth). Already the three R's are taught on this basis.

The loose experimentation with various methods (Dalton plan, project method, and others) was carried so far as to endanger the elemental acquisition of general knowledge. According to the statement of a leading educator (Shumsky) the graduates of many seven-year schools even in the big cities had received such inadequate preparation that they often were not able to follow the lectures in the *Vus*. The resolution of the Central Committee, quoted above, proposed to the commissariats of education of the Soviet Union that they proceed immediately to "the drawing-up of scientific Marxian courses of study." The revised courses should make *provision for an exactly defined body of systematic knowledge* of the native tongue, mathematics, physics, chemistry, geography, and history. But the Committee did not touch the basic principles of the studies at all. There are three such basic principles: 1) *a communistic outlook upon the world;* 2) *emphasis on labor;* and 3) *immediate connection with life*.

An analysis of the revised course in any subject shows an all-permeating spirit of dialectic materialism. The new program for grammar, for instance, although it still uses in part the traditional categories (noun, verb, and so forth), is treating the language as a medium of class struggle. New words and forms, created under the Soviet régime, are referred to and studied as an expression of the revolution. The textbooks contain stories, essays, and poems directly related to the struggle of the proletariat in the Soviet Union or abroad.[14] Literature is studied as a form of class struggle. After a period of neglect, carefully selected classics have been reintroduced as a means of giving insight into the life of the bourgeois classes. The commissariat of education of the RSFSR decided, in the fall of 1933, to publish, for the use of school children between the ages of thirteen and fifteen, special abridged editions of the Russian pre-revolutionary writers (Pushkin, Lermontov, Gogol, Nekrassov, Tourgenev, Tchekhov, and others) and of foreign classics (among them Mark Twain, Jack London, Longfellow, Walter Scott, Charles Dickens, and others). A series of classics for the primary schools is being published at present. But revolutionary literature, both Russian and foreign, occupies the central place. As for mathematics, there is a strong effort to treat it dialectically, and the problem which this purpose raises is continuously discussed in special publications. Numbers should be treated as results of a process; six, for instance, may mean three plus three, or four plus two, or ten minus four, or

[14] The *Story of the Great Plan*, a textbook for the primary schools, is an example. It is translated under the title, *New Russia's Primer*.

two times three, or be the result of an infinite number of processes. The dialectic relation between "quality" and "quantity" forms a part of the studies: for instance, the nth power of one-half in its relation to one or zero, transition from a circle to an ellipse, from a polygon to a circle, or from a trapezoid to a triangle. The problems are taken from surrounding life and are anything but abstract. The pupils in the primary school have to solve arithmetical problems about tractors, the collection of grain, taxes, and the like.[15]

Natural sciences as well as physics, chemistry, and astronomy, are studied for the purpose of controlling nature, and used also for anti-religious propaganda. An introduction to chemistry states boldly: "chemistry in school must be communistic, and reflect the ideas of the working class and serve its purposes." Somewhat more comprehensible is the requirement of the study of chemical warfare, poison-ous gases, explosives, and the like. The study of geography is based on Engel's hypothesis that the "geographical environment affects mankind, not directly, but mainly by means of the given relations in the productive process." It is connected with economics and includes the rational exploitation of natural resources, socialistic reconstruc-tion in the Soviet Union and world struggles for oil, copper, rubber, and other commodities. Furthermore, it describes foreign countries with a special reference to possible intervention, and touches some military subjects. Among other things the study of geography is in-tended to lead pupils to the conclusion that "the existence of the bourgeois class is incompatible with a rational development of so-ciety and mankind."

The new tendency is emphasized in the joint decree issued in May, 1934, and signed by Joseph Stalin, general secretary of the Com-munist party, and Vyacheslaf Molotoff, President of the Council of Commissars. According to a dispatch of the Associated Press pub-lished in the *New York Times,* May 17, 1934, the decree ordered that beginning in the next semester, ancient and modern history and ele-mentary geography be added to the subjects taught in primary and

[15] The story goes that a class was offered the following problem: A merchant buys grain from a peasant at fifty cents a bushel and sells it in the city at a dollar a bushel. What does he get? Before the little folk could think it over, smart Peter gave a prompt reply: "Five years in prison."

secondary schools. Previously these subjects have been taught only with relation to their revolutionary significance.

The *Pravda*, chief Communist party organ, explained:

Abstract sociological themes up to now have been substituted for a coherent exposition of historical facts. . . . Our school children know very little about the actual facts of ancient and modern history. . . . A knowledge of historical events and personalities is of exclusive importance for the future constructors of socialist society. . . . Similarly, the study of geography has been nothing but abstract themes and sociological generalizations. Our textbooks are over-filled with figures and statistical material. . . . Students have been taught to ignore the names of rivers, cities, states and mountains and have been taught socialist economics instead of pure geography.

The decree ordered the immediate replacement of the present textbooks.

Foreign languages are considered "first of all as an instrument of contact with the revolutionary working class of the West." Foreign literature is used for comparing the sufferings, humiliation and struggle of the revolutionary proletariat in the West with its life in the country of victorious socialism. At the same time, acquaintance with the technical literature in foreign languages is encouraged as a powerful lever for realizing the *idée fixe* of "overtaking and passing the capitalistic world." Correspondence of the pupils with comrades outside Russia is fostered as a good opportunity both for improving knowledge of language, and establishing closer ties with the revolutionary West.

From what has been said, the peculiar character of the social sciences, as they are studied in the Soviet schools, should be clear. The Soviet schools temper, in theory, the volume and character of studies to the age of the pupils. But even in the first years of the secondary school (fifth and sixth years of schooling) when the boys and girls are from thirteen to fourteen years old, they have to study, and to write papers and make speeches on, such topics as: the dictatorship of the working class and the dictatorship of the bourgeoisie; the labor policy of the party; its national policy; the last thesis of Joseph Stalin; anti-Semitism and nationalism as an expression of counter-revolution; perspectives of the world revolution; trade unions, Soviets and coöperatives as the main driveshaft from the party to toiling masses; planned economy. The axis about which the study of social sciences revolves is the problem of two worlds, two systems (capitalistic and Soviet), between which there can be nothing but struggle ending with the inevitable victory of the world revolution.

The other two characteristics in the Soviet educational system are labor and contact with life. It would be somewhat artificial to treat these two elements separately, since, according to the Soviet attitude, to live means to work, and physical work is as honorable as mental work. As a matter of fact, there can be observed now and then an inferiority complex among the intellectuals in the Soviet Union, under the influence of incessant praise for manual workers. "He who does not work shall not eat" has become reality in a country with some 165,000,000 people. Work is a social duty, but it is supposed to give the greatest satisfaction to a conscientious citizen. School is also a place of work. Pupils are working for themselves and for the community. Labor establishes the most effective contact with the environment through the exercise of senses and reason; labor processes secure real knowledge of things, and, more than that, they lead to the reconstruction and remodeling of the environment according to a higher design. This attitude of the Soviet school towards labor suggests the gulf which separates the Soviet labor school from the "labor school" in the West. Even for the most progressive defenders of the "labor school," like Dewey, in this country, or Kerschensteiner, Lay, Oestreich, and others, in Europe, labor is one of the pedagogic methods, a purely educational matter not connected directly with the surrounding life of the community, a means to an end. In a Soviet school socially useful labor is an end in itself. The method, thus conceived, is a reflection of the rôle of productive labor in life, and aims not at the preparation of a perfect human being in general, but of a toiling citizen, who commences in school, in forms adapted to his age, what he will continue to do when the school period is over—not more and not less. Different methods such as the Dalton plan, the project method, or the Montessori scheme are all of them subordinated to the supreme principle just sketched. He who does not realize this attitude cannot understand the Soviet system of education. He is like a man who tries to unlock a door with the wrong key.

The life of any school of any grade in the USSR is saturated with concrete, productive, collective labor adjusted to the peculiarities of age, season, and region. The materials and forms of labor are taken from the environment and adapted to the requirements of instruction. Very small children in preschool institutions practice collective labor, their individual bias being taken into consideration. They dress and undress themselves; they are taught to wash dishes in turn and to arrange dining tables; they cultivate plants and get knowledge of colors and numbers in the course of work; they decorate their rooms and arrange festivals, always proceeding from the psychologically simple forms to those more complex. Their awakening emotions are directed as early as possible along the line of a materialistic outlook upon the world. They are trained to fear nothing, to respect and love the red banner, to prefer collective work to individual, to sacrifice their personal desires for the sake of the common interest. As a rule, no fairy tales embellish their leisure: illustrated poems and stories about the real forces and beauties of nature and the great aims and deeds of man (those of Lenin being greatest) displace them. Their imagination is directed toward an active and rather utilitarian approach to the environment.

The work in the primary school is linked up with the life of the surrounding village, town, or factory, as the case may be. The pupils study their working environment and take active part in the life of the local Soviet, "reading hut" or coöperative store; they perform useful tasks such as distributing notices of meetings, and selling stamps. They work in the school garden or orchard, and what is produced is used for the needs of the school. The school workshops prepare furniture for the school or for the next kindergarten. Frequently the children teach the three R's to their illiterate parents. They bring home new moral standards and criticize their parents' old-fashioned views and manners of life. They have their own clubs and meetings for the discussion of politics and current problems.

The secondary schools vary in the character of their activities—especially in industrial districts where they are linked up with the so-called "mother-enterprise." This may be a textile plant, a metallurgical factory, a coal mine, a lumber mill, or any other type of large industrial undertaking. Their workshops produce useful things for the school, or the products may be sold for money with which to improve the school. Wherever possible they spend a part of their time in the factories, the educational result being a rather thorough acquaintance with the fundamentals of the main industrial branches. The "schools of peasant youth" are similarly adjusted to agriculture. During recent years the majority of schools have made an important step toward a closer contact with life by concluding special agreements with the neighboring industrial enterprises or collective (or state) farms. A formal agreement is usually concluded between all the workmen and administrators of a factory and the general body of pupils and teachers of the school. The agreement contains a long list of mutual obligations. The factory undertakes to delegate workmen to the school council, to check the accomplishments of the school and to take care of its material needs, to provide the school workshops with tools and scrap, to grant scholarships; the school in turn undertakes to fulfill conscientiously the prescribed program, to strengthen discipline among the pupils and teachers, to look after sanitary conditions in the school, to liquidate illiteracy among the workmen and their families, and to provide the workmen and the rest of the population with amusements, such as theatrical performances, concerts, and revolutionary festivals.

It is hardly necessary to point out that any approach other than the Marxian simply does not exist in these schools except as a target for criticism. Dialectic materialism is regarded as the only scientific outlook upon the world, and the only scientific method as unshakeable as the discovery of Copernicus. Moral education is not based on religion. Kant's "categorical imperative" is, for a Soviet school, only a misleading formula which assumes a universal code of ethics and suggests the reconciliation of classes. The only accredited ethics is that which reflects the interests and ideals of the struggling proletariat. This is the sole measure of good and evil, of moral and immoral, of justice and injustice.

Sex education is not a special subject of instruction in schools. The system of universal coeducation is supposed to foster more natural relations between boys and girls. Open discussions, stressing the social duties as the highest end of life, are held whenever they appear to be necessary. This orientation is designed to help children to overcome the sex difficulties which arise during the period of adolescence. Redirection of the sex interests into socially useful channels (manual work, club life, excursions) together with manifold physical exercises is considered a reasonable solution of this difficult problem.

Physical education holds an important place in the schools. It starts with an emphasis on hygiene and sanitary measures in the nurseries and occupies a considerable portion of the time in the schools of all grades. Like all other phases of education, it is subordinated to class interest and is not regarded as an end in itself. It is a means of strengthening the working class bodily, of fostering social instincts and team spirit, and of serving eugenic and military purposes. School schedules provide special hours for physical culture. Various sports and excursions belong to the regular educational program.

Formal military training does not exist, but the idea of defense is introduced in various forms: questions of defense of the Soviet state are discussed whenever opportunity offers; courses of studies, as mentioned above, frequently include sections devoted to military preparation; some physical exercises have a military form; and the glorification of the Red Army is incessant.

The widespread belief that aesthetics are neglected in Soviet education is not supported by the facts. According to Marxian doctrine there does not exist any universal system of aesthetic values. The proletarian conception of beauty differs from the bourgeois conception. Art must be freed from the decadent influences of the dying class, and become a creative element in the formation of new life. This part of Marxism is not highly developed. The aesthetic element permeating Soviet education, however, caused John Dewey, after his visit to Russia, to remark: "There is no country, unless it be possibly Mexico, where the aesthetic aim and quality so dominates all things educational as in Russia today."[16] Only in preschool institutions is artistic education not made a separate subject, but even here the activities of the children have a conscious artistic character. Special hours are devoted in the schools to plastic arts, singing, music, and rhythmics. Artistic education varies from play to collective cre-

[16] *Soviet Russia*, p. 43.

ative work. The walls of the schools are decorated with posters, drawings, and models made by the pupils. Choruses, orchestras, dramatic performances, processions, celebrations of revolutionary holidays, of "days of harvest" (in villages), and of industrial achievements (in towns), absorb a considerable portion of time, and introduce an element of joy and enthusiasm into the pupils' lives. The development of manual and mechanical skills, too, takes into account the artistic element. New forms, new standards of beauty arise. The museums of old art are frequented by children, the interpretations made by the accompanying instructors being, of course, of a strictly class character.

The stimulation of national cultural development among the numerous minor nationalities is a striking feature of Soviet policy. The All-Union Academy of Sciences supervises the tremendous work of creating new alphabets for nomadic tribes which have had none, and of Latinizing the Arabic alphabet—an example followed recently by Turkey. All the numerous nationalities which compose the USSR have not only the opportunity of developing their own culture, but are encouraged and generously supported in their cultural growth by the dominant Russian nation, in direct contradiction to the ruthless Russification which characterized the "Dark Ages" of the old régime.

In the control of the pupil's work, the grades "satisfactory" and "unsatisfactory" are used as measures of efficiency, concentration, formal knowledge, and abilities. The grades are discussed with the pupils at special meetings at the end of each term; dissensions arising between the "pupils' collective" and the teacher are submitted to the school council in which the pupils are represented by delegates. As a matter of fact control is continuous, since the daily program is filled with active work and problems to be solved by collectives of pupils. The schools check not only the theoretical knowledge, but also the abilities and skills of the pupils. Thus children graduating from the primary schools usually are required to know how to use electricity, to make minor repairs, to use simple tools, to work in a garden or in an orchard, to wash and repair laundry, to prepare simple meals. They also are expected to be able to draw a simple sketch, to orientate themselves in space and time, to use different means of communication and transportation, and, last but not least, to report events, to read papers intelligently, to take minutes, to preside at meetings, to discuss current politics, to prepare wall-newspapers, posters, and small exhibitions, to organize children's clubs and festivities. Gradually the artificiality of stuffing small children's brains with politics is becoming evident to the Soviet authorities. They realize the danger of the fatigue and dullness that follows overdoses of abstractions in school activities. In April, 1934, the Central Committee of the Party ordered a radical limitation of political studies, especially in the primary schools. The decree reprimands the school superintendents for imposing incomprehensible political themes and discussions upon the children and prohibits in particular the study of Marxism and Leninism, as well as any discussion of the Party affairs, in primary schools. Similar topics are to be strictly limited and supervised in the secondary schools to avoid fatigue of the children.

Within the limits drawn by general legislation and the decrees of the Party and Soviet authorities, each school forms a self-governing body with three participating elements: teachers (the principal of the school and the school council), students (students' committee), and the surrounding community (local council of assistance). The activities and forms of students' self-government vary according to the age of the pupils and the character of their environment, but the common underlying purpose is to make the children coresponsible for the school and to educate them to the feeling that the school is their home. The student body is not atomized; it lives and functions in numberless circles and groups devoted to specific purposes: study, sport, discipline, children's clubs. Children's courts, displacing the disciplinary measures of the teacher, have lost their prestige and are being abolished, since they developed an unhealthy affection for trials and punishments and were creating a spirit of mutual suspicion and distrust. Punishments in the old sense are generally avoided, collective discussions of individual misconduct and persuasion being substituted for them.

There is no question in the Soviet school life that is not discussed with the pupils as with an equally interested element of the school, whether it be the schedule of studies, the need of equipment, or social work.

It is impossible to give an account of a Soviet school without men-

tioning the Pioneer and Comsomol organizations. The discerning
reader may realize their importance if it is pointed out that the relation between the students' self-government on the one hand, and the
Pioneer (or Comsomol) organizations on the other, is parallel to the
relation between the Soviet government and the Communist party.
Inspired by the idea of the Boy Scouts, the Pioneer movement was
called to life at the initiative of the Comsomol in the year 1921. Both
forms of youth movement are, so to speak, the younger branches of
the Party, the members of the former being in age from ten to sixteen, those of the latter from fourteen to about twenty-three. Children under ten years may become "October girls and boys" (*Octi-
abriata*), if they show a special interest in communistic ideas. These
organizations penetrate the whole life of youth in the Soviet Union.
They have been created according to the slogan: "Down with political apathy; down with neutralism in education."

The Pioneers are not merely preparing themselves for the noble
rôle of warriors and builders of communism. They *are* the younger
guard of the actual fighters for communism. Wherever there are
children there exists a Pioneer brigade. There is no school without
the so-called Pioneer "outpost." Special representatives of the Comsomol supervise and instruct the Pioneer movement. Like the workmen's clubs and the collective kitchens, the youth organizations are
consciously cultivating the broader spirit of communism as against
the traditional family ties—"the most conservative stronghold of
the dying old world, the monster of individualism and selfishness."
They also tend to head and direct all the activities of the children
inside and outside the schools, encouraging them to various forms
of socially useful work and politically useful forms of leisure. They
are the faithful knights of the Party and of the State.[17] They are
fiery agitators against religion, and take part in antireligious processions. They help to accomplish the *Piatilietka*. At the same time
they are helpful in the struggle against small nuisances, for instance, in the control of animal pests that would otherwise ruin the
crops. Recently they were given by the government the task of kill-

[17] In a city near Moscow the Pioneers made and put on the roofs of some factory
buildings huge posters: "We fight against our drunken fathers," and the story goes
that their propaganda for temperance led to the closing of the neighboring saloons.

ing annually five rats, ten mice, and ten field mice each. They help in discovering new supplies of natural resources and organize "poultry days," and "forest days." In schools they are the guardians of communism, and as such are tirelessly active. They are frequently the instigators of "socialistic competitions" between schools; they take part in the formation of shock brigades (*Udarniki*) and in the so-called "cultural attacks"—meaning campaigns of propaganda for literacy among adults. Besides all this, they are the eyes and ears of the Party, and watch non-partisan teachers who adhere to old methods and systems.

A similar rôle is played by the Comsomol—Lenin's union of communist youth—in the schools of higher grade. It is constantly at war against such "bourgeois prejudices" as religion, idealism, "obsolete" modes of life, and oppression of women. There are over five million registered members of the Comsomol and their number is growing steadily.[18] In a brilliant speech at the Comsomol congress of 1921, Lenin advised them first of all to study. They are fulfilling his will, but do much more than that: they raise new problems, they criticize, they investigate; they support the Party and the State and are a powerful source of new initiative.[19] The schools of working apprenticeship in the industrial districts and the "schools of peasant youth" owe their existence to the Comsomol propaganda. The Comsomol contributes considerably to the liquidation of illiteracy. Its members supply several million members to the well-known "Union of the Godless."

Numberless conflicts between the communistic youth organizations and the teaching staffs of the schools became at one time a serious obstacle to educational work. The problem was how to find and establish a reasonable equilibrium between the propagandistic and pedagogical aims of the school. The majority of the teachers not being members of the Party, their position was often precarious. At one time the authority of the teacher was undermined and discipline disappeared. The disorganization of the schools reflected the

[18] Seventy percent of all juvenile workers are members of the Comsomol.

[19] They are constantly used in the struggle against the incursion of red tape. Forming so-called "squadrons of light cavalry," they meddle frequently in bureaucratic affairs. Educationally there is given at the same time a useful outlet for the natural overflow of young energy.

troubles in economic life, which were due to a similar confusion between the functions and authority of the specialists and those of the
representatives of the Party. The above-mentioned resolution of the
Central Committee applied to education the new principles proclaimed by Stalin in 1931. Its unequivocal intention is to strengthen
the authority of the teacher at the expense of the other elements in the
Soviet school, to replace collective by individual responsibility. At
the same time the scope of the pupil's self-government is clearly restricted to "the improvement of the quality of school work and raising school discipline." The former all-embracing, often chaotic, right
of pupils to meddle in everything is now being curtailed. This shows
a growing confidence in the teacher and will undoubtedly (when
fully realized) become beneficial to Soviet education.

2. *Vocational and Adult Education*

Vocational education is divided into three grades. The lower
grade, corresponding in age to the first cycle of the secondary school,
includes vocational schools, "schools of working apprenticeship,"
"schools of peasant youth," and some other minor types. They are
based on primary-school education and prepare workmen for the various skilled occupations. The chief form of the vocational school of
the second grade is the *Technicum*; it prepares specialists of middle-
grade qualification and entitles its graduates to enter the *Vus* (the
Russian abbreviation for all institutions of university grade).

The above-mentioned *Rabfaks,* worker's faculties for adult workmen (usually of the ages eighteen to thirty-five years), are designed to
enable adults who have failed to get higher education, but have finished the primary schools and are politically literate, to enter the *Vus*.
As a rule the *Rabfaks* are connected with universities. They have a day
division for workmen who are sent by organizations and who devote
their time exclusively to study, and an evening division for workmen
who are occupied by day. The *Technicums* are specialized according to
industrial, agricultural, pedagogical, medical, art, and socio-economic
lines. The practical work forms the core of the studies.

The *Vus* form the last link in the Soviet school system. They have
two distinct aims. They must create new intellectual leaders of the
country from the ranks of the workmen and peasants, to replace the

former intelligentsia. They also must provide the various branches of Soviet life with qualified specialists. The selection of students according to class principles, which characterizes the whole system of education, reaches its climax in these institutions. By the year 1933 the proportion of workmen's and peasants' children among the students in the *Vus* had reached 50 percent. Within a few years the ratio is expected to reach 75 percent, since the proportion of workmen's and peasants' children among the new registrants has grown from 28.7 percent in 1926-27 to 68.4 percent in 1930-31. Not less significant is the proportion of the members of the Party and the Comsomol among the students; it increased from 11.4 percent in 1923-24 to 53 percent in 1933. Among the aspirants, i.e., students selected for scholarly work, the proportion grew from 8.8 percent in 1926-27 to 71 percent in 1929-30. This shows how persistently the Soviet state is working toward the elimination of non-proletarian scientists and teachers in the higher schools. The special institute in Moscow which trains "red professors" (like some other special institutes) admits only members of the Party.

The study of general subjects (except social sciences) is reduced to a minimum in the *Vus*. The USSR, unlike the United States of America, has no colleges. A few years ago there was a tendency to divide the universities into highly specialized institutes, but this process has now ceased on account of the great additional expenses which it involved. In accordance with the lines of specialization in the *Technicums,* there exist the following faculties (partly united in universities, mainly in the form of special institutes) : industrial, agricultural, pedagogical, medical, art, socio-economic, but also some other as for instance the recently created geographical and historical faculties. Most of the students receive full scholarships (thirty-five to one hundred ninety rubles a month) from the state or from various organizations in need of qualified specialists. They live usually in dormitories, and are completely occupied with their studies. As a matter of fact, the Soviet student is not a respected intellectual, but is rather a workman who temporarily enriches his scientific equipment in order to return as soon as possible to practical work. About half of his time is spent in factories and other institutions suited to his specialization. Lecturing is reduced to a minimum and takes not more than a fourth of his time. Prescribed courses of study call for supervised individual or collective research in seminars and libraries. The students of course participate in the whole organization of the *Vus* through their delegates and various bureaus, and are closely connected with the trade unions which correspond to their specialized fields of work. They have no worries about getting work, since a job usually is waiting for them even before they have finished their studies. This situation gives them a feeling of security unknown in the West nowadays. The students, led by the Comsomol, take the most active part in satisfying the economic and cultural needs of the country. They are the chief participants of the so-called *subbotniki*: i.e., days of voluntary work for the state. They send delegates to the remotest parts of the Union to fight on some new "front." At the same time they are omnivorous in their appetite for learning, and their sincere love of knowledge is matched only by their willingness to live without even elemental comfort. In some places they live in communes on a collectivistic basis, property being owned in common. In these communes they try to create the new forms of life, of morals, and of mutual relations.

Social sciences are an essential ingredient of all the curricula. They are, of course, treated from the Marxian standpoint only. It is significant that there is no "academic autonomy" in the sense of a privileged form of self-government in the *Vus*. That dream of the Russian universities prior to the revolution has not been realized under the Soviet régime. The presidents of the *Vus*—"rectors" or "directors"—are appointed by the commissariat of education, as are also the members of the faculties. Deviations of the professors from the official Marxian philosophy are persecuted, and no qualifications or scholarly merits are sufficient to save the guilty professor from the wrath of the government or the Party. The *Vus* are the highest cultural centers in the respective districts and their connections with the life of the country have wide ramifications.

In the case of any other country, the description of the educational system would be complete at this point. In the case of the system in the USSR, an account must be given of adult education, which is supervised mainly by the Chief Committee for Political Enlightenment (*Glavpolitprosviet*).

Before the October revolution, "out-of-school instructions" existed in Russia in forms similar to those in other countries. But the activities of the Soviet state are not comparable with those of the rest of the world. It extends its influence to all forms and manifestations of life, and is directed toward the most rapid possible transformation of the mind, the creation of a new man. The western governments usually follow the policy of a "passive policeman" with regard to the education of grown-up citizens. The "bias" of our libraries, museums, theatres, movies, and other channels of instruction and recreation manifests a passive acceptance of prevailing values rather than a conscious and active political purpose. In the Soviet Union all of these agencies are owned and controlled by the state, and serve its ends and ideals. It is not possible to describe all the activities of this character. The entire leisure, as well as the intellectual interest, of the Soviet citizen is exploited by the state for its political and social purposes. There are no exceptions to this principle and this policy. Institutions for the liquidation of illiteracy, schools for adults, reading rooms, libraries, museums, Red corners, clubs, exhibitions, excursions, theatres, concerts, movies, radio, the entire press, lectures, traveling libraries, itinerant bookstalls, posters, special peasant papers, all kinds of education by correspondence, sport performances, even circuses and variety shows, are controlled, supervised, directed, and inspired by the state. They also are linked up with the communistic faith, as well as with current policies and problems such as *Piatilietka* or the danger of intervention. The state satisfies all spiritual needs of the population, but the "food" has a constant political ingredient which is openly admitted or inconspicuously introduced. The glorification of socialistic constructiveness in contrast to the decaying world of capitalism constitutes the central theme. A special section of the commissariat of defense called *Pur* accomplishes the same work for the Red Army. The coöperatives, the trade unions, and other organizations take care of the political education of their members. The public opinion which is molded by the state creates a uniformity of views whenever they are expressed in public. Anti-Soviet attitudes are a crime, and even neutralism is tolerated less and less: its strongholds—literature and art—feel the growing strength of the Soviet state, and become, willy-nilly, its agencies.

Soviet education attempts to breed an intelligent and enthusiastic warrior and builder of communism—a new species of *homo sapiens* for the new world to come. That it will come is an article of faith of the "élite" in the Soviet Union. In its view the new spirit is already permeating the life of the civilized world through the triumphant march of the machine. Capitalism uses the high technique but resists and fights its inevitable social and economic consequences.

To expect, within a short decade, a complete success from the educational system of a country as large and as inert as Russia, would be unfair and unreasonable. A fair statement of the question of accomplishment would be: Has there been any elevation of the general cultural level of the people, and has there been definite accomplishment toward education along lines prescribed by the communists?

With respect to the general cultural level there is noticeable a conspicuous success. The previously mentioned resolution of the Central Committee states with justified pride:

The number of pupils in the primary and secondary schools has increased from 7,800,000 in the year 1914 to 20,000,000 in 1931. The social composition of the schools has changed radically. Children of the workers and of the masses of toilers in the village, who formerly had no educational opportunities, constitute at present the chief contingent in our schools. The culturally most backward peoples of the Soviet Union are given instruction in their native tongues; this involves the use for educational purposes of seventy languages. ... During the last year alone the number of pupils in the primary and secondary schools increased from 13,500,000 to 20,000,000.

Universal primary education has been almost achieved—especially in the RSFSR. Universal education on a seven-year basis (primary school and the first cycle of the secondary school) is expected by the year 1934. Illiteracy has been liquidated in the last four years among over 20,000,000 adults (as compared to the 8,500,000 scheduled in the cultural *Piatilietka,* for the five years ending 1933) . The circulation of newspapers and other periodicals increased from about 2,700,000 in 1913 to 35,000,000 in 1932. In 1914 a record total of 130,000,000 copies of books was published in the area of Imperial Russia. In 1931, in a much smaller area of the USSR, about 800,000,000 copies (mass publication of pamphlets included) have been published according to the reports of the *Voks* (All-Union Society of Cultural

Relations) .[20] The character of the Russian newspapers and periodicals is of a much higher educational value by comparison with pre-war Russian or modern western newspapers. There are, according to the most recent data, 470,000 students in the universities and similar institutions, and 797,000 students in the *Technicums*—and these figures represent only a half of the "hungry applicants." In the whole area of the USSR the proportion of literate persons increased from about twenty-five or thirty percent in the year 1913 to about sixty percent at present (according to other sources to seventy-five percent) .[21] The second Five-Year Plan (1933-37), approved by the Congress of the Communist party of the USSR in January, 1934, requires and expects the following pace of development:

During the second Five-Year plan period not only is the liquidation of the illiteracy of the entire population of the Union, the liquidation of the semi-literacy of the adult, able-bodied population, and the introduction of universal, compulsory elementary education to be completed, but universal compulsory polytechnical education embracing the seven-year course is to be introduced in the village as well as in the town, this task having been basically completed as far as the town is concerned during the first Five-Year Plan period. The total number of students (in primary and secondary schools, workers' faculties, factory schools, technicums—and universities) is to increase to 36 million as against 24.2 million in 1932, or to 197 per 1,000 inhabitants, as compared with 147 per 1,000; not counting pre-school institutions, which in 1932 embraced 5.2 million children. . . .

The plan prescribes also:

Extensive development of mass extra-mural education, closely connected with the organization of the leisure time of the toilers for purposes of cultural advancement; increase in the number of clubs in town and village from 6,800 to 10,900 (the increase in towns amounting to 10.5 percent, in the villages to 130 percent), and in the number of public libraries from 15,000 in 1932 to 25,000 at the end of 1937.

Yet the qualitative achievements are less striking. The Soviet leaders are aware of this, and "struggle for quality" is one of the most pop-

[20] Joseph Freeman, *Soviet Worker*, p. 320.
[21] In a recent conference devoted to the second cultural *Piatilietka* (1933-37), a member of Gosplan stated that the entire adult population up to the age of fifty was already literate; including even the most backward nationalities of the Soviet Union. Unfortunately this general statement was not accompanied by a statistical analysis.

ular slogans. In every field of education may be found samples of a very high standard, but they do not represent the general level. Soviet publications display a severe self-criticism with regard to these short-comings. Great amounts of unfavorable evidence are stated daily with courage and bitterness. With reference, for example, to the level of instruction, a report[22] shows that in Saratov (a big industrial city on the Volga River) pupils of the seventh grade (about fourteen years old) were not able to figure twenty percent of forty-five, many of them believed that the Volga flowed into the Black Sea, and that Don (a river) was a sea. Another report states with regard to discipline: "Often children do anything in school except study." A pamphlet issued by the organization of Pioneers declares: "Our schools are called labor schools. But how many of them possess this character? The truth is that such schools constitute a small minority."[23]

The teaching staff is very far from being adequate, the difficulty lying chiefly in the fact that there is need for new hundreds of thousands of teachers. Short summer and winter sessions try to pre-pare new contingents of teachers, but in so far as this is accomplished, it is done at the expense of the quality of their instruction. The new stress on the polytechnization of the schools forces teachers to study various crafts in order to be able to check the work of the pupils. This serves to make the situation more difficult.

The teachers as well as the pupils are overloaded with a great variety of "socially useful work" in addition to the routine of studies in school. Only recently, the number of nervous breakdowns among pupils and teachers became so alarming that new instructions were issued in an attempt to create less abnormal conditions. The equip-ment of the schools is very often unsatisfactory; worn-out buildings, filth, lack of textbooks, and shortage of tools and materials for the polytechnical work, are common in many schools especially in the country. To make it easier for the children to reach the schools there are running now in Moscow special buses bringing children to school and home, but this comfort remains a dream for the country, and the absentees in the primary schools amount sometimes to twenty per-cent, in the Caucasus even to forty percent, because of the distances,

[22] *Na Putiach K Novoi Shkole,* January, 1932, Moskva.
[23] *Nakas,* Moskva, 1931, p. 43.

according to a report by Mr. Bubnov, the commissar of education in the RSFSR.[24]

The teachers are still in many cases suspected of anti-Soviet tendencies and suffer greatly under these suspicions. Only a few years ago there took place a "purging of the teaching staffs" of the universities with the purpose of eliminating the "infidels." Members of the faculties were compelled to undergo a public "examination" of their political creeds. The trials were led by party commissions and participated in by students.

Methodological experimentation on a large scale is still going on. Methods frequently are changed overnight. This was, for example, the case with the "project method." In the summer of 1931 the commissariat of education of the RSFSR advised, in a special decree, an increase of the number of hours spent by pupils of the primary and secondary schools in the workshops and factories. This increase was to be made at the expense of their curriculum in the schools. A few months later the previously mentioned resolution of the Central Committee declared that this proposal was wrong, and it was rescinded.

Such illustrations and criticisms could be multiplied; but it would be unfair to convict the educational system on the basis of such shortcomings. The Soviets may be right in calling them "maladies of growth."

3. The Products of the Soviet System

The ultimate issue is whether there is emerging in Soviet Russia a new species of citizen with a communistic mind and pattern of behavior, such as the educational system tries to breed and to cultivate.

In contrast with political party practice in the West, the membership of the Communist party, "WKP," and of its younger branch, the Comsomol, is consciously restricted by dint of severe prerequisites, tests, probations and merciless periodical purgings (*Tchistka*). The communists are tireless in their efforts to reforge the mind and will of the population. As often as not their over-

[24] It seems worth while to note the success of the Soviet labor colonies in reëducating young criminals, including the vicious "homeless children" (*besprisornye*) and turning them into useful citizens.

zealous, reckless treatment of the non-partisan citizens causes set-backs, especially among the peasants. But the strong organization, the discipline and the intelligent leadership of the Party have been able to overcome the numerous "crises of confidence." It is impossible to estimate closely the number of people sincerely in sympathy with the main principles of the Soviets, but various observations indicate that it is growing. The system of education accounts directly for this growth.

What are the outstanding characteristics of this "élite" which is leading "Red Russia" toward her new destiny? The *chevalier sans peur et sans reproche* is first of all a selfless and tireless warrior and herald of the communistic millennium, as full of enthusiasm as the first crusaders. He is the legitimate heir of the century-old, humble Russian pilgrim who wandered all his life in search of final truth.[25] He is also the heir of the pre-war peasant with his strong affection for the *mir* (community) who applied to himself the collective pronoun *we* rather than the consciously individualistic *I*. The roots of his fervor may be found in the fanatical Russian sectarians who, in the seventeenth century, committed mass suicides at the stake while defending the glory of their creed. But at the same time the new man is a cold, rationalizing politician, modeling the world after the pattern set up by Marx and Lenin. He possesses some characteristics of the early founders of Christian communes, yet also some traits of Nietzsche's superman.[26] He is free of the so-called bourgeois prejudices. He has no pity for class enemies. The idea of profit-seeking is abominable to him; he scorns material comfort and wealth until they are secured for everybody. He suppresses individualistic feelings and ambitions and desire for self-display: the interests of the class absorb his personality. The world is for him divided into communists, who are his brethren all over the globe; exploiters, who

[25] Interestingly enough: the two Russian words for truth are: (a) *istina,* a derivative of the verb *iskat,* to search; and (b) *pravda,* meaning both truth (intellectual value) and justice (moral value).

[26] Block's famous poem "Twelve" written in 1918 in Leningrad ends with the startling picture of *twelve* Russian "Reds" with guns in their hands and holy faith in their hearts. Ahead of them marches Jesus Christ adorned with a white garland of roses.

are his irreconcilable enemies to be conquered; and the unconscious remainder, who are to be converted. He works eighteen hours a day, always a soldier of the Revolution on duty, a pawn on the chess-board of class war; he lives for the Party and is ready to die in its defense.

It would be incorrect to suppose that the educational system alone could produce this "new mind." The whole set of Soviet institutions continuously revolutionizes life from top to bottom (collectivization of the farms!); the motivating effect of these institutions, despite their short existence, is growing, especially in view of the intellectual isolation of the Union from the rest of the world. The redirection of life goes on incessantly; a huge dam is built against the old, while a magnificent dynamo drives life and mind into the channels of communism.

But an extremely important question arises. Education in the Soviet Union is inseparably tied up, even chemically alloyed, with propaganda. The distinction between these two weapons is subtle so far as technique is concerned, yet their goals are different. The end of education is a personality; the end of propaganda is an adept. Education is to equip men for further growth and for critical searching after truth; propaganda claims to possess the truth and is anxious only to persuade of its goodness. For the educator human material is an end in itself; it is only a tool for the purposes of the propagandist.

The *Communist Manifesto* states unequivocally that it conceives of universal welfare in a classless society as the prerequisite and basis for a free development of the socially minded personality. The *Manifesto* apparently underrated the length of time required for the "jump from the realm of necessity to the realm of freedom." The experience in Russia shows that the renowned "jump" may take several decades. The "transitional state" has lasted seventeen years, and nobody can foretell how many more economic and cultural *Piatilietkas* it may require. Therefore we must speak for the time being of a "jump" from a "bourgeois necessity" to another "proletarian necessity." The Bolshevists expect a gradual transformation of the Soviet régime into a communistic "realm of freedom" under their leadership. Does this mean that they are going to take away the "scaffoldings" gradually and in the same degree as the remnants of capitalism are erased and the parts of the communistic structure accomplished? This seems probable judging from some recent tendencies of the Soviet policy.

The educational system of the proletarian dictatorship faces the necessity of developing builders and members of the classless society, while as a matter of fact it is wholly absorbed by the urgent needs of maintaining the dictatorship. Bolshevists usually apply the dialectic law to the contradictory character of the problem, and thus hope to overcome the antagonism. This notion may be consistent with theoretical consideration, but does not necessarily provide an effective solution of the educational dilemma "Eng ist die Welt, und das Gehirn ist weit. Leicht beieinander wohnen die Gedanken, doch hart im Raume stossen sich die Sachen."[27] At any rate the spiritual freedom of a critical, intelligent personality—a substantial element of the communistic society—can hardly be discerned in the Soviet Union. It is confined to a hothouse in the Kremlin and does not blossom outside. The millions of Soviet citizens are brought up with a conception of freedom arbitrarily delimited by the ruling party.

The overwhelming majority of the toiling masses in the Soviet Union enjoy freedom of thought in school as well as in life so long as they think along the basic lines of Marxism and Leninism sanctioned by the party. The educational system has to contribute to the maintenance of this concept of freedom and to defend it as the only reasonable, desirable and legitimate one possible. It admits only those mistakes in leadership which have been recognized by the leaders themselves. But Lenin was never wrong. If his writings reveal contradictions, it is the duty of the learned commentators to reconcile them, to show that they are apparent rather than actual. In case they disagree, the Party's official interpretation claims infallibility and must be accepted unconditionally as the final truth. An opinion supported by references to Lenin's theories and even to his

[27] "The wold is narrow, and wide the brain of man. Thoughts dwell easily together, but things jostle each other in space."—Schiller.

incidental remarks and notes gets credit and prestige. At present, Stalin is sharing Lenin's unshakable authority.

Such dogmatism and intolerance often creates simulated faith. Two striking instances may illustrate what is meant. Before Stalin's famous article "Dizziness from Success" was published in February, 1930, no paper in the Union uttered a word of criticism against the heartbreaking speed in the collectivization of the farms, and all praised its remarkable tempo. *After* Stalin gave the signal, the papers "discovered" overnight hundreds and thousands of the most reckless and stupid violations of the law, and outdid one another in demands for punishment of the the the men who were in charge of its enforcement. Another instance is in point. As soon as the previously mentioned resolution of the Central Committee of the party had been published, the official organ of the commissariat of education of the RSFSR suddenly "burnt the idols it worshipped yesterday," and disavowed the "project method" and other "heresies" which it had defended previously.[28] What can be the educational effect of such moral deeds? An alarming servility spreads all over the country and sometimes frightens the communist leaders themselves. *Pravda,* the central organ of the Party, published crying illustrations of overardent efforts to introduce dialectics in various branches of science and instruction.[29] It reported indignantly about papers and articles concerning the "Dialectic of a Diesel-Motor," "Marx-Lenin Theory in the Locksmith Trade," "The Principles of the Party in Mathematics," "Venerology and Dermatology from the Dialectic Standpoint," and so forth. The central organ of the Party stated with justified disdain: "Isn't this a mockery at dialectics to treat it as a universal pass-key?" No doubt it is. "Mais tu l'as voulu, George Dandin!" This overzeal is an inevitable result of the educational policy of the Party itself.

J. B. Watson has given a bitter picture of the modern religious man:[30]

He is a deeply religious man. What does that mean? It means that the individual goes to church on Sunday, that he reads the Bible

[28] *Sa Politechnitsheskuiu shkolu,* No. 10, 1931.

[29] *Pravda,* June 4, 1932.

[30] J. B. Watson, *Behaviorism,* New York, 1930, p. 273.

daily, that he says grace at the table, that he sees to it that his wife and children go with him to Church, that he tries to convert his neighbor into becoming a religious man. . . .

This picture applies to many Russians displaying their devotion to the Soviets. The Party leaders sincerely condemn and hate such lip service and the periodical purgings serve to get rid of these elements which seep into the Party. However, it is mere self-deception to disregard the fact that the root of the evil lies in the character of education. The right of the Soviet citizens to criticize current evils, "minor defects of the mechanism," does not compensate at all for the "tabu" on more substantial criticism.

Dialectic materialism recognizes the existence of "absolute" or "objective" truth, and welcomes the progress of science as a means of approaching it.[31] But that implies that the most brilliant theories are subject to change. How can Soviet education secure a further movement towards the "objective" truth if it puts a halter on thought about fundamentals?

The general notion that the Soviets deny personality is not correct. Soviet education struggles against individualistic habits conflicting with the common good of the masses. With this reservation, personality is fostered and encouraged. The institution of *vydvishenzy*—workmen promoted to the highest position in industry and in the government—is proof of this, as is also the intense inventive and exploring spirit noticeable all over the country. But full agreement with the official creed is a condition *sine qua*. Whether one is a teacher or a carpenter, a scholar or a clerk, he is required to show his colors, to declare whether he is for the Soviet régime or against it, and he knows the penalty for being against it. The intellectuals suffer, of course, more than the rest. Such is education proper for hypocrisy or political apathy in the long run, but not for a free and conscious fellowship. "There lives more faith in honest doubt, believe me, than in half the creeds."

One might easily increase the number of instances which show the inconsistency of Soviet education with its own avowed end: "preparing members of a communistic society" which will not know class divisions but will undoubtedly have some other divisions, since,

[31] Lenin, "Materialism i Empiriocriticm," *Sotshinenia*, XIII, 83-84.

according to Marxism, "without divisions there is no progress."
Here lies the vulnerable point of the Soviet educational system.
Marxism pleads for a full liberation of the mind. Bolshevism
equipped with the best inheritance of pedagogical science eradicates
the old backwardness with an unheard-of speed. The traditional
gulf between mental and manual labor, between the intellectuals
and "kitchen-maids" is dwindling and giving way to a homogeneous
mass of conscious citizens. But if curiosity and doubt are *incidental*
traits of the human mind, the Bolshevist restraints may become detrimental to further growth by depriving man of the strongest factor
of progress. If these traits are deeply rooted, then a vigorous struggle
against the spiritual monopoly of the leaders may become inevitable
in securing the blossoming of human thought in the future commonwealth of mankind. This seems to be the dialectic drama of Soviet
education, and a momentous lesson for the world.

About twenty-five centuries ago Plato tried to break the vicious
circle which Dewey formulates in the words: "Education proceeds
ultimately from the patterns furnished by institutions, customs, and
laws. Only in a just state will these be such as to give the right education: and only those who have rightly trained minds will be able
to recapture the end and ordering principle of things."[32] Plato's
way out was to discover genuine philosophers and to let them be
kings. The rulers of the USSR are not professional philosophers,
but they have a clear-cut philosophy indeed, and satisfy Plato's requirement of establishing in outline the proper pattern of true existence. They very likely realize the above-mentioned basic contradiction in their educational policy, but extra-educational factors, like
the fear of foreign intervention and counter-revolution, precluded
so far any substantial change—and the argument is not to be entirely
discarded.

This criticism, however, cannot lessen appreciation of the remarkable practical achievements of the Soviets in the field of education,
amounting to a cultural revolution, nor can it obscure their marvelous
attempt at putting unified and consistent social objectives in the
very center of the entire educational work of a nation.

The statement that "Christianity has never been tried" may offer

[32] J. Dewey, *Democracy and Education*, New York, 1916, p. 103.

a consolation to some pious soul, but it is in fact an inexorable condemnation of our civilization as it stands. Dewey starts one of his recent publications[33] with the significant words: "It is unnecessary to say that we are in the midst of a great educational uncertainty, one probably unparalleled at any past time. There is nothing accepted as axiomatic, nothing beyond the possibility of questioning and few things that are not actually attacked." But Dewey is hardly right when he states: "Confusion is due ultimately to aimlessness . . . only new aims can inspire educational effort for clarity and unity. They alone can reduce confusion."[34] The aimlessness of western education is not immanent: it reflects the confusion in modern life and in our social ideals. The school of the nineteenth century had definite aims, though they were seldom expressed in laws or decrees. England has been reluctant to organize education as a rigid public service. And some outstanding Englishmen like Samuel Coleridge suggested a system of education that would "train the people of the country to be obedient, free, useful and organizable subjects, citizens and patriots living for the State prepared to die for its defense."[35] As a matter of fact the schools of England, like those of the whole western hemisphere, were (sometimes inadvertently) working toward this very end: they faithfully followed the unwritten organic demands of their stable social environment.

All human culture is, at present, in a critical phase of development. The unparalleled violent tide of technical and industrial progress has begun to threaten its creator. "Die ich rief, die Geister, werd' ich nun nicht los." The entire social mechanism got out of gear, so to speak. The accompanying mental confusion is obvious. People are separated by divergent ideals of individualism and socialism, of nationalism and internationalism, of pacifism and militarism, of religion and science. . . . A craving for unity is growing daily. Some deplore the "lost paradise" of the Middle Ages, others confidently look forward to ə new more perfect unity. In education the renowned wisdom of teaching "to know the good and to

---

[33] "Way out of Educational Confusion," *Harvard Bulletin*, 1931, p. 1.

[34] *Ibid.*, p. 41.

[35] M. Sadler, "English Philosophy of Education," *International Educational Review* (1931-32), p. 352.

do the bad" is attacked. There is little harmony between our changing basic concepts and our institutions. In such times an "ostrich" policy may be fatal. The urgent necessity of far-reaching socio-economic readjustments must be courageously declared. Moreover, they must be effectuated. Then a new consistent set of social objectives might be generated, planned, and embodied in education, and open a brilliant period of human history indeed. The race is not between "education and catastrophe"—it is between reconstruction and revolution.

THE OBJECTIVES OF EDUCATION
IN FASCIST ITALY

BY
SHEPARD B. CLOUGH

X

FASCISM AND ITALIAN LIFE

A correct understanding of the objectives of education in Fascist Italy cannot be obtained by a study of Italian education *in vacuo.* That "schools are a part of the life of a nation and mirror that life," a statement by Benedetto Croce, the well-known Neo-Hegelian philosopher of Naples, is a self-evident truth. Only an obscure conception of a nation's educational problems and pedagogic aims may be had without some notion of the nation's economic conditions, its social structure, its intellectual heritage, its historical traditions, and its political institutions. Therefore, it would seem wise to place upon our canvas some bold strokes indicative of the major peculiarities and characteristics of Italy before attempting to draw a picture of the objectives of Italian education.

1. *Background*

Perhaps the most fundamental factor in Italian life is the economic, and if a correct impression of the economic conditions of Italy may be had, much will have been done to give an insight into the contemporary problems of the nation. Only in the light of such information can a clear conception of educational problems and of pedagogic objectives be envisaged. From the outset it should be definitely understood that Italy is relatively a poor country. Her total national wealth has been estimated to be only $25,000,000,000, while that of her neighbor France has been judged to be $60,000,000,000, and that of the United States $320,803,000,000. Italy is practically devoid of the raw materials essential for an industrial civilization—coal, iron, oil, and cotton. Her main source of wealth is agriculture, but even in this branch of economic activity she is handicapped by the fact that only about one-half of her land is arable. Her over-seas commerce, which enjoys the use of several good harbors, is at a disadvantage because of the industrial weakness of the country and the limited national hinterland of the ports,

and her labor, of which she has a superabundant supply, is forced
to accept a standard of living that is three and one-half times lower
than that enjoyed by workers in the city of Philadelphia. Nor
is the wealth that Italy does have equally distributed over the
entire country. Broadly speaking, the North is wealthier than the
South; it is more highly industrialized, more fertile, and more given
to the arts of commerce. Southern Italy, Sicily, and Sardinia are, in
truth, abjectly poor districts.

The poverty of Italy, and particularly that of the South, is the
cause of one of the nation's greatest educational difficulties—the task
of providing the necessary physical equipment for education. So
poor is Italy, in fact, that all her cities, provinces, and her central
government spend less on education per annum that does the city
of New York.[1] As might well be imagined from this astounding
fact, school buildings in Italy are not of the best, and some towns,
especially in the South, are without educational establishments of
any kind. Illiteracy is therefore rife; twenty-seven percent of all the
Italian people cannot read, and, in some of the poorer southern
provinces, the proportion of illiterates is as much as fifty-three percent of the population. The general poverty of Italy also means that
a comparatively small number of the population can afford the
luxury of more than elementary school instruction and that even
this education must needs be largely vocational training for the very
practical purpose of enabling them to gain a livelihood after graduation. Furthermore, poverty results in extremely low salaries to teachers—elementary school teachers being paid from $191.20 to $492
a year, plus bonuses that may vary from $15.60 to $67.60—salaries
which militate against the teachers' developing themselves by extra
study or travel, especially travel abroad.

These problems are aggravated by Italy's social structure. The
country is steeped in a tradition of class distinction—of frigid sepa-

[1] This may be explained in part by the fact that retail price levels are lower in
Italy than in New York, by the inflated prices of New York real estate, by high
salaries in New York, by political graft, by extensive building programs, and by
teachers' retirement schemes. Even when all these items have been taken into
consideration, however, the foregoing statement still seems astounding.

This and all subsequent information of a monetary nature are computed according to the rate of exchange existing prior to March, 1933.

ration of the aristocracy and the high bourgeoisie from the industrial and agricultural proletariat. In industrial and commercial centers and in agricultural districts, where the large landed estates, the *latifundia,* are still in the hands of the aristocracy, there is little evidence of an altruistic willingness on the part of the wealthy classes to shoulder the heavy financial burdens of adequate educational facilities for the poor. The industrial worker is, for the most part, class-conscious enough not even to attempt to lift himself out of his class by taking the expensive road to knowledge, and the dispersed agricultural employees find the physical hindrances to education of long distances, sparse attendance, and expense too great to warrant more than an "academic" interest in education.

This separation of the two classes tends to the creation of an intelligentsia which is snobbish and of a proletariat that is unconscious of its ignorance. And this unfortunate condition is still further fostered by the intellectual heritage of the nation. Ever since the Italian Renaissance of the fifteenth and sixteenth centuries emphasis has been placed on learning and culture that are far beyond the reach of the common people. In the Renaissance period the *literati* established Ciceronian Latin as the means of literary expression *par excellence,* a medium that only a chosen few could hope to master; the humanists stressed the importance and beauty of classical history and literature, which were far removed from the knowledge of the man in the street; and artists produced large and expensive paintings and statues, which could only be acquired, and hence only seen, by the few possessors of great wealth. The succeeding centuries witnessed a continuance of Renaissance ideals, and modern Italian culture, although the democratic movement of the nineteenth and twentieth centuries has effected considerable change, tends to be of such a nature that it is only for the few. So high above the common people are things intellectual in Italy that the masses are left to grope about in the dark valleys of incomprehension, while the self-centered intelligentsia basks benignantly upon the peaks of culture.

The poverty of Italy, the great divergence between the social classes, and the continuance of the classical and philological traditions of the Renaissance, condition and complicate Italian education.

But they are by no means the only factors at work. Religion plays an important rôle in the life of the Italian people and *ipso facto* in the life of the schools. Italy has been traditionally Roman Catholic, and the Church has developed in large measure in the Italian peninsula. Its administration has been carried on from Rome, and Italians have been most often chosen as its pontiffs and are most numerous among its saints. The Protestant revolt in the sixteenth century, by estranging large sections of the world from Catholicism, made the Church more Italian than ever before, and the Italians came to look upon it as a semi-national institution. The paganism of the Renaissance, the religious skepticism of the eighteenth century, and the scientific threat to established doctrine in the nineteenth century were not, however, without their impress on the serene surface of Italian Catholicism. Yet no serious anticlerical movement developed until the Church endeavored to block the aspirations of Italian nationalists to effect a territorial unification of Italy. The seizure by these nationalists of the temporal possessions of the Pope, including the Eternal City itself, gave rise to animosity between the Church and the State, and in 1870 the Pope, in protest, withdrew to the Vatican as a voluntary prisoner, turning only a deaf ear to the State's overtures for peace. For some time the Church ordered Catholics to refrain from politics; while they did, several anti-Catholic laws were enacted, civil marriage was made legal, divorce was permitted, and religious instruction was barred from public schools. In the early twentieth century signs of the dissipation of the bitterness between Church and State were numerous, nationalists regarding the Church as one of the essential and traditional forms of national culture, the Catholic Socialists considering political action in the name of Christianity as the only solution of social problems, and the Idealists, led by Gentile, looking upon Catholicism as part of the spiritual life of the people. Fascism, however, inherited the political hostility of Church and State, and, although it effected a technical settlement of the problem, discovered that Fascism and Catholicism were rivals for the supreme loyalty of the Italian people—a rivalry that is nowhere more apparent than in the education of the youth.

The educational system and Italian life generally are further conditioned by the nation's historical traditions. The glory of an-

cient Rome, when Latins carried the torch of civilization throughout the western world, still survives. The magnificence of the Italian
Renaissance, when Italy gave the tone to the cultural and cultured
life of Europe, is in the minds of all educated Italians. But perhaps
more vital than either of these memories are the regionalist loyalties that grew up during that long period from the fall of the Roman
Empire to the latter half of the nineteenth century, when Italy, for
the most part, was divided up into several small states, each with its
own separate government, its own traditions, and its own customs.
The unification of Italy meant the political amalgamation of these
entities and, although the union was accompanied by a wave of
nationalism, it was not sufficient to down regional differences. Today
provincial feeling is so strong that a northerner resents being called
a Sicilian and provincial differences in dialect are so great that a
Turinese can hardly understand a Neapolitan. Despite these local
variances there has been, ever since the early part of the nineteenth
century, a very important nationalist movement in Italy—a movement which aimed first at effecting the unification, then at consoli-
dating the power of the new nation, and finally at achieving national
glory at home and abroad. Under the pressure of this movement,
Mazzini's nationalist phrases became household maxims; Garibaldi's
red shirt became a national symbol; and Cavour's astute diplomacy
was held up as a model of statesmanship.

The most talked-of factor in modern Italian life, however, is
neither poverty, illiteracy, class separation, intellectual snobbery,
religion, regionalism, nor nationalism. It is Fascism—a force that has
given a peculiar complexion to public life in Italy and that has
molded the educational system to its own liking. It is a force without a knowledge of which an understanding of the objective of
Italian education is impossible.

The beginnings of Fascism are closely connected with the person
of Benito Mussolini. The father of this romantic figure was a black-
smith of Forlì Romagna; his mother was a school teacher. From
the former the future dictator of Italy received his early political
ideals—international, revolutionary socialism; from the latter he got
a taste for music and learning. After a rather meager education Mussolini attempted to teach school, but, being exiled to an isolated

hamlet, he decided to try his fortune in Switzerland. There he earned a living at manual labor and became a labor agitator and journalist. Upon his return to Italy he continued these latter pursuits, violently opposing the Italian war with Tripoli in 1911 (an action which resulted in his imprisonment) and becoming editor of the Italian Socialist paper, the *Avanti*. His confirmed pacifism however, was destroyed by the events of 1914. From the first he opposed Italy's entrance into the war on the side of her Triple Alliance partners, Germany and Austria-Hungary, and advocated her joining the Allies. For this stand he was expelled from the Socialist party. Not disheartened he organized a small band of nationalist socialist followers into the *Fascio* (club) of Revolutionary Action at Milan (1915) and established a newspaper of his own, *Il Popolo d'Italia*. Subsequently *Fasci* sprang up in other cities, preaching nationalism, socialism, and "interventionism"[2] at one and the same time. After Italy had entered the war, Mussolini served (as a corporal!) in the trenches and was wounded (by the explosion of a trench mortar!) in 1917. He then returned to his paper to continue his nationalist and socialist campaign.

Upon the conclusion of the World War the Fascist group was still small and insignificant; the majority of the Socialists still dreamed of a communist world order with international brotherhood prevailing for all mankind. This majority group launched a revolution in 1919, and at first received the blessings of the Fascists for their action. Soon, however, Fascist praise changed to censure, for while the Fascists agreed with the Socialists in the desirability of changing the social order, they did not approve of destroying the Italian nation or of joining foreigners in an internationalist socialistic state. This defection from the revolutionary cause did not prove to be a real impediment in the red movement, but a serious obstacle did shortly present itself. The Socialists found that, whereas they could seize factories and run them satisfactorily, as long as the supplies of raw materials lasted, they could not get credit for the purchase abroad of new supplies. For this reason the realization of a collectivized economic system in Italy failed. But the failure irritated the revolutionaries to such an extent that they resorted to

[2] Italy's entrance into the war.

desultory civil war for no other purpose, seemingly, than the aimless destruction of property. It was against this disorder, rather than against the revolution, that a definite opposition formed, an opposition which was to be the basis of the future Fascist party. To the ranks of Mussolini and his followers, nearly all of whom were young men, veterans of the war, and ex-Socialists, who were deeply imbued with love of country, came at this time members of the bourgeoisie, who were anxious to do everything possible to protect their possessions; came nationalist intellectuals, who wanted to save from destruction the nation that had contributed much to the culture of the world; came patriotic workers, led by a former I.W.W. organizer from New York, Edmondo Rossoni, who still nourished revolutionary ideas, but who wanted to realize them on a national scale. These strange bedfellows, members of all the social classes in Italy, had one thing in common—love of country. It was in the name of this love that the "Fascists" suppressed Socialist disorders; and nationalism, indeed, has remained the touchstone of common action among them.

Fascists came together to prevent the destruction of the means of production and to preserve Italy. They soon learned that these ends could not be accomplished by the simple crushing of the Socialists and they became convinced that, if their ambitions were to be realized, it would be necessary for them to take over the reins of government. Italy was confronted at the time of the Fascist party's formation with general governmental incompetency. The budget showed a large annual deficit; the railways were in a snarl; and production was greatly reduced. Hence, when a parliamentary crisis developed in 1922, which threatened to lead to further anarchy, the Fascists marched on Rome and without the formality of discharging a "whiff of grapeshot" took control of the state. They then established themselves firmly in the political saddle by forcibly eradicating all opposition, an undertaking which was not completed until 1925 (when the last of the hostile political parties was either absorbed or crushed), and which left them dictators of Italy. They improved the economic situation by balancing the budget, straightening out the railway tangle, and stabilizing the lira, and they added to internal peace by effecting a technical, if not an actual, settle-

ment of the sixty-year-old conflict between Church and State. But
they desired to do more than simply restore calm in the country;
they desired that Italy become a nation of the first magnitude—a
nation that would be reminiscent of ancient Rome and that would
fulfill the dreams of the great patriots of the *Risorgimento*. To accomplish this admittedly great task the Fascists believed that the
talents of all Italians and the resources of all Italy would have to
be made to yield their best fruit—fruit that could be produced only
under the paternalistic supervision of the Fascist dictatorship. Under the benevolent care of the régime, then, Italy girded her loins
for the struggle upward. A "Battle of Grain" was instituted by the
government to increase the production of wheat; subsidies were
offered to key industries in order to make Italy economically more
self-sufficient; exportation was encouraged to strengthen the position
of the lira; and strikes and lockouts were prohibited in order that
the Italian labor supply might be utilized to the maximum. The
state established itself as the arbiter of the struggle between capital
and labor, and the Labor Charter of 1927 definitely stated that all
Italians *must* contribute to the economic growth of their country—
capitalists with their capital, workingmen with their labor, and intellectuals with their brains. In this nationalist crusade the educational system was enlisted to do its share—the elementary schools to
overcome illiteracy and to give vocational training, which might
help to avert some of the effects of Italy's poverty; secondary schools
and universities to hold high the banner of scholarship and to attain a scientific excellence, which might alleviate the hardships
caused by Italy's natural poverty; and all educational institutions
to win Italians to the great cause of national destiny and to Fascism.

2. The Educational Ideals of Fascism

There was really little that was new in the educational ideals of
Fascism, but the Fascists declared their purposes so vociferously, ve-
hemently, and enthusiastically that old educational ideals took on
an entirely new aspect. Serious attempts had previously been made
to overcome illiteracy: in 1877 gratuitous public elementary education
had been made compulsory until the age of twelve; and in 1911 it
had been placed under the strict supervision of the state. Nationalism

had been propagated by the schools throughout the entire pre-Fascist period; and just prior to the advent of Fascism plans had been made to rejuvenate the whole educational system. To the credit of Fascism, however, it must be said that the new régime brought with it the dynamic drive necessary to turn good resolutions, that so frequently provide pavement to the nether regions, to living realities.

The philosophy underlying the Fascist educational plans was a fusion of Neo-Hegelianism and ardent nationalism, and had for its chief exponent Giovanni Gentile, a follower of Croce and Minister of Public Instruction in the first Mussolini cabinet. From the first he expressed the belief that the schools should be employed for strengthening the nation and for "making Fascists":

We affirm our belief that the State is not a system of hindrances and external juridical controls from which men flee, but an ethical being which, like the conscience of the individual, manifests its personality and achieves its historical growth in human society. Thus it is conscious not of being hedged in by special limits, but of being open, ready, and capable of expanding as a collective and yet individual will. The nation is that will, conscious of itself and of its own historical past, which, as we formulate it in our minds, divines and delineates our nationality, generating an end to be attained, a mission to be realized. For that will, in case of need, our lives are sacrificed, for our lives are genuine, worthy, and endowed with incontestable value only as they are spent in the accomplishment of that mission.

The State's active and dynamic consciousness is a system of thought, of ideas, of interests to be satisfied and of morality to be realized. Hence the State is, as it ought to be, a teacher; it maintains and develops schools to promote this morality. In the school, the State comes to a consciousness of its real being.

And again:

Fascism is a party and a political doctrine. But above all . . . it is a total conception of life. It is impossible to be a Fascist in politics and not in the school, not in one's own family or office. . . . Thus Fascism embodies what may be called its own characteristic, namely, taking life seriously. Life is toil, effort, sacrifice, and hard work; a life in which we know perfectly well there is neither matter nor time for amusement. Before us there stands an ideal to be realized; an ideal which gives us no respite. We have no time to lose. Even in our sleep we must give account of the talents entrusted to us. We must make them yield fruit, not for us who are nothing, but for our land and country, for this Italy that fills our hearts with her memories and aspirations, with her joys and labors, that rebukes us for the centuries our fathers lost, but that comforts us by recent events when Italian effort produced a miracle, when Italy united in a single thought, a single sentiment, a single desire for sacrifice. And it was precisely the young men, the young Italy of our prophet, that were ready, that ran to the sacrifice and died for the country. To die for that ideal by which alone men can live and by which men may feel the seriousness of life.

And further:

Hence the school cannot be confined to grammr ʻ to mathematics, or to any other material that is a mere ornament or adornment of the intellect. The intellect can be developed only by developing personality. Hence we must seek to understand all things and to love all things so far as it is true that to understand is to love. But love must always set out from a center and return to it; a center that is a point of view, a faith, a pillar on which the conscience may safely lean. . . . For this reason we need today a national Italian school, governed by a lively conception not so much of the rights as of the duties of the Italian people, and that is of every Italian. A conception not strictly and foolishly chauvinistic. But nevertheless firm and religious. And this is politics, a holy politics, and we intend that those who deny it be considered not as champions of broadmindedness and liberal-mindedness, but as vulgar and miserable profaners of that temple which we must jealously guard.

The implications of this idealistic philosophy are obvious. The real mind of the child develops by action and not by the mastering of abstract forms of verbal knowledge. The schools, therefore, should furnish an opportunity for the mental activity of its pupils and should teach them the meaning of their acts. All bodies of knowledge, all sciences and their laws are abstractions from action, and by the process of education must be transformed into knowledge. It follows that education should focus its attention on the pupils rather than upon the subject matter to be imparted to them, and that from the elementary school through the universities stress should be placed upon the development of the talents and upon the discipline of individual personalities. This is to be accomplished in part by vocational training, in part by the study of the traditional subjects of the curricula, and in part by the students' participation in all the institutions and traditions of the Italian people. Moral personality is achieved by the identification of the individual with the culture of his nation. To be sure, culture is universal; but it is formed by a combination of national cultures. Each individual must do more than steep himself in this national culture; he must learn to create and hence widen his own and his nation's experiences and culture. Politically the Gentilian educational philosophy implied that freedom is a people's participation in the cultural and traditional life of the nation and is not a liberty to act without authoritative restraint. This liberty can be obtained only if citizens serve the national will (in Italy as expressed by the Fascist party) and the chief means of winning them to this service is a unified system of national education. Religiously Gentile believed that the individual can live in the universal spirit only through the national spirit and that the Church is a national institution. Hence religion must be taught in the schools, the elementary-school children receiving instruction in the traditional religion with all its myths and superstitions. In the secondary schools and universities the "critical element is introduced, and traditional religion becomes transformed into a self-conscious, national Idealism"—the philosophy in which Gentile is a staunch believer.

3. *The Gentile Reform and the Elementary Schools*

The first step in the practical application of these theories was the issuance in 1923 of a series of decrees which comprises the so-called Gentile Reform. In the first place, these decrees provided for certain changes in the state's educational administration which aimed to bring the schools more directly under the control of the Fascists. To this end the Minister of Public Instruction (or, as he was to be called later, of national education) was given the right to appoint members of his own choice to the formerly elected Superior Council of Public Instruction, a body whose function it was to assist the minister in determining general educational policy; he was given the power to choose the persons who would execute the Fascist educational plans; he could select the superintendents of schools for each of the nineteen educational districts into which Italy was divided; and he could name the members of the superintendents' advisory councils—the Scholastic Council and a Disciplinary Council for elementary schools and the Council for Secondary Schools. He could thus impose a complete Fascist personnel in the central organs of educational administration, and, even in the large cities that enjoyed educational autonomy, he could maintain a stringent oversight.

The matter of control and inspection having been dealt with, it was necessary to take steps to extend elementary education. New pressure was brought upon local communities to provide adequate elementary-school instruction, and the state reserved funds for assisting the poorer districts, particularly in the South, to meet this requirement. Then the age to which school attendance was compulsory was advanced from twelve to fourteen years, and the school year was decreed to be ten months, or at least one hundred eighty school days. Furthermore, elementary education was divided in a new manner into three grades: the Preparative Grade of three years, which was designed for children between the ages of three and six; the Inferior Grade of three years for pupils between six and nine; and the Superior Grade of two years for pupils between nine and eleven. The Reform provided that after the completion of the fifth grade, presumably at the age of eleven or after the completion of the fourth grade and upon passing special examinations the child might choose one of many courses. In rural districts, where there are no secondary schools, he might complete the minimum requirement of education to the fourteenth year by taking the *corsi integrativi,* which are a continuation of elementary instruction in the three R's plus general vocational training. In urban districts he might go, as opportunity permitted, into more specialized trade schools,[3] into technical institutes, or into gymnasia, all of which were classified as secondary schools. Thus a serious attempt was made to offer children from an early age special instruction in their chosen fields of endeavor, but, it should be remarked, no effort was made to provide a way whereby the majority of Italian youths might obtain a higher education. The Fascists believed in the French adage, *"Il faut que chacun soit dans sa place,"* and that every one should have training suitable for his "place," thus giving impetus to the traditional aloofness and snobbery of the intellectual class. Furthermore the Fascists were convinced that specialization should begin early, in order that the student might, by the time he had completed his formal training,

[3] Complementary schools.

be equipped to transcend the accomplishments of the past by creative acts.

The Gentile Reform also altered the curricula in the hope that the Fascist theories of individual development by accomplishment, of the propagation of nationalist culture, and of philosophy might be realized, and that the goal of a literate country, an enlightened intelligentsia, an economically powerful state, and an intensely nationalistic Italy might be attained. The most fundamental innovation in the curriculum was, according to the Fascists, its elasticity. A distinct effort was made to extend curricular autonomy to administrative officers and to teachers, in order to enable them to adapt the subjects taught to the particular needs of the students of their region and to allow them to develop the children's educational "instruments." Nevertheless, a standard program was suggested which was approximately as follows:

TABLE V

ITALIAN ELEMENTARY SCHOOLS

SUBJECTS	Pre-para-tory	I	II	III	IV	V	Sup-ple-men-tary[a]
	HOURS PER WEEK, BY YEARS						
Religion	1	1½	1½	2	2	2	2
Singing, drawing, and recitation	4	2½	2½	4	5	5	3
Reading and writing	..	7	6	5	5	4	3
Orthography	..	..	2	2	..	..	..
Arithmetic	..	4	4	4	3	3	2
Various recreative intellectual occupations	6	4	4	4	1	1	1
Gardening, manual training, gymnastics, hygiene, and domestic training	24	6	5	4	4	4	..
Natural and physical science	..	..	..	..	2	2	3
History and geography	..	..	..	..	3	3	2
Civics and economics	..	..	..	..	..	1	1
Professional work	..	..	..	..	..	..	8
Total	35 Thursday included	25	25	25	25	25	25

[a] Corsi integrativi.

From this schedule it will be seen that emphasis is placed upon the Italian language in the first five years, for the pupil can do little educationally until he has learned to read and write. The stress on reading and writing placed this early in the school years means that many persons become literate, but do not continue their education far enough to develop tastes for refined literature or to obtain a critical attitude toward the things they read. They are made literate, but then fall victims to whatever is placed within their reach. Even in the schools they become the object of indoctrination of subjects they are given little opportunity to discuss.

Of still more importance is the wholesale inoculation of Italian children with nationalist ideas, not only after they have learned to read and write, but even from the time they can remain quiet and listen to stories—an inoculation that makes them immune to internationalism or to an appreciation of the accomplishments of other states. "In the school the State [must] come to a consciousness of its real being."

In the second year, during the time allowed for various recreational intellectual occupations, the teacher must "relate episodes of civil, religious, and military valor . . ," explaining the faith necessary for making sacrifices for the country. In the third year the teacher must develop their historical and national consciousness, relying for his theme on the lives of great men (Garibaldi and Battisti among others) ; and in the fourth and fifth years he must give a series of readings to illustrate the regional contributions to the life of the nation, especially during the period of Italian unification. During the courses of gymnastics the life of a soldier must be portrayed as an example of strength, discipline, and courage. During the geography lessons especial attention must be given to a study of the city, historical places in the region, the physical and political nature of Italy, and of foreign countries, especially those to which Italian emigrants have gone. The study of history begins in the third year with Italian history from 1848 to 1918, the general course being supplemented by the readings of the most significant proclamations, letters, and memoirs of national martyrs, and the orders of the *condottieri*. In the fourth year ancient history is prescribed with emphasis on ancient Rome. In the fifth year the pupils study Italian history during the period of foreign domination (with emphasis on the history of the province), the works of Italian artists (especially local ones), events of Italian history during the nineteenth century, the Italian army and navy, the great heroes and brilliant episodes of the Great War, the great public works undertaken after the unification of Italy, and a comparison of the national wealth with that of other countries. After the fifth year (in the *corsi integrativi*) the pupils must read at least one popular but well-known history, study the Italian colonies, and get some "notions" of foreign countries. Even in religious instruction especial attention must be paid to *Italian* saints. In addition to all this there are the reading lessons, which from the programs might not seem to be nationalistic but which are in reality extremely patriotic.

XI

THE THEMES OF FASCIST EDUCATION

1. *Nationalism in the Elementary Schools*

From the first the Fascists realized that a new arrangement of the curricula would have to be accompanied by the creation of Fascist textbooks and the selection of Fascist teachers. As a guaranty that the instruction should be of the Fascist kind, a textbook commission was appointed to weed out all books that were not of the approved political and nationalist views. This commission investigated 1,710 readers, 317 histories, and 114 books for religious instruction, but so severe was its censorship that it approved definitely only 32 readers, 125 histories, and 11 religious manuals. Those books which received the stamp of approval were thoroughly nationalistic. An analysis of one of the history books will make this clear:

Franco Ciarlantini, *Storia Italiana*. Milan: Mondadori, 1925.

This text is for first-year history classes, that is, for the pupil's third year. It is one of a series prepared for all classes. It has the approval of the state. The interpretation of Italian history in this book is very nationalistic. It covers the nineteenth and twentieth centuries, but almost all the space is devoted to the *Risorgimento* and the World War. The book is filled with minor but dramatic anecdotes (pp. 17, 24, 48, 49, 53, 54, 58, etc.). Especial emphasis is placed on the heroes of the *Risorgimento* (S. Pellico, Mazzini, Garibaldi, and Cavour) and of the World War (Generals Cadorna and Diaz, Cesare Battisti and Nazario Sauro, the last two being Austrian subjects who deserted to serve for Italy but were taken prisoners and killed). The book begins with these words:

"Italy, our Country, has not always been a united and free nation. Our grandfathers remember the sad times when foreigners were masters in our homes, when the Country was divided into many little states and the citizens were subjected to all sorts of outrages and did not have the right to protest.

"Those were sad times, children!"

The book ends with this passage:

"In Eternal Rome, on the historical hills of Campidoglio, rises the monument of Italian Independence in the center of which is erected the statue of the Gentleman King.

"At the foot of the statue there is an altar called the Altar of the Fatherland. There an urn of pure marble contains the bones of one of the thousands and thousands of soldiers who fell without leaving a trace of their names.

"This is the Tomb of the Unknown Soldier who represents all the dead of our War and to whose memory has been awarded the Golden Medal with this inscription:

" 'This worthy son of a valiant race and of a rich civilization held without flinching those trenches most bitterly contested, displayed courage in the most cruel battles, and fell fighting for no other end than that his Country might be victorious and great.' "

In one of the religious books one will discover this quotation:

As there is only one official religion of the State, the Catholic, so today there must be only one political faith, Fascism, which is synonymous with the Italian Nation. As the Catholic must have a blind belief in the Catholic faith and obey the Catholic Church blindly, so the perfect Fascist must believe absolutely in the principles of Fascism and obey the hierarchical heads to whom he owes allegiance without reserve.

Religious dogmas are not discussed because they are truths revealed by God. Fascist principles are not discussed because they come from the mind of a Genius: Benito Mussolini. . . .

Nevertheless, the Fascists believed the textbooks to be of an unsatisfactory nature for their purposes and undertook the preparation of new ones written according to their lights. Several of these books have now made their appearance, and it is possible to glean from them a general notion of the desired brand of "spirit." All of them proclaim the glory and greatness of Italy, her wonderful accomplishments, her contributions to civilization, and her natural beauties; many of them stress the history and nature of the region in which they are to be used, making it clear, however, that the region is an integral part of Italy; all of them describe the achievements of Fascism; and all of them pay homage to Benito Mussolini. In many of them *Il Duce's* picture is reproduced, and frequently there is placed beside it a young Italian lad, dressed in shorts and the Fascist black shirt, giving the Dictator the Roman salute. A second grade reader, which endeavors to explain the wonders of Italy by describing the voyages of such a little boy, Marco, has this characteristic passage:

Marco thus saw all Italy. A country great and beautiful, industrious, and powerful. In his little heart he felt swell up a love for her, a love stronger than for any person he had ever loved; a love which he had never experienced before. "Italy, Italy," he exclaimed, and opened his arms as if to embrace her.

Now he understood: it was too beautiful. This was why foreigners wanted to hold it in their power. Thus he understood why Garibaldi and so many other heroes had loved it so much and had given their lives to liberate it from foreigners.

In this process of making Fascists the teachers naturally play a vital rôle. In spite of the best curriculum imaginable and ultra-nationalistic textbooks, education in Italy would not be nationalistic, if the teachers were not nationalists. Hence, Fascists have given special attention to the selection and training of their teaching personnel. By a law which permits the dismissal of teachers who profess political opinions contrary to those of the régime, wholesale "purifications" of teaching staffs have taken place, the victims usually having been charged with incapability. The appointment of teachers is based upon competitive examination, but among those who qualify by passing these tests preference is given, first, to those who were decorated in the World War, secondly, to those who have passed other competitive examinations, thirdly, to those who have published books, and fourthly, "to those who have other [perhaps even political!] qualifications." The examinations for elementary-school teachers place emphasis upon the most nationalistically stirring phase of Italian history—the *Risorgimento*—and, in instructions to candidates, warning is given concerning the necessity of reading certain of the most patriotic works of Italian literature. And once the teacher enters upon his meager incumbency, he is hounded by Fascist propaganda. He is encouraged to join the National Fascist Association of Primary School Teachers which aims, "first, to encourage the general cultural education of the teachers and, secondly, to expound the new concept of life, of history, and of the Nation, which Fascism has affirmed to be the keystone of its action and of its future." And he is also encouraged to subscribe to a Fascist educational journal, *La Scuola Fascista, Educazione Fascita, Annali dell' Istruzione Elementare,* or *Educazione Nazionale.* Italian teachers must have the correct inspiration, if they are to mold into perfect Fascists the clay which is given them.

In addition to the nationalist influence of textbooks and of Fascist teachers, provision has been made for providing a nationalist environment for Italian children both inside and outside the schools. The school building must breathe the spirit of Italy: every new educational structure must have the lictor's rods, emblem of Imperial Rome and of Fascism, worked into it and every classroom of both elementary and secondary schools must have a crucifix, a picture of the king, and a picture of Mussolini. The Fascists desire that every day's work begin with a prayer and a national anthem, that the schools have pictures of the heroes of the *Risorgimento,* of the Great War, and of the masters of Italian culture, that every school have its flag, and that on the eve of every vacation a patriotic speech be made and that the children respond with the Roman salute and the Fascist song whose chorus runs:

> Adolescence, Adolescence,
> Springtime of Youth's effervescence,
> The Fascists are the essence
> And salvation of the free. . . .

Out of school the Fascist supervision of the children's development continues. Here the Fascist party comes into direct competition with the Church, for the latter organization also seeks to win the allegiance of the youth. Thus an intense rivalry exists between the temporal and spiritual powers in Italy, and, as long as this rivalry lasts, there will undoubtedly continue to be ill-feeling between Church and State, despite such evidences of a complete settlement as the Vatican Accord of 1929 and Mussolini's visit to the Pope in 1931. Thus far in the struggle between the two powers for the youth, the Fascist party seems to have been victorious. In 1928 the Catholic Boy Scouts organization was dissolved, and later all Catholic youth organizations which did more than give religious instruction were suppressed. In their places were set up as part of the educational system the Fascist youth organizations: Balilla for boys between the ages of six and fourteen, the Advance Guard for those between the years fourteen and eighteen, Piccole Italiane for girls eight to fourteen, and Giovani Italiane for those fourteen to eighteen. In these organizations about 3,000,000 of the youth of Italy are enrolled for the purpose of being trained physically and morally for the new order of Italian life. Both boys and girls in these groups have distinctive uniforms, suggestive of the dress of Mussolini's adult

cohorts. The boys are given considerable military and physical training both during the winter months and at summer camps. And both
boys and girls are the objects of continual Fascist propaganda. The
girl is taught:

1. To fulfill her duties as daughter, sister, student, and friend, with
   cheerfulness and joy even though they be fatiguing.
2. To serve the Nation as her other and greater mother, the mother
   of all good Italians.
3. To love the *Duce* who has made the Nation stronger and greater.
4. To obey her superiors with joy.
5. To have the courage to repulse those who give evil council and
   deride honesty.
6. To educate the body to withstand physical fatigue and the spirit
   not to show pain.
7. To abhor stupid vanity but to love beautiful things.
8. To love work which is life.

The boy learns from his director, who is always a member of the
Fascist Militia, not to question Mussolini's dictum, *"Libro, moschet-
to: Fascista perfetto."*[4]

Thus the objectives of elementary-school education come into relief. The Fascists have increased vocational training in an effort to
equip the youth with techniques which will aid them to overcome
the poverty with which Italy was endowed by nature and to provide
something practical in the hope of breaking down the opposition
of those parents who, by necessity or conviction, send their children
to fields or factories instead of to school. The Fascists have also taken
long strides in the direction of extending elementary education in
their drive on illiteracy, which, they feel, is a great handicap to a
greater Italy. But most important of all they have improved the
methods whereby Italians are steeped in national tradition. In the
Gentilian manner moral personality is achieved by the identification
of the individual with the culture of his nation. Instruction in
Roman Catholicism, the Italian language, Italian literature, and
Italian history is given, therefore, to the exclusion of instruction in
the culture of any other state, for the greater glory of the individual, and in order that he may help Italy to transcend all other
nations. The universal spirit, which Gentile holds can only be obtained through the national will, is entirely lost sight of. Fascist
elementary education in practice is strictly nationalistic.

[4] A book, a musket, a perfect Fascist.

2. Secondary Schools

To the elementary schools most of the youth of Italy (4,029,066 of the 4,574,362 children who were legally required to attend elementary institutions in the school year of 1928-29) go for this nationalist instruction. Only a few of them continue their education to a point where, in Gentile's scheme, they might develop a critical attitude. In the school year 1928-29 only 327,228 students were registered in public and private secondary schools, a very small enrollment when one considers that students enter these institutions at the age of eleven, after having completed the fifth grade, or at the age of ten, after having passed entrance examinations. And of this 327,228 some 148,662 were registered in art, music, naval, commercial, agricultural, or industrial institutes or in trade schools. The other 178,566 were divided among the classical *ginnasi,*[5] the classical and scientific *licei,*[6] the technical institutes,[7] normal schools,[8] or girls' finishing schools.[9] Thus it is apparent, first, that specialization begins at an early age in Italy, and, second, that beginning with secondary schools education is limited to a chosen few—a condition which the Gentile Reform of 1923 looked upon as highly desirable.

If the objective of Italian secondary education is not to illuminate and edify the masses, what is its purpose? The vocational training of the secondary schools aims, as does the vocational training in elementary schools, to improve the material welfare of Italians, or, more specifically, to train skilled workers. The classical and scientific training, on the other hand, aims to prepare students for institutions of higher learning—to help to train the future leaders of the nation. And all secondary training intends to continue the process, begun in the elementary schools, of making nationalists. The first two objectives are self-explanatory; the last requires some elucidation.

In discussing religious education in the elementary schools and

[5] The period of study in the *ginnasi* in five years.
[6] The period of study in the *licei* is three years.
[7] The courses are for either four or eight years.
[8] The preparatory course in the normal schools lasts four years. The advanced course, three years.
[9] Three years' course, to be completed after four years in a *ginnasio.*

philosophy in secondary education, Gentile has pointed out that, whereas the aim of the lower schools is uncritically to teach national institutions, the aim of the secondary school is to develop a critical spirit among the students. It would naturally follow that, if this spirit of criticism were developed, it would be necessary to give nationalist education more subtly than in the primary grades. And Fascists provided for other ways of nationalist instruction than direct indoctrination. This is obvious from even a cursory survey of the curricula of secondary schools. In almost all kinds of secondary institutions studies of the Latin language and literature, of Greek culture, of Italian history and culture, and since 1929 of Catholicism are given a prominent place. In other words, emphasis is put upon the culture of the Italian peninsula, irrespective of whether it is strictly Italian or not, with the idea of creating a great tradition that is believed to be *Italian*. The classical ideal of the Renaissance period is thus given a new lease on life, perhaps because it is in itself admirable, but at least incidentally because it is national. So much time is thus taken up that little is left to devote to a consideration of other contemporary cultures. This nationalist character of secondary education is still more clearly brought into relief by an investigation of the subject matter treated. In the courses of general history, for example, only cursory consideration is given to the internal history of foreign countries; their history is studied, as a rule, only when it has a direct bearing on Italian history. And, as though this were not enough, there is the extracurricular but very vital youth organization, the Advance Guard, whose appointed task it is to make Fascists of the youth between fourteen and eighteen years of age.

In the secondary schools, as in the elementary, evidence is to be found on every hand of the attempts of the idealist philosophers to make of education not a cramming away of undigested and unconnected facts but a molding of the student's personality by a lively interest in his work and an understanding of the material treated. The chief burden for the success of such a system falls on the shoulders of the teachers, and to the selection of teachers the Fascists have given their earnest care. At first, their solicitude in the matter took the form of eradicating the "incompetent," who by an interesting coincidence were usually anti-Fascist, about five hundred of the total teaching corps of ten thousand being dismissed. But later their surveillance was extended to the choice of new teachers. Appointments they controlled through the Ministry of National Education, their choices being made on the basis of competitive examinations and *other qualifications*.[10] But, being extremely cautious in the matter, the Fascists require that a new incumbent for a vacancy serve a probationary term of three years before receiving a permanent appointment. In this period of trial it is hoped that the candidate will become affiliated with the Fascist secondary-school teachers' association, subscribe to Fascist educational magazines, and otherwise display approval of the present Italian political régime and its educational policies—hopes which are tantamount to orders. Teachers must be qualified to do their share in attaining the objectives of secondary education. They must be able to perform their professional services satisfactorily. They must be able and willing to make Fascists.

3. University Education

Italian youths are graduated from secondary schools on the average at the age of eighteen, and, if they have taken courses preparatory to entering a university, they are eligible for entrance to such an institution. The number of those who continue their education is, however, relatively small, only 47,090 being enrolled in institutions of higher learning during the school year 1928-29—a figure which includes students in higher normal, architectural, veterinary, higher commercial, agricultural, and pharmacy schools, as well as those in law, letters and philosophy, and medicine. And in this same year only 2,378 students were registered in faculties of letters and philosophy, while 8,835 were registered in law schools, and 8,985 in schools of medicine and surgery. The relatively small enrollment in the humanities may be explained in part by the fact that few Italians can afford to send their sons to universities in spite of the relatively low tuition fees of between $40 and $86 per annum. But a more adequate explanation is to be found in the tradition, mentioned in the early part of this study, that higher education is not for the masses or the lower bourgeoisie; it is for a financial and cultural

[10] Secondary-school teachers are paid between $440 and $705 *per annum.*

élite. To maintain this tradition was one of the avowed purposes of the Gentile Reform.

The limited number of students in higher education indicates the highly professional (one might say, the highly pragmatic) character of university instruction. Practically all of the students are registered in professional schools and the few in the faculties of letters and philosophy are there for the most part for the purpose of securing a training that may allow them to enter the teaching profession. Instruction is thus both more highly specialized and further advanced than that of the American college and is loosely comparable to that of American graduate faculties. The only degree given by Italian universities is the doctorate, which is analogous to the master of arts in America, a fact which further indicates the advanced degree of higher instruction. It is therefore evident that perhaps the main objective of Italian higher education is to train leaders of the various professions. And the motive underlying this objective is to be found in an investigation of the *Weltanschauung* of the Italians. When such an investigation is made, it becomes evident that the Fascists seek, first, to provide a better material existence for themselves and their nationalists, and, second, to create a stronger and more glorious state.

To make Fascists is primarily the task of the lower schools; to make the makers of Fascists and of the new Italy is the work of institutions of higher learning. That this work may be satisfactorily accomplished Fascists maintain a careful oversight of the universities. By retaining for the Minister of National Education the power to appoint rectors of the universities, deans of the faculties, and directors of schools of higher instruction, the Fascists have created a system in which the directing personnel, which is responsible for the political tenor of the instruction, is Fascist. And, although they have given the universities autonomy for the regulation of local and internal affairs, they insist that all professors be sympathetic to the Fascist cause, every professor being required to swear an oath of allegiance to Italy, to the King, and to Fascism.[11] This is especially significant, for, although the Italian university professor is

[11] Failure to swear such an oath results in dismissal. Five professors were discharged on this ground in 1931.

poorly paid, a full professor after fifteen years of service receiving only $1,297.50, professors have always played an important rôle in Italian politics, counting among their number such distinguished politicians of recent date as Orlando, Salandra, Scialoja, Gentile, Rocco, and De' Stefani. Selection of university professors, as of secondary-school instructors, is in the hands of the Fascists. The Minister of National Education appoints new incumbents from lists of those who have passed competitive examinations or, if politically satisfactory men cannot be obtained in this way, he may select any one who has achieved scholarly distinction to teach as a *libero docente* (free instructor). To this latter prerogative the Fascists have had frequent recourse in order to secure the desired personnel for the exposition of Fascist doctrine.

The indoctrination of students with nationalism in Italian universities is limited to those students who enroll for instruction in the humanities, law, economics, or political science. They are subjected to an advanced nationalization process. The technique employed, like that of the secondary school, is subtle, but it is real. In faculties of letters and philosophy the curriculum stresses nationalist culture. Courses in philosophy place emphasis on Italian philosophy; courses in literature, on Italian literature; and courses in history, on Italian history. Instruction in history in most universities consists of one course in ancient history, one in medieval history, sometimes one in the history of the *Risorgimento,* and one in general modern history. The history of foreign countries, as in the secondary schools, is practically never studied unless it has a direct bearing upon Italy. Students in the humanities, then, get not crass nationalist instruction but nationalist instruction by implication. They obtain a wide knowledge of things Italian, and, because they know little of non-Italian cultures, they may consider foreign things inferior.

In law schools nationalist education is much more in the open. Here courses are given in Fascist political, economic, and social theory, usually by outstanding members of the Party, who have been selected to act as *liberi docenti*. However direct Fascist instruction may be in the law schools, it is neither as extensive nor as flagrantly flaunted before the students as in the faculties of political science, which exist in the universities of Rome, Pavia, Padua, and Peru-

gia, and as in the Superior Institute of Economic and Social Science
at Florence. The express duty of these institutions is to train officials to man the new Fascist ship of state. A pamphlet of the Fascist
Faculty of Political Science of Perugia, founded in 1928, explicitly
states that:

The Faculty which has been created fulfills a great need of the
régime. Fascism, having become national and having synthesized
the historical character of Italian civilization, has need of a methodi-
cal study of its doctrine and its political, economic, and juridical
institutions by the young men who enter administrative, syndicalist,
or corporative, diplomatic, or colonial careers.

The State, which the *Duce* is creating and forming every day and
every hour, must have in its arteries—in the lowest and the highest
positions—the sentiment and consciousness, as well as the science,
of Fascism. For this reason, according to the wish of the *Duce,* graduates of the Fascist Faculty will be given preference in the various
administrative, syndicalist, diplomatic, and colonial positions.

In these institutions, as well as in the law schools, courses in
Fascist political theory stress the conception, which is the pivot of
Fascist political thought, that the welfare of the individual is subordinate to the welfare of the state, and that the state comes to a
realization of its being through the fusing of the individual will with
the will of the nation. Other courses deal with the machinery for
the accomplishment of this theoretical ideal. The Fascist party, the
Grand Council, Fascist administrative bodies, and the corporate
state, with its elaborate system of syndicates and its central organs,
are the objects of close study, minute criticism, and profuse praise.
In economics classes the student is taught the Fascist theory that,
because production is the basis for national economic strength and
welfare, labor in all its forms is a duty; that private initiative is
preferable to state socialism, and that the state must control and plan
by means of the corporate system the production of the state. And,
because of the interest in nationalist political thought, dictatorial
government machinery, and nationalist gild economics, research has
been conducted in the problems raised by them. The Fascist government places emphasis on the importance to the régime of the find-
ings of scholars, and maintains that it is amenable to constructive
criticism. How self-repairing Fascism will be, however, history only
can tell. At the present it is only safe to state that Fascism will do no

more than surrender its forms: It will never surrender its ideal of nationalism.

The Fascists' efforts to win university students to their cause have not been limited to activity within scholastic walls. They have also aimed to surround the students' extracurricular life with Fascist phenomena. To this end Fascist University Groups have been founded in all universities. They serve as social centers, organize sporting events, and give their members financial aid in case of need, medical assistance, and reduction on railway fares and for other public services. It is claimed that 27,000 students, or over half the total enrollment, belong to these Groups and it is generally admitted that they are doing much to overcome the traditional cynicism and the disintegrated university life of the Italian student. But more important, perhaps, than the action of these groups, are the Fascist ceremonies for the youth of university age—ceremonies which do much to capture the imagination and stir the enthusiasm of the students. The most important of these is the *Leva Fascista*—the event by which members of the Advance Guard are inducted into the Fascist party. All Fascists attach great importance to this Levy, for, since 1927, the doors of the Party and hence of the Fascist armed force, the Militia, have been closed for the most part except by the process of promotion into it from the Advance Guard. The Levy is accompanied by great celebrations and displays, with Mussolini usually addressing a body of the youth. Entrance to the Militia, which is optional, affords the youths another Fascist thrill. When they are admitted to it, they take this vow: "I swear to obey the orders of the *Duce* without question and to serve the cause of the Fascist Revolution with all my strength and, if necessary, with my blood." Having sworn this oath, each boy receives a rifle as a symbol of his faith and as a means of fulfilling his "duty." To these initiation rites the university student, like any novice, responds with emotional enthusiasm.

Thus,

the University of today (in Italy) believes that its objective is not only of a cultural but also, and first of all, of an ethical and political nature; that a people progresses not only by virtue of its thinking but also, and above all, by its action; that culture ought not to be separated from life; and that Italian life is a new life, in which the genius of a single mind has disclosed a brilliant course toward the greatest heights—heights which the entire people strives to reach. . . .

Fascism has constructed the new edifice of the State—a construction built on Roman lines and with Roman strength. To preserve this edifice, to make the people understand its essence and its *raison d'être,* its function and its ends, to assist its future development, is an essentially political task which, in its highest forms, the University must perform. The University must train the ruling classes who will conscientiously assume responsibility for tomorrow.

The non-political and agnostic University has no *raison d'être.* The true University is the purposeful one. The University is given by its very nature a political task.

Thus let us consider [the University] in its entirety as the molder of the mentality and of the character and as the natural educator of the youth who are entrusted to her. . . .

The University will thus work with a spirit cemented by ever higher aspirations and with a heart full of passion for the greatness of the *patria.*[12]

4. *Summary*

The objectives of education, whether in the elementary, secondary, or higher branches, in Fascist Italy are, first, to improve the material welfare of the people; second, to train Italians for leadership in all branches of intellectual life; and third, to make nationalists. The success of present-day education in attaining the first objective is meager. In attaining the second, it is satisfactory; but in attaining the third, it is eminent. The Italian educational system fuses regionalism into a love for all Italy; it adopts Roman Catholicism as a national institution; it carries on the cultural traditions of the Renaissance; it praises the ideals of the *Risorgimento;* and it glorifies the nationalist sentiments of Fascism. Italian students are so surrounded by nationalist ideas both in the class room and out of it that it would be contrary to all our notions of environment, if we were to believe that these ideas do not leave their imprint on the minds of the youth. In nationalism all else is made dim—the class struggle, the poverty of the country, and the achievements of other states. Italian education, if it does not accomplish anything else, makes Fascists.

[12] Discourse by Professor A. Bruschettini, Rector of the University of Naples.

SOCIAL OBJECTIVES IN DANISH EDUCATION

BY
JOHN H. WUORINEN

XII

DENMARK AND FOREIGN COUNTRIES COMPARED

1. *Denmark and the Danish Tradition*

The conditions and circumstances which have determined in the past the development of educational enterprise in Denmark, and which operate even today to modify the heritage of yesterday, include many factors not susceptible to satisfactory analysis and others that yield more readily to specific appraisal. Among the latter are some of general significance which, while sufficiently obvious to require no extensive treatment, invite at least passing comment.

Denmark is a small country; the total area is in the neighborhood of fifteen thousand square miles. It is about one-third the size of New York, and one-fourth the size of Iowa. The state of Texas is nearly twenty times as large as Denmark. Most of the area, or almost ninety percent, is productive. According to recent statistics (1930), approximately eighty percent of the land is actually under cultivation. In comparison with agriculture, the other natural resources of the country are of distinctly subordinate significance. A substantial part of the industry which has sustained a slowly growing industrial class for fifty years and more is intimately connected with the broad agricultural foundation upon which present-day Denmark rests.

The Danes as a people probably represent one of the most homogeneous nationalities in Europe. While any one mindful of the multitude of sins intellectual which the term "race" is likely to cover will abstain from speaking of a Danish "race," the people of Denmark do attain pretty closely to the unity implied by the conventional, though perhaps meaningless, concept of "race." Certainly the linguistic unity of the nation is complete. The persistence, even today, of certain local dialects does not mean that Danish is not the mother tongue of the nationals of Denmark. The provincialisms and minor linguistic divisions that do exist fall far short of exerting the decentralizing or disruptive influence usually associated with the existence of national minorities or of stubborn cultural separatism found in one form or other in most of the major European states. No strained interpretation is necessary for the classification of the present 3,540,000 inhabitants of Denmark as Danish, for they are Danes in the full sense of the word.

Of this total about 1,980,000, or well over fifty percent, were classified as urban in the census of 1930. The portion of the population actually living under conditions that are rural rather than urban, however, is considerably greater than is indicated by Danish population statistics. Denmark's population is, in fact, overwhelmingly rural, particularly in view of the number of people who obtain their living either directly from the soil, or from occupations dependent upon agriculture. For example, roughly eighty percent of the total exports of Denmark are derived from agriculture. Denmark is a nation of farmers.[1]

It is not necessary to labor the point that those intangible things which distinguish the Danes from their northern neighbors—which make them, say, Danes and not Swedes, Norwegians, or Finns—are not primarily a consequence of geography or of the natural resources which have made Denmark an agricultural commonwealth. The generalization may be hazarded that the Dane is more the product of historical, human, cultural forces, than of the concrete physical environment in which he lives. It is in accepted modes of thought, in ways of perceiving and interpreting the past of his country, and in the content and meaning of a patriotism which, especially in times of national crises, transcends differences of party, profession, and social cleavage, that the Dane stands out among his fellows of the North. A national tradition handed down from generation to generation enables the Dane to experience sympathetic responses to countless aspects of his country and people which leave the foreigner cold and indifferent, and makes it possible for him to devote his deepest loyalties to his own country and no other.

In the perpetuation and enrichment of this national tradition, the schools have played an important rôle. In schools high and low, instruction in Danish, the history and literature of Denmark, and other related subjects has long been designed not only to place the

[1] For pertinent statistics, see Danish *Yearbook*, 1931, Tables, pp. 16-17, 19.

heritage of the past within the reach of the chosen few, but to enable the common man as well to participate in it. Putting it in very general terms, the Danish educational system has been designed, for at least two generations, to produce an intelligent, enterprising, and patriotic citizenry sustained by a deep appreciation of the national heritage. It might well be contended that this has been, and still is, the fundamental social objective of Danish education. This social objective, thus broadly stated, and the success with which it has been realized serve to explain a good deal of the marked homogeneity in social customs, usages, viewpoints, language, and the like which obtain in Denmark. That much of the national tradition rests, in the last analysis, upon no more concrete foundation than literary convention in no way decreases its significance as a unifying force.

In the "Introduction" to his *Denmark, A Coöperative Commonwealth,* published a decade ago, Frederick C. Howe remarks that

Denmark seems to me to be quite the most valuable political exhibit in the modern world. It should be studied by statesmen. It should be visited by commissions. . . . Denmark is one of the few countries in the world that is using political agencies in an intelligent, conscious way for the promotion of the economic well being, the comfort and the cultural life of the people.

The story detailed by this enthusiastic commentator shows how an intelligent utilization of the limited resources of a small nation has made possible a type of economic, political, and social organization in which the State controls, to a considerable extent, the distribution of wealth; in which the farmer has long since demonstrated that agriculture can be made pleasant as well as profitable; in which education is the possession of all the people; in which a multitude of social agencies are amply financed. Nor have these results been obtained, he points out, through the instrumentality of an efficient bureaucracy or a benevolent plutocracy; Denmark "is a demonstration of the average man, and especially of the man farthest down."

Howe is but one of the many foreign students of Denmark who reflect the admiration that the Danes have won abroad, especially during the past twenty or thirty years, by the success with which they have forged ahead. Nearly all foreign students of Denmark comment upon the resourcefulness of the Danish farmer, or sing the praises of Danish educational experiments. While it may be difficult to accept without qualification the claims that Denmark has been completely successful in increasing the economic security of the farmer, or in creating the kind of group attitudes that serve best to further relevant and vital group interests, it must be admitted that even a critically minded observer cannot well escape the conclusion that the Danes have indeed wrought mightily, and that they appear to have come fairly close to success in their efforts to relate at least a very important part of educational work and processes to social ends intelligently conceived.

It is probably unavoidable that no analysis of Danish educational aims and accomplishments during the past fifty or sixty years can be carried very far before the discovery is made that the subject is tantalizingly complex. The background against which Denmark's educational effort must necessarily be projected; the extravagant claims concerning the results obtained which mar much of the available material; the many contradictions and uncertainties encountered as soon as the attempt is made to appraise the meaning of "Danish education" or of "Danish national characteristics," as shaped by school or university experience; the task of evaluating the degree to which institutionalized education has contributed, say, to the active interest in the manifold problems of society manifested by the Danes, probably most strikingly illustrated by the ramifications of the coöperative movement—these are but a few of the problems that must be at least partly solved if the analysis is to establish contact with reality. Only a student "without fear or research" can hope fully to solve them; an ordinary mortal can only attempt to indicate their nature and offer suggestions which are more often tentative than final.

2. *Elementary, Secondary, University, and Vocational Education*

The elementary schools in Denmark do not differ radically from elementary schools in other lands which have a primary-school system worthy of the name. They seem to be well adjusted to the needs of a predominantly rural life. Instruction is simple, direct, and free. Attendance is compulsory from the age of seven to fourteen, although many children enter at the age of six. The enrollment in 1930 was about 493,000, divided among 4,479 schools. Speaking in general

terms, the work of the elementary schools is organized in such a manner as to emphasize three main objectives: thoroughness in fundamental subjects, an understanding and appreciation of the environment in which the pupils live, and a reasonable familiarity with subjects of more or less immediate practical significance. The extent to
which these objectives are realized is suggested in a general way by
the fact that Danish, history (largely national), religion, arithmetic,
and gymnastics loom large in the primary-school curriculum. The
objectives mentioned are not typically Danish, of course. They apply
to Sweden, Finland, and Norway no less than to Denmark. It is
pretty well agreed, however, that in Denmark, at least, they are attained to a notable degree, and the suggestion is often made that the
emphasis on the Danish language, literature, history, and geography
—Danish alone is given about one-fourth of the hours of instruction
—is responsible for the result. Mention should be also made of the
excellent corps of teachers found in the elementary schools. They
are well trained and well paid, and enjoy a social prestige and esteem
quite uncommon in the United States. Incidentally, this statement
applies equally to secondary-school teachers and to the faculties of
the universities and higher technical schools.[2]

The elementary schools are administered jointly by the local
authorities, the Church, and the national government. In matters of
general import, administrative supervision is vested in the ministry
of ecclesiastical affairs and public instruction. Control by the central
government assures unity, but extensive authority is left in the
hands of the local commune, whose taxation provides the main support of the schools. The general boards of education found in each
deanery, constitute the link between the ministry of education and
the local unit. Most of the work of the ministry is actually done
through the deanery boards, and various parish boards. A corps of
inspectors and advisers connected with the ministry constitute the
agency through which the observance of educational laws and or-
dinances is assured, and the competence of the teachers controlled.

[2] See H. W. Foght, *Danish Elementary Rural Schools*, U. S. Bureau of Education, Bulletin No. 29 (1914) ; H. M. Hegland, *The Danish People's High Schools*,
U. S. Bureau of Education, Bulletin No. 45 (1915), chap. iii; Howe, *op. cit.*, chap.
x.

Secondary education begins as a rule at the end of the fifth year of school work, when the pupil is eleven years old. It embraces, first, the middle school of four years; second, the one-year *Real* course; and third, the four-year *Gymnasium*. The latter offers three courses: classical, linguistic, and scientific. Each of these leads to university work, upon the successful completion of the course. While nearly all elementary schools are owned and directly controlled by public authorities, many of the secondary schools are not state-owned. About fifty percent are communal, and a considerable number private. Communal and private schools thus play a very important part in Danish secondary education. The fact that private schools appeared before the state began to make adequate provision for secondary education, and other circumstances that may be omitted here, account for this situation. The secondary as well as the elementary schools, however, are under the supervision and control of the ministry of education.

Many students in Danish secondary schools do not continue beyond the middle school. The enrollment in 1931 was about 4,100. Few middle schools or *Gymnasia* are boarding schools. Some latitude is allowed in the middle-school course of study to meet local needs and conditions, but considerable uniformity prevails throughout. Danish, history, geography and mathematics constitute about one-half of the curricula of these schools. Two foreign languages are also included. Speaking in general terms, the middle school course is considered sufficient for an ordinary career in business or industry, and, obviously, admits the student either to the *Gymnasium* or the *Real* course.

The *Real* course is in a sense a kind of finishing year for those students who do not intend to continue their studies in the *Gymnasium*. It is often found attached, as it were, to the middle schools, or is a part of the complete secondary schools which offer instruction in the whole range of secondary education, the middle school to the *Gymnasium*. The content and character of the *Real* course manifest considerable latitude. Danish, two modern languages (usually English and German) , and electives represent about fifty percent of the curriculum. The successful completion of the *Real* course opens the doors to certain minor positions in the civil service—such as clerkships in the postal or railway service—and admits the student to certain technical and commercial schools. In 1931, the *Real* course enrollment was slightly over five thousand.

The student who enters the *Gymnasium* is confronted by three alternatives. He may choose to devote his three years to one of the following courses: classical, linguistic, or scientific. The weekly programs of the three courses have much in common, in that subjects like Danish, history, religion, and French are about equally emphasized. Sciences constitute a major subject only in the scientific course, but have a place in the language division also. Attendance upon the various courses during the past few decades indicates a considerably smaller enrollment in the classical division than in the others. Indeed, only a few of the *Gymnasia* maintain the classical course, while nearly all of them—state, communal, and private—offer the other two. As early as 1910, the enrollment in the classical course barely exceeded one-tenth of the total number of *Gymnasium* students. The *Gymnasium* closes with a comprehensive examination which admits all successful candidates to studies at the University of Copenhagen.[3]

The University of Copenhagen, founded in 1479, tops the edifice of the Danish educational system. This institution, which has functioned for well over four hundred years, has exerted a tremendous influence upon Danish life. It is probably correct to say that the Danish national university has been the agency of nearly all the important cultural trends and influences which have shaped the intellectual development of the country. A like degree of influence can hardly be claimed by any one of the universities in the leading European countries, where greater resources and other factors have made possible the maintenance of several institutions of higher learning. A recognition of the fact that the University of Copenhagen is, in a very real sense of the word, the nerve center of Denmark's academic life, and has long since become an integral part of the warp and woof of Danish intellectual and scientific life and accomplishment is of fundamental significance for an understanding of the nation as a whole.

The work of the University is organized under five faculties: the-

[3] The University at Aarhus, established in 1928, is left out of consideration in this survey because of considerations of space. In general, its work corresponds to that of the older and more important institution in the capital.

ology, law, medicine, philosophy, and science. It is not altogether
safe to appeal to statistics of enrollment as an indication of the relative importance of the five faculties, but it may be said that those of
medicine, philosophy, and science are the largest, in the order named.
During the first year, all students at the University pursue the same
introductory course, which is completed, as a rule, at the end of the
first year. The subjects required are logic, psychology, and an elementary course in the history of philosophy. The length of the different courses—which, by the way, may be called professional—varies
a good deal. Four years and eight years represent, in the main, the
shortest and the longest periods of study necessary for the attainment
of a university degree (in arts and medicine, respectively). The
yearly attendance is about forty-five hundred. A high degree of freedom in the student's choice of subjects, in the management of his
work by the professor, and in the government of the university, has
long prevailed at the institution. For example, the rector or president, whose office rotates among the professors, is chosen by the
faculty, and the consistorium, composed of members of the faculty, is
the highest administrative organ of the University.

Some of the other higher institutions may be briefly mentioned.
The State College of Engineering (Polytechnic Institute) is another
Copenhagen school of university rank. With respect both to entrance
requirements and quality of work, the College of Engineering is fully
on a par with the University of Copenhagen. It offers courses extending over five or six years, which are designed to train chemical,
electrical, construction, and mechanical engineers. The Commercial
High School, also located in the capital, is organized to give one- or
two-year courses in conventional subjects in the field of business. The
Pharmaceutical College and the School of Dentistry are other important specialized institutions. Mention should also be made of
other professional or semi-professional schools, such as those of fine
arts and navigation. The naval and military academies provide the
army and the navy with necessary specialists.

Of great significance for Denmark is the Veterinary and Agricultural College, likewise located in Copenhagen, for its work touches
most intimately upon many of the problems of a predominantly
agricultural commonwealth. The institution was founded in 1856,

and has trained for decades not only specialists for Denmark, but a considerable number of Norwegian and Finnish veterinarians and agricultural experts as well. The courses range, roughly, from two to five years. They include theoretical, experimental, and practical work in veterinary science and the various aspects of agriculture, animal husbandry, forestry, and horticulture. In connection with the institution there are maintained chemical and bacteriological laboratories for food and soil testing, the investigation of animal and plant diseases, and the like. Just as the University of Copenhagen tops the so-called academic educational institutions of Denmark, so the Veterinary and Agricultural College tops the schools devoted primarily to agricultural education. The lower agricultural schools, because of their close connection with the folk high schools, will be discussed together with the latter.

Rather definitely outside of the system of institutions mentioned thus far, are certain other schools designed to aid the moderately schooled average citizen in his chosen vocation or trade. Particularly important are the trade or industrial schools. They number over one hundred fifty and have a total yearly attendance of some twenty thousand. Most of them are evening schools attended by students over fourteen years of age. The courses offered include Danish, algebra, geometry, bookkeeping, one or two foreign languages (usually English and German) , and a considerable variety of more specialized work in masonry, carpentry, wood turning, blacksmithing, and other trades. Many of the trade unions also support, for the benefit of their members, a wide variety of evening trade schools in which instruction is concentrated upon subjects designed to turn the student into an expert in his chosen trade. Probably the outstanding individual institution among these two groups of industrial schools is the Technological Institute, which offers short courses for mechanics and manufacturers, and also gives instruction in the use of machinery for farmers. Some fifty-three hundred students attended in 1929.

Schools of housekeeping and domestic science have shown a rapid growth during the past quarter of a century. The subjects studied are primarily of practical importance, but include also elementary theoretical and liberal studies. These schools are largely attended by girls from middle- rather than lower-class homes. The latter furnish most of the students who attend the Servant Girls' Union in Copenhagen, which offers special training in cooking, serving, and other domestic arts. These vocational schools for women, and the trade and industrial schools mentioned above, testify to the existence of important educational work designed to lead the individual to a more successful mastery of his work, however unpretentious it may seem, and thereby to make him a more valuable member of society.

XIII

DENMARK'S UNIQUE CONTRIBUTIONS TO EDUCATION

1. *The Folk High Schools*

The above summary description of elementary schools, secondary schools, and universities, and of some of the vocational and other non-academic educational institutions of Denmark has been compressed to the dimensions of a bare outline. In the pages that follow, an effort will be made to describe and evaluate an educational institution of peculiarly Danish origin and significance, which appears to be largely responsible for Denmark's success in solving a substantial part of her rural problem. It is in the solution of this problem, primarily through the instrumentality of the folk high school, that Denmark has made her outstanding contribution in the field of education.

Prior to the early years of the nineteenth century, Denmark was a state of considerable importance, especially in the affairs of northern Europe. Holding a strategic position at the entrance to the Baltic and possessed of a substantial navy, Denmark was able to exercise an influence out of proportion to her geographic extent, population, or other resources. The upheavals of the Napoleonic period reduced Denmark to one of the smallest countries in Europe. The nation having sided with Napoleon, her fleet was lost to England in 1807, and Norway was ceded to the King of Sweden in 1814. Territorial losses were matched by other disasters. Trade and commerce were ruined, and the public debt reached crushing proportions. Nor did the body politic and social present an inspiring picture in the early decades of the century: an absolute monarchy, a privileged landed aristocracy, an unimportant bourgeoisie, and a peasantry which, while it had been freed from serfdom in 1788, still lived in a state far removed from the condition of a free and prosperous peasantry. To make a bad situation worse, agriculture, the mainstay of the nation, suffered

for years after 1815; for example, more than one-third of the large
estates were disposed of in bankruptcy sales between 1823 and 1825.
Some decades later, Denmark suffered additional reverses. The loss
of Schleswig-Holstein to Prussia (1864) was interpreted by many as
the beginning of a process which would end only with the disappearance of Denmark from the political map of Europe.

When all seemed lost [says a writer in commenting upon this
period of Danish history] and the nation was sinking into lethargy
and despair, new voices were heard in the land. A new philosophy
was promulgated; it taught that education must become universal,
practical and democratic; that hereafter Denmark's defense must be
built on the foundation of broad intelligence, rooted in the love of
God and home and native land.[4]

This statement may seem to be an exaggerated generalization, but,
making allowance for the limitations that ever tend to mar even the
most carefully phrased generalizations, it represents a fairly accurate
summary of a good deal of the background and spirit of Denmark's
most original effort to infuse education with a definite social objective. The folk high-school idea was formulated under the stress and
strain of the difficulties to which reference was made above. It was
designed from the beginning to provide a solution for a problem of
national significance.

The man responsible for the folk high schools was Bishop N. F. S.
Grundtvig (1783-1872). Grundtvig was one of the men who sensed
keenly the degradation of Denmark during the first half of the century. A strongly religious nationalist, he made repeated efforts long
before 1830 to arouse his countrymen to a realization of the need of a
spiritual and intellectual revival which would lead the nation to a
new era of economic prosperity and political progress. The consequences of the revolutions of 1830, which led to a slight modification
of the prevailing unlimited monarchy in Denmark, in that advisory
assemblies were created for the purpose of counseling the king, gave
Grundtvig an oportunity to urge upon his fellow Danes the necessity
of a system of instruction designed to educate the lowly masses rather
than the privileged few. He argued that when peasants and burghers
were called upon to sit in the advisory assemblies, it was imperative

[4] H. W. Foght, *The Danish Folk High Schools*, U. S. Bureau of Education,
Bulletin No. 22 (1914), p. 15.

that their educational equipment be equal to the occasion. The representatives ought to know enough of their country's history and social problems to enable them really to assist in the making of the laws of the land. His contention was, briefly, that a high school designed to aid the sons of the common people in the mastery of important contemporary and other questions was urgently needed. The school he had in mind would not train politicians, in the narrow sense of the word, but would develop and enrich the life of the whole people by training the youth of Denmark in the difficult art of useful and intelligent citizenship.

It is pertinent to note that Grundtvig's educational scheme was given its first opportunity in connection with a situation strongly colored by nationalist elements. It was only after the appearance of the nationalist struggle in Schleswig, where the Danish peasantry stood in opposition to the German bureaucrasy and nobility and was in danger of being Germanized, that attention began to be paid to Grundtvig's agitation. The first school embodying his principles was actually established in North Schleswig in the year 1844. The real purpose of the school was to strengthen the Schleswig Danes in their contest with the German elements; the general aim, however, was stated in words that may be considered a fairly accurate characterization of the later folk high schools as well.

The aim set is to found an institution where peasant and burgher can attain useful and desirable arts, not so much with the purpose of immediate application to his particular calling in life, as with reference to his position as a native son of the country and citizen of the State. We call it a high school because it is not to be an ordinary boys' school but an educational institution partly for young men past the age of confirmation, partly for full-grown boys and men. We call it a people's school because persons of every station may attend it, even if it is specially arranged for the rural class and expects its students from that source.[5]

The beginning once having been made, a number of other folk high schools were established, especially in the course of the fifties. However, the opposition to them among professional educators, as well as other difficulties which naturally attended upon a novel educational experiment, made most of them short-lived. Curiously enough, they began to prosper only after the loss of Schleswig and

[5] *Ibid.*, p. 25; cf. H. M. Hegland, *op. cit.*, pp. 85-86.

Holstein in 1864 served to arouse the nation to a keen realization of the necessity of new objectives boldly conceived and persistently carried out. "Outward loss inward gain" became the motto. In the words of a Danish writer, "Everything seemed to depend upon educating a new generation which could, by firm will and industry, rebuild what had been demolished by the war."[6] New men, most of whom were disciples of Grundtvig, and among whom Christen Kold was perhaps outstanding, appeared in the high-school movement. They were leaders who not only reflected the determination suggested by the words quoted, but were mindful of the demands placed upon the masses by the liberalization of Denmark's political institutions which had taken place since the decade of the forties. New and more exacting demands of citizenship, as well as the dangers to the continued existence of the kingdom which seemed to inhere in the territorial mutilation of 1864, spurred the educators who began to labor with renewed zeal for the Grundtvig ideal. By the close of the seventies, the folk high schools were rapidly increasing in numbers, and by the turn of the century they had come to exercise a profound influence upon the Danish nation.

The folk high-school idea meant a radical deviation from conventional educational practice. The mission of the schools was conceived, not in terms of specific, nicely adjusted courses or curricula, but in terms of instruction designed to contribute to a spiritual and intellectual awakening of the bulk of the nation. Such an ambitious purpose cannot be described in phrases applicable to ordinary educational institutions; it defies schematic presentation and facile summary. It is significant that Grundtvig never formulated a definite plan for the work of the schools. The following statement indicates some of the aversion which he felt toward conventional education, and which led him to urge a new departure.

We must be born before we know what caps will fit our heads, to say nothing of how high a destiny we shall reach and what knowledge we may be able to acquire. . . . [We have] become so perverted [in ordinary schools] that we can scarcely imagine a school whose life is not mapped out before it begins. This can be easily done with the bookish art, which consists in memorizing a certain

[6] H. Bergtrup in H. Bergtrup, H. Lund, and P. Manniche, *The Folk High Schools of Denmark and the Development of a Farming Community*, p. 107.

number of glossaries and rules, and at its best in studying and imitating such unchangeable things as books. But just as this method is impossible of application to life, which precludes stagnation and can follow no rules but those of nature, so also is it impossible to apply it to education, which must adjust itself to life as it really is.

The folk high schools, Grundtvig maintained, should perform a "life-giving, light-spreading, heart-warming function," and instruction should give the student

a clear notion of civic society and the conditions of its welfare, and appreciation of the national characteristics of his people, sincere devotion to "King and fatherland," ability to express himself orally in his mother tongue, with ease and vigor, freedom and propriety, and finally a definite knowledge of what we have and what we lack, based upon reliable reports on the conditions of the country.[7]

In other words, the folk high schools were to serve, literally, as "schools for life" and not as institutions in which a specific amount of vocational or other narrow training could be acquired. Founded on the rock of nationality, designed to arouse and maintain a strong spirit of nationalism and religious faith, they were intended to offer instruction of broad "cultural" content. While a certain amount of vocational training soon became a part of their program, it has never assumed proportions that would turn them into stereotyped continuation or vocational schools.

Grundtvig and many of his followers envisioned a school for all classes of the population without reference to geographical or vocational distribution. Yet the folk high schools soon came to be attended almost exclusively by the rural population. For the past fifty years, they have ministered primarily to the farmer class—a fact worthy of some emphasis if we are not to conclude that the direct influence of the high schools has reached the butcher, the baker, and the candlestick maker in the same degree as the tiller of the soil. The schools got their start in the country, and began their work among the farmers, and early came to be known as "peasant schools." Furthermore, a city mechanic or laborer as a rule had no opportunity to enjoy the seasonal leisure which conditions in the North impose on the farmer, thus permitting him to enjoy the offerings of the schools.

[7] The quotations are from H. M. Hegland, op. cit., pp. 79-80. See also ibid., pp. 73-79.

The religious aspect of their work, and the relative lack of diversion in rural communities, may also have contributed toward making the schools markedly sectional as regards the students' antecedents.

The high schools may be called short-term boarding schools or part-time schools. From the very outset, they have existed as private institutions. Private and not state initiative brought them into being, and they have retained their private character down to the present. Some of them are owned by various high-school societies and corporations, but the majority are owned and controlled by the principal. In either case they represent coöperation applied to education. They are inspected by the state. When they meet certain requirements as to number of students, equipment and the like, they are recognized by the ministry of ecclesiastical affairs and public instruction and receive annual grants from the national treasury. Such public aid has been granted since 1852 and has been important in enabling the schools to carry on at the least possible expense for the student.

TABLE VI

DANISH FOLK-HIGH-SCHOOL WEEKLY CURRICULUM

	AVERAGE WEEKLY HOURS OF INSTRUCTION	
SUBJECTS	Boys' Course (5 months)	Girl's Course (3 months)
Danish	8.0	7.7
History and Civics	9.5	9.3
Penmanship	1.1	0.8
History of literature	5.2	5.9
Geography	2.4	2.3
Sciences and Hygiene	4.2	3.8
Arithmetic	5.0	3.6
Drawing	2.5	0.8
Singing	1.1	1.3
Gymnastics	5.4	5.6
Household arts	..	9.6
Agriculture	4.2	..
Other subjects	1.5	1.0
Total	50.1	51.7

The students are as a rule between eighteen and twenty-five years of age. Most of them are sons and daughters of farmers, and have completed the elementary school three or four years before entering the high school. Most of the institutions offer two courses of study: a five-month course in winter for young men and a three-month course in summer for young women. Instruction consists in part of a review of more important elementary subjects. Danish, history, and literature, however, are the subjects of greatest importance, and it is chiefly through them that the folk high schools attempt to accomplish their aim. The general range of subjects in the average high-school curriculum is suggested by Table VI on page 226.

The table indicates in part the effort made to imbue the students with the national tradition of Denmark. As a matter of fact, instruction in Danish, history and geography, and in literature, serves to emphasize national elements and interests. Probably one-third of the subjects included may be said to be of direct aid in the transformation of the student into an actively nation-conscious citizen. Singing, a subject of much greater importance than the curriculum suggests, markedly contributes to this end. The school day begins with song. As a rule, patriotic folk songs are sung at the beginning and at times at the close of every class or hour of work. The songs are varied in character but deal often with patriotic, religious, and historical subjects.[8]

The methods of instruction are more remarkable than the subjects taught. Ordinary schools attempt to impart to the student a given body of formal knowledge. The assumption is that after the student has amassed a certain fund of information, and has attained the stage of intellectual maturity necessary for the ability to generalize, his fragmentary knowledge will coalesce into a unified whole. This procedure, whatever may be its defects or advantages, requires more time than the folk high schools have at their disposal. Their approach and procedure must necessarily be different.

The method may perhaps be best illustrated by the treatment of history, especially national history. History in general is interpreted as the purposeful experience of peoples and nations. As such it has a

[8] For various types of folk high-school curricula, see Hegland, *op. cit.*, pp. 113-27, and L. L. Friend, *The Folk High Schools of Denmark*, pp. 12-14.

greater significance than any philosophical system. Historical evidence has an authority which cannot be challenged. Properly considered, history reveals its own laws, and those of nature, which show that what has happened in the past has come about not by chance, but inevitably. History teaches by example: the Greeks were able to withstand the Persians because they were morally superior. By the same token a small nation today can pit its strength against the pretensions of a larger one, if its citizens are animated by a desire to live free, rich lives, not only for their own good, but for the benefit and glory of their country. The noble and the fine in the past should challenge the student to his best efforts in things great and small. It is the function of the teacher to interpret the past in this general spirit, and to furnish the interpretations necessary to give significant relief to the object lessons of history.[9]

It is obvious that history instruction along these lines requires something more elevating than laborious recitations out of textbooks. It demands nothing less than the inspired spoken word of the teacher. Inspirational lecturing not only in history but in other important subjects is in fact the main characteristic of the teaching in folk high schools. Books and the like are considered useless and paralyzing aids in the work. As one close student of the folk high schools has put it, the high schools

are concerned with people whose intellectual level must be called primitive in comparison with the materials with which they deal. They must therefore appeal not so much to the understanding of the students as to their hearts and their personalities. For this, vivifying human speech far surpasses the "dead words" of books.[10]

Nor do the students take notes, as a rule. Notes are likely to be useless in the folk high-school scheme of things, which does not include examinations of any kind. No effort is made to measure the student's accomplishment by means of anything even remotely resembling examinations; the student need never be paralyzed by the fear that he must give periodic evidence of information properly digested. He comes to the school to absorb as much as his powers permit, and in the process becomes immersed in matter presented by a corps of in-

[9] See H. M. Hegland, *op. cit.*, pp. 120 ff., and H. Bergtrup, *op. cit.*, pp. 112 ff. and *passim*.

[10] H. M. Hegland, *op. cit.*, p. 122.

spirational teachers who rely on the efficacy of the "living word" and repudiate the authority of the printed page in the teaching process.

2. The Agricultural Schools and the Coöperative Movement

Almost from the beginning of the folk high-school movement, forces were at work which threatened to turn the high schools into agricultural schools. Perhaps the main reason for this tendency was the fact that the folk high schools drew nearly all of their students from the agricultural population whose main concern and interests were closely connected with farming and its problems. Many have contended ever since the establishment of the first folk high school nearly ninety years ago, that these schools should offer instruction only in agriculture. The supporters of this contention have said, and still say, that any other type of instruction is useless because only vocational instruction can be understood by the more or less untutored peasant youth, and unprofitable because it will not contribute to more efficient cultivation of Denmark's farms. Others have championed mixed schools—that is, schools partly agricultural and partly devoted to the aims of Grundtvig, Kold, and other defenders of the folk high schools—and still others have favored the establishment and maintenance of separate schools of both types. Especially in recent decades, the combined schools have come to occupy a conspicuous place, partly, it seems, at the expense of the other two types of institution. This seems to be suggested by the following figures. In 1930, there were sixty-one folk high schools whose combined attendance was 6,380; eighty-three combined high and agricultural schools attended by 9,366 students; and twenty-two agricultural schools with an enrollment of 2,986.[11]

The agricultural schools began to appear in the eighteen sixties. They were founded primarily by former students of the folk high schools. While their specific purpose differed from that of the folk high schools, they reflected the general aim and spirit which characterized the folk high schools. The connection between the two schools has remained close down to our day, and there is a good deal of truth in the statement that the agricultural school is the child of the folk high school.

[11] Statistisk Aarbog, 1931, Table 15.

The growth of the agricultural schools became rapid in the course of the seventies and the eighties—a period in the history of Denmark marked by profound disturbances in the economic life of the country which seemed to threaten the material foundations of the Danish nation. These years of economic stress and strain constituted, it has been said, the first real test of the soundness of the folk high-school idea and instruction. Both stood the test and contributed immeasurably to the making of modern progressive Denmark.

The appearance shortly after the middle of the nineteenth century of the United States, Russia, and the Argentine as important grain-exporting nations had a disastrous effect upon the small-scale production of Denmark. Against competition with these countries, the Danish farmer found it impossible to make any headway. The adoption of protection by Germany, by seriously limiting the Danes' opportunities in German markets, had the effect of making a bad situation worse. During the early years of the decade of the seventies, it seemed that insurmountable difficulties were being heaped in the way of Denmark's economic development, and that the whole agricultural basis of the nation was beginning to yield under the pressure of conditions over which the Danes had little or no control. By the close of the century, however, not only had the Danish farmer been saved from the economic misfortunes that threatened him, but the general level of agricultural efficiency had been raised to a degree which enabled him to become a prosperous and progressively minded member of society, and made Denmark the subject of enthusiastic comment abroad.

The details of the Danish agricultural revolution need not detain us. It will suffice to say that within the space of a score of years, Denmark abandoned her traditional farming and emerged as a leading dairying country, whose export of butter, eggs, cheese, and the like brought her prestige and substantial profits in foreign markets. The value of agricultural exports grew by leaps and bounds—from about twenty-five million dollars in 1881 to about one hundred fifty million dollars in 1912. Other indications of this economic revival might be mentioned; live stock increased from 1,470,000 in 1881 to 2,460,000 in 1914; the average yield of butter per Danish cow was eighty pounds in 1864, 116 pounds in 1887, and 220 pounds in 1908.

These results, and a host of others closely connected with them, were achieved through schools of agriculture and through the possibilities for the growth of the coöperative movement which the folk high schools had created. The contention that the agricultural schools and the folk high schools were of fundamental importance in making this all-important agricultural change—that, in other words, the Danish peasant could not have been transformed from an inefficient tiller of the soil into a progressively minded farmer except for the ideals and objectives on which the folk high-school movement rested—appears to be supported by a body of evidence that can hardly be brushed aside as irrelevant. Both "statistics and popular judgment," says a Danish writer, emphasize the fact that without the instruction obtained in these schools the farmer would not have found the way to prosperity. The folk high school, says he, "put a new spirit, a new sense of independence, into the peasant class. It stimulated activity and promoted perseverence because it awakened them to the possibilities of their position."[12] Nearly all writers on Danish agricultural development during this critical period emphasize the connection here stressed. Although detailed proof cannot readily be presented in its support, the unanimity of Danish and foreign opinion may perhaps be accepted in the place of statistical evidence.

The coöperative movement is perhaps the thing for which Denmark is most widely known. For approximately half a century, the Danish rural population in particular has adopted and applied the coöperative idea to a degree which pretty fully justifies the title "coöperative commonwealth" which is frequently applied to the country. It is probably no exaggeration to say that coöperation is the most pervasive form of enterprise in Denmark today, and that it has modified to a marked degree the system, or lack of system, which we call capitalistic. Capitalistic agencies of the familiar kind play almost no part in many all-important undertakings of the Danish farmer: through his coöperative organization, he does his extensive dairying; kills and sells his hogs and cattle; imports fertilizer for his farm and food for his live stock; obtains his insurance; does his banking and establishes his credit; buys many if not most ordinary articles of

[12] H. Lund in H. Bergtrup et. al., *op. cit.*, p. 41.

consumption at wholesale; and sells to himself at retail prices. In a word, he does most of his business through coöperatives. Coöperative retail stores alone number upwards of two thousand, and the total number of various coöperative societies exceeds four thousand. Approximately two hundred fifty thousand farmers who represent some forty percent of the population of Denmark, support them by active membership.[13]

In attempting to explain the notable success of the coöperative idea in Denmark, one is forced to a recognition of the work of the folk high schools in this field also. Statements by Danes familiar with the situation will suffice to indicate the part played by the folk high schools in the coöperative movement. Mr. Hans Lund of the Rodding Folk High School maintains that it is

not too much to claim that general opinion in Denmark favors the view that the most important reason for the triumph of the coöperative ideas among the peasants is to be found, not in the social and political sphere, but in that of the spiritual influences which emanate from the Danish folk high schools.

Mr. H. Hertel, a writer on the history of coöperation in Denmark, states that

these schools awakened in the young men and women a yearning for knowledge and a desire for work; the character of the pupils was strengthened, and they left the schools with a much enlarged view of life. To satisfy its yearning for knowledge a current of youth flowed from the folk high schools to the agricultural schools, and when it afterwards passed out into life it did so with a strong feeling of fellowship, and a desire to work for common progress. Youth thus gained some of the qualifications necessary to the success of a coöperative movement.

The third appraisal comes from the pen of Mr. Anders Nielsen, a leading figure in the coöperative movement in Denmark. Speaking of the folk high school, he holds that

It has filled and levelled the clefts in society, and thereby paved the way for working together. It has sent students out into life with an added love for the country and its achievements, riper and more thoughtful, more receptive to life's teachings, and therefore well equipped to understand and make their way where less developed run aground. This significance of the folk high school has . . . been emphasized and affirmed so often, and from so many sides, that it can well be stated as a fact that not only the coöperative

[13] Cf. F. C. Howe, *op. cit.*, chap. iv.

movement, but the cultural position of the Danish farmers as a whole, rests on its foundation; and when we thus consider the social importance of the coöperative movement, and its economic contribution . . . we must acknowledge with gratitude the great religious and school leaders Grundtvig and Kold, and their many coworkers and followers who have called forth a higher culture and feeling of solidarity among the people, and who taught the people to think and use their powers so as to develop their lives in such a way that the united efforts of all ensure that not only the individual but the whole community is benefited.[14]

3. Past Accomplishments and Future Prospects

In bringing this discussion to a close, no attempt will be made to enlarge upon the more or less conventional aims of the Danish elementary, secondary, and higher educational institutions. To them may be applied most of the broad generalizations applicable, say, to the corresponding segments of the German educational pyramid. An effort will be made, instead, to state some of the conclusions toward which the writer has been driven by the treatment accorded in these pages to the folk high school and the objectives of this distinctly Danish educational experiment.

It has been pointed out that the folk high schools represent an endeavor to mold educational effort to fit the needs of that majority of the Danish people to whom ordinary educational opportunities have either been closed or but moderately available. Something has been said of the rejection, by the men responsible for the appearance and accomplishment of the folk high schools, of most of the conventional system and procedure because it was deemed useless and even pernicious. A new system, considerably removed from the tested and the tried, was evolved by them: entrance requirements, formal curricula, and examinations were thrown overboard, and such study aids as books given only a very subordinate part in the new scheme of things. It has been shown that, according to a fairly wide variety of Danish and foreign opinion, the folk high schools have realized, to a marked degree, the somewhat intangible and pretentious social and cultural objectives which sustained Grundtvig, Kold, and scores of other leaders of the folk high-school movement. We have also noted that presumably well informed students of Denmark agree that the

[14] The quotations are from Howe, *op. cit.*, pp. 47-49.

folk high schools should be accorded a good deal of the credit for the developments which have made Denmark one of the most progressive dairying and farming nations of our day. It seems, therefore, that the folk high schools have been remarkably successful in accomplishing the ambitious task which they were intended to perform.

The assertion may be made, furthermore, that these schools have contributed much toward the transformation of the Danes into a strongly nationalist-conscious nation. By their emphasis on the Danish language, and the history and literature of Denmark, they have instilled in their students a deep love of the fatherland. Indeed, it is the opinion of not a few Danes that at least some of their progress in agriculture should be explained in terms of a competitive feeling, stimulated by patriotism, which "cannot bear to see Denmark fall behind in the race of nations in those lines of activity in which she is in any way qualified to compete."[15] In the field of politics likewise the influence of the folk high schools has been considerable. It is pretty well agreed, for example, that the persistence of the demands for democratic reform which characterized Danish politics during the closing decades of the last century was largely sustained by farmers whose capacity for active participation in public affairs had been aroused and developed by the folk high schools; when the reformed parliament of 1901 convened, some thirty percent of the membership of both houses of the legislature was composed of former students of these schools. That the folk high schools have been responsible for a good deal of the cohesive force which has enabled the farmers of Denmark to unite in a wide variety of coöperative enterprises can hardly be denied in view of the opinions held by leading men in the Danish coöperative movement.

The long and impressive bill of particulars which can thus be drafted in defense of the folk high schools discloses at least one important omission. These schools minister almost exclusively to the needs of the rural population. For reasons that defy satisfactory analysis, they have failed to attract the allegiance of the industrial, urban working class. The Danish Social Democrats, for instance, have not embraced the folk high-school objectives, and only a small number of working-class students are found in them. The folk high

[15] H. M. Hegland, op. cit., pp. 139-40.

schools have become farmers' high schools; they have failed to develop into real people's high schools. They have at best bridged, but not filled, the gap which separates town and country, the landowning farmer and the organized industrial wage-earner. This observation would hardly be worthy of mention were it not for the fact that Social Democracy represents a force of growing importance in the Danish body politic: the first Socialist ministry assumed office in 1924, and the present Socialist Stauning cabinet has presided over the destinies of Denmark since April, 1929. It is perhaps permissible to say that however much the folk high school has accomplished in the past, its future will depend in no small degree upon its success in making new conquests among the industrial workers and the less prosperous small farmers and agricultural laborers. Down to the present, the folk high schools have failed to become important agencies in the elevation of the industrial proletariat—a significant fact in judging the usefulness of the folk high school for a predominantly industrial civilization.

A final word of caution must be uttered. The attempts made in these pages to appraise the work of the Danish folk high schools fall short of giving a satisfactory answer to the question: How far have the objectives of these schools been actually lifted from the stage of ambitious aspirations to the stage of results concrete and measurable? Strictly speaking, nearly all the evidence pertaining to the educational system of Denmark is only opinion. This is particularly true of the extensive material dealing with the folk high schools. It is perhaps equally true of most sources of information dealing with schools in other lands which attempts to penetrate beyond the obvious and the unimportant. That is to say, as soon as we pass from the statistical record of school and university attendance, literacy percentages, and the like, and proceed to formulate conclusions as regards the larger social significance of a given school or system of schools, gratuitous assumptions begin to lead us imperceptibly but steadily from the realm of fact into the world of the probable. It is the contention of the present writer that in view of the imperfections of the existing mechanism for recording the more fundamental consequences of educational enterprise, so-called facts must ever be liberally sprinkled with the spice of hesitance and caution. Even when the evidence seems to indicate, as it certainly seems to in the case of Denmark, that education of the folk high-school type is productive of important, socially advantageous results, it fails fully to expose all of the pertinent facts and compels us to be satisfied with capturing the meaning of tendencies and of general implications while failing to establish contact with truth ultimate and final.

EDUCATION IN CANADA

BY

J. BARTLET BREBNER

XIV

THE INTERPLAY OF CANADIAN
SOCIAL ATTITUDES

1. *Particularism*

In the sense in which we understand the phrase "French education" there is almost no Canadian education.[1] Canada itself and its peoples are so diverse in so many particulars, that only since 1900 has there been any notable development of a national character in education. The local and the particular have been dominant, but now they are being affected by certain general characteristics which, naturally enough, owe more to Canada's North Americanism and to her response to contemporary world conditions than to her heritages from France and Great Britain. Ten million Canadians (predominantly French and English) occupy a strip of land seldom more than two hundred miles wide which stretches from Atlantic to Pacific but which is three times interrupted by large areas almost without population. The urban centres, which have grown with great rapidity since 1900, and the more densely populated areas are close to the United States. Every province except Prince Edward Island has its great empty spaces and its fringes of thin population, which form cultural frontiers to which education must reach out feebly. It is no

[1] The standard book of reference is the *Annual Survey of Education in Canada*, Ottawa, King's Printer, which is supplemented by the *Annual Report of the Technical Education Branch of the Department of Labour, Canada*. Among useful recent commentary articles are: R. La Roque de Roquebrune, E. Montpetit, and Sir Robert Falconer, "Cultural Development," in *Cambridge History of the British Empire*, Vol. VI, New York, 1930; P. Sandiford, "Canada," in *Comparative Education*, New York, 1918; W. E. Macpherson, "Canada," in *Educational Yearbook of the International Institute of Teachers' College, Columbia University, 1924*, New York, 1925; a series of articles on the separate provinces in the monthly, *The School*, Toronto, 1923-28; Sir Robert Falconer, "English Influence on the Higher Education of Canada," and "American Influence on the Higher Education of Canada," *Transactions of the Royal Society of Canada*, Third Series, Vol. XXII (1928), Section II, pp. 1-16; Vol. XXIV (1930), Section II, pp. 23-38; several articles in *The Year Book of Education*, London, 1932-34; and G. M. Weir, *The Separate School Question in Canada*, Toronto, 1934.

wonder that the Canadian polity is a federation, which, from its beginning in 1867, has recognized particularism by making education
the almost exclusive concern of the provinces, now nine in number.

Canadians are differentiated among themselves by geography, language, race, and creed—not only the descendants of the eighteenth
century French- and English-speaking colonists, but the flood of
European immigrants who rushed in to get the last free land of
North America after 1896. Prince Edward Island lies in the southern Gulf of St. Lawrence. Nova Scotia is almost an island, connected with the mainland by a narrow isthmus at its northern end.
New Brunswick is separated from the other two Maritime Provinces, and all three form an eastern cornice of the Dominion cut off
from the populous heart of Quebec and Ontario by the whimsical
northern projection of the state of Maine and by the impassable
block of mountains and rough country in northern New Brunswick
and the Gaspé Peninsula. The St. Lawrence River both divides and
unites the people of Quebec, depending on the seasons. Ontario
merges with Quebec on the east, but its northern and western regions are part of the Laurentian Shield, a district of rivers, lakes,
muskeg, and thin soil which supports a scant population and which
in the past diverted the westward flow of Canadian and American
population to the regions south of the Great Lakes. The western
prairies have no natural divisions, but Manitoba, Saskatchewan, and
Alberta lie in a fertile basin between the barriers of the Laurentian
Shield in Ontario and the Rocky Mountains in British Columbia. In
the habitable valleys and wooded coastal shelves of the westernmost
province, Canadians are persuaded by topography to look west to the
Pacific instead of east to Ottawa. The *genius loci* operates as effectively in Canada as elsewhere in the world, but its greatest strengths
have been local rather than national.

Race, language, and religion coincide with some of the geographical divisions and run across others in confusing ways. The main
division is between English and French, Protestant and Roman Catholic, but each of these divisions is subdivided again. Quebec is overwhelmingly French and Roman Catholic, but the Acadian French
who form about a fifth of the population of the three Maritime
Provinces have been conscious of their difference from the French

of Quebec ever since the seventeenth century. The French-speaking
inhabitants of the prairies, with their substantial fraction of *métis,*
have carried down from the days of *coureurs-de-bois* and *voyageurs*
a pride in their superiorities over the more sedentary French in the
East. English-speaking Canada has been recruited from Loyalist and
quite unpolitical immigrants from the Thirteen Colonies and the
United States, from the mass migrations out of nineteenth-century
England, Ireland, and Scotland, and from the Canadianized children of Continental European immigrants. But English-speaking
Canadians have been sometimes sharply divided by religious affiliation. The Church of England, favored as it was from 1760 to 1840
by the old British colonial policy, fought a long and ultimately unsuccessful battle against the Roman Catholics, the Presbyterians, the
Methodists, and the Baptists to entrench itself in a privileged position with regard to state and religion and education. Seeds of bitterness from that struggle still subsist, although they can be forgotten if
circumstances seem to demand that Protestantism wage the old war
against Catholicism—French, Irish, and Scotch. The Continental
European immigrants have also contributed religious differences.
Such sects as the Mennonites and the Doukhobors have caused disturbances (notably in relation to education) far out of proportion
to their numbers, and other groups which have settled in blocks on
the prairies have resisted stubbornly the educative processes of their
new country. By reaction, however, they have stiffened the resolution of the communities among which they are minorities.

Even the external influences on Canada have worked in contradictory ways, now to effect persuasion, now revulsion. Of them
the influence of the United States has been by far the most powerful.
For a hundred and seventy-five years British North America has seen
the United States forge ahead in exploitation of the continent at a
rate which Canada did not attain until the twentieth century. Two-
thirds of the Canadian people live in the wedge of Quebec and Ontario which runs far into the United States south of its most northern boundary, and most of the others (in the West) are separated
from the United States by a political boundary which has meant less
to population movements in North America than the geographical
barriers which break up Canada. In a continent whose riches have

raised exploitation to an almost systematic popular philosophy, the attitude of the less successful exploiter toward its neighbour has inevitably been sensitive and defensive, and that of the more successful largely blandly ignorant. Canada has been drenched with influences from the United States; she has borrowed consciously and unconsciously all kinds of techniques, goods, and ways of thinking; and she has resented many even of the appropriate evidences of her North Americansim because they seemed to represent Americanization at the hands of a colossus that seldom admitted her existence except to suggest from time to time that her destiny lay in losing her identity in the United States. Denied the chance of anything approaching economic equality with the United States, and frequently bruised by irresistible American economic policies, Canada has characteristically fallen back on a feeling of moral superiority which has salved some wounds and fortified some fruitful policies of self-discipline.

Hardly less confusing has been the influence of France. When French Canada became British in 1763, it contained an odd blend of central paternalism and sturdy local self-reliance. In 1774 the British government threw its weight on the side of paternalism by reëstablishing the Roman Catholic hierarchy and the seigneurial system. Fifteen years later the French Revolution and the advent of the French bourgeoisie to power opened a deep and widening chasm between France and French Canada of early eighteenth-century mould. That gap was seldom crossed until about 1865, when it was bridged, paradoxically enough, by French-Canadian adoption of the nineteenth-century British liberalism which had also won adherents in France. When the French anti-clericalism of the opening years of the twentieth century proceeded to separate Church and State and expel the congregations, New France was shocked again, and this time almost into a rejection of France in favour of considerate Great Britain. *"France notre cœur, Albion notre foi"* was a not unfair summary of the situation. Since that time the recognition of Canadian autonomy and of Quebec's own considerable autonomy within the Canadian federal system has created greater self-reliance, and during the last twenty-five years French-Canadians have been engaged in a highly selective process of *rapprochement* with some French circles and ideas. Even yet much of French life, thought, and education is held to be corrupting and nefarious, although some emotional and cultural affiliations are very strong.

One has only to remember the various reasons for which emigrants from the British Isles came to Canada in order to appreciate their contradictory effects on Canadian society. To begin with, there was the official class, whose Anglicanism and authoritarianism found welcome and emulation among its ambitious natural acolytes in the colonies. The evictions of tenants by Scottish landlords in their hasty efforts to imitate English improvements in agriculture at the end of the eighteenth century sent out hordes of Scots who clung to their Presbyterian Churches and their history, but had little reason for gratitude to any government save the democratic one which they began to assist in creating in the new lands. The "hungry forties" sent out thousands of the English rural population, but in Ireland they took the form of actual famine and transplanted whole villages from scenes of despair in Ireland to apparently boundless opportunity in North America. The raids of the Irish Fenians from the United States against the British colonies were spectacular evidence of what, in altered degree, was the attitude of many Irish immigrants in those colonies to "British," if perhaps not to more purely Canadian, institutions. Finally, there came the mixed flood of British immigrants after the South African War, many of them less vigorous and self-reliant than their predecessors. Some of these by their ignorant assumption of superiority and of the right to special consideration were themselves responsible for the Canadian advertisements for employment which included the phrase "No Englishman need apply."

2. Nationalism

Inevitably all of the particularisms which have been listed above have modified one another and have been modified by an overriding sense of Canadian nationality. The successful defence of the colonies in the War of 1812 gave a marked self-consciousness to the Maritime Colonies and actually made for an identity of interest and self-consciousness between English Upper Canada and French Lower Canada. Those local integrities were sorely strained by the divisions incidental to the colonial struggle for self-government, by the

Canadian rebellions, and by the great immigrations between 1825 and 1850. Following the concession of colonial autonomy about 1848, healing and uniting processes got to work and had eventuated by 1873 in the daring, if shaky, structure of a federation which stretched from the Atlantic to the Pacific. Fear of the United States, British interest in Canada as a route to the East, a Canadian sense of mission in the development of the West and the prevalent atmosphere of nationalism combined with other forces to make British North America a single political entity, with the exception of Labrador and Newfoundland. By 1885 the Intercolonial and Canadian Pacific railways had given the federation some actual unity and the several political defections and two western rebellions had been successfully dealt with.

During the next thirty years Canada led the way in the British Empire towards that combination of political independence and voluntary imperial association which is known as "dominion status." Naturally, that political progress was the product of other forces in the national life. Canadians became increasingly conscious of themselves as such, of their mission in North America and of the rights as well as the responsibilities which were involved in it. Anglo-American diplomacy which seemed to slight Canadian interests, the slow realization of the relation which exists between military effort and a share in foreign policy, and, above all, the swelling tides of immigration and national prosperity made it natural to think of Canada as a nation. Eastern Canada had sent its sons in thousands to the West, and by their early arrival there, and the instinctive Canadianism which they carried with them, they were able to give the West at least a Canadian core before immigrants poured in from the United States and Europe.

It was the war of 1914-18, however, accompanied and followed as it was by an astounding increase in Canadian productivity, which really established Canadian nationality. The remarkable war effort, the share in the peacemaking, and the national position in the League of Nations were speedily followed by legal and constitutional recognition of a new status. Great Britain announced her intention of becoming a dominion in 1926, but as *Punch* pointed out, decided not to secede from the Empire, and the Statute of Westminster in

1931 sealed the bargain. Canada and the other Dominions became legally and constitutionally equals of Great Britain within the Empire. Yet it should be remembered that during the same years French-Canadian opposition to the war and to military conscription split Canada into two parts and that breach is still not entirely healed.

Indeed, there are several kinds of separatism in Canada at present, although Canadian nationality has been vigorously fostered by the prevailing economic nationalism of our day, particularly by the ruthless tariff discriminations by which the United States has successively either destroyed Canadian export enterprises or forced them to seek world markets. The Maritime Provinces, for instance, which originally repudiated federation only to be bribed and manœuvred into acceptance of it, have become a sort of economic backwater in Canada, shut off from their natural economic affiliation with New England and geographically cut off from the Canadian centre at Ottawa. Quebec's particularism is very strong in most of its aspects, and the emigration of French-Canadians to enter upon a minority rôle in other provinces has increased her sensitiveness. Ontario, which is the industrial centre of Canada, is protectionist. The agricultural prairies want freer trade. British Columbia has discovered the Far East and asks that Canadian policies be modified in terms of her interests there.

3. *Conservatism*

There is also an interplay of conservatism with a very small amount of radicalism in Canada which should be taken into account in estimating the effects of national and local attitudes. Measured by world criteria, North America still stands as the champion of individualism and *laissez faire* against the advances of various kinds of state socialism, Bolshevist, Fascist, or Fabian. In North America, Canada has very good reasons for being (with exceptions to be noted later) on the whole more conservative than the United States. Her weaker position in relation to the United States encourages a defensive psychology whose manifestations in unenterprising complacency and maintenance of things "as they are" have recently seriously perturbed acute Canadian observers. The conservatism of authority in Quebec is still very strong and finds expression in ways too numerous to be detailed here. In Ontario the analogous if less effective force is the surviving United Empire Loyalist and Tory tradition which makes that province in many ways the most anti-American in the Dominion. There is a small amount of radicalism among industrial workers, and among the farmers of the Prairie Provinces when wheat prices are low, but west of the Rockies it is pretty continually held in check by the conservatism natural to a large group of retired English naval and military officers and civil servants.

Moreover, Canadian development has proved to be subject to a time lag which has had curious conservative effects. Sometimes it has meant that Canada has belatedly taken up some idea or technique or article which other parts of the world have tested and found good. An omnibus example might be industrialization or the provision of normal schools. Sometimes Canada has imitated the United States before the United States has decided that it has made a wrong move. Examples of this are harder to find because they are blurred in advance and retreat, but unrestricted free election of subjects in higher education hurt some Canadian universities before its limitations had become widely apparent in the United States. Sometimes Canada has held back long enough to avoid making a false step. Probably Quebec's refusal to follow the sweeping North American example in the prohibition of alcoholic beverages and the subsequent gradual agreement with her of the remaining provinces provide the most striking recent example of this beneficial effect of the time lag.

Mention has been made of exceptions to conservatism, individualism, and *laissez faire*. The most conspicuous have been Canada's large-scale public enterprises in the ownership and operation of hydro-electric enterprises and railways. These and lesser enterprises of the same sort in other fields have always been subject to substantial domestic criticism. Some of these social experiments, like telephone service, state banks, and state-aided coöperatives, have failed to survive, yet Canada is often held up as an example of successful state socialism. In general, there is good reason for believing that practical considerations in a pioneer country have been more responsible for Canadian state socialism than allegiance to new political philosophies. Radicalism, as radicalism, has had little to do with it. Canada, like the Australian states and New Zealand, wanted to catch up with the world's technical progress in public utilities before individual or private corporate enterprises, unaided, could find it profitable to do so. Part of these public services was secured, as in the United States, by lavish state subsidy of private enterprise, notably in the field of railways and canals, the backbone of Canadian unity. The present nationally owned railways, however, represent a combination of the bankruptcy of several publicly aided private enterprises and of the public demand that the railway services be maintained. Canada has always had rather more public services than conservative business standards would indicate that she could afford.

As further evidence of Canadian conservatism it might be added that there has been, until recently, no substantial radical political party in Canada, and that past radicalisms have been brief protests against intolerable political and economic discriminations. Canada's one original contribution to political science has been the invention of autonomy within an empire. Aside from that, she has been imitative and conservative.

XV

THE GROWTH AND OPERATION OF THE CANADIAN EDUCATIONAL SYSTEM

1. *Educational Backgrounds*

The complex of generalizations about Canada which has been elaborated above is arbitrary and inconsiderate of many substantial modifications in fact. Generalizations about Canadian education must be inconsiderate of even more exceptions and limitations. It is fair, however, to begin by saying that Canadian education has generally been conceived to have three principal tasks: namely, to train social servants such as doctors, lawyers, and clergymen; to improve and adapt the exploitative processes suitable to Canada and to train men in their use; and to Canadianize new arrivals and their children. One can easily surmise the differences in emphasis on the three tasks which would exist, say, in Saskatchewan and Quebec. Education as self-cultivation has been a luxury reserved for a very small fraction of the Canadian people.

The principal matrixes of Canadian education have been French, British, and American. New France of the eighteenth century was administered by the same machinery as any province of France itself. There was no system of public education, because education was the affair of the Church. The parish priests were the first, and often the only, teachers the *habitants* knew and they naturally were not pretentious in their educational programmes. The Jesuits had set up a classical college at Quebec as early as 1635. The Sulpicians taught advanced subjects in their seminary at Montreal. The Ursuline nuns, the Hospitallers, and the sisters of Notre Dame had founded schools for girls. In 1763, aside from the higher education available to candidates for holy orders, and craft schools in Quebec and Montreal, education for nearly all Canadians meant nothing or "the three R's" as learned at the parish church or presbytery. Amplification of the structure, when it came, had a way of being in accordance with the aims of the Roman Catholic Church in Canada. The classical colleges, to which reference will be made, were conservative and retrospective. Only today are such worldly institutions as technical and commercial schools and colleges being asked for and received outside of the urban centres: Montreal, Three Rivers, and Quebec.

The heritage from the British Isles and the British American colonies seemed superficially to be the creation of colonial replicas of the English public schools and universities, for, from the founding of King's College and its school at Windsor, Nova Scotia, in 1790, down to the middle of the nineteenth century, the British government and colonial governors coöperated with the Anglican official groups in the colonies in setting up such institutions with generous state support. Popular demand for practical education, locally available to the children of the less privileged, could not be denied, however; and although no one can measure the proportions, it is certain that the village schools of Scotland, New England, and the middle continental colonies played an overwhelming part in determining the character of that element in British North American education. Then when these elementary schools came to serve as the foundation for a policy of secondary, normal-school, and higher education more in keeping with circumstance than Anglican monopoly, the architects of the new structure turned to Prussia and the United States for the integral design, to Ireland for textbooks, and to Edinburgh University, Trinity College, Dublin, and the University of London for alternatives to Oxford and Cambridge.

The borrowings from the United States are difficult to measure because a substantial number of them were the result of an inevitable gradual infiltration which it occurred to no one to observe and record, and because Canadian sensitiveness in the matter of indebtedness to the United States meant that more formal adoptions went almost or completely unacknowledged. Yet any salesman in Canada of school supplies and books from the United States or indeed any manufacturer of them in Canada could easily demonstrate the debt in education which Canadian national feeling made it politic to forget. Perhaps the most convenient demonstration of the force of North American models was the Canadian provincial adoption of the state university so characteristic of the United States. That idea

of New England emigrants to Michigan was framed in 1817 and
began to function in 1841. It was amplified in later years in Wis-
consin and elsewhere. The purest Canadian emulation of it is to be
found in the young universities of the West: Saskatchewan, Alberta,
and British Columbia, but it has operated to modify in varying degree the characters of the universities of Manitoba, Toronto (Ontario), and New Brunswick, and even independent foundations like
McGill (Montreal) and Dalhousie (Halifax).

2. *Primary and Secondary Education*

Canadian educational institutions fall fairly conveniently within
the usual classification of western education. Primary and secondary
public education in rural and urban public schools are usually provided for children from the age of five or six onward to thirteen or
even to as late as twenty-one, but it is characteristic of a country with
a large agricultural population that compulsory attendance for other
than urban children begins at seven years of age for seven provinces,
and at eight for another. Quebec has no law of compulsory attendance, but forbids the employment of children under sixteen years of
age unless they can read and write. In many districts throughout
Canada school vacations are arranged to fall at times most convenient for rural populations. School attendance is not entirely satisfactory in a country of great distances, and even the possible measure-
ment of it is not conclusive. From the figures which are available it
would appear that Alberta, Saskatchewan, and British Columbia
manage to get about eighty percent of pupils of ages five to nineteen
into some kind of school in a given year, Ontario about seventy-five
percent, and the remainder from the seventy percent of Manitoba
down to the sixty-one percent of Prince Edward Island. In the percentage of the total enrollment in average attendance only Prince
Edward Island falls below seventy-four percent. The proportion of
pupils in private schools is very small, and such schools find it necessary to follow public standards for examination purposes.

The problem of reconciling French and English, or Roman Catholic and Protestant, aims for children in the schools has been solved
in a fairly practical way. Except in Quebec, public schools are as a
rule undenominational. In Quebec the provincial secretary controls

special types of education, but the ordinary structure is controlled by the provincial educational council, which is bifurcated. Two committees, Roman Catholic and Protestant, each with a deputy minister as secretary, regulate the two kinds of schools. In some other provinces such as New Brunswick, the religious minority provides its own schools. In Ontario, Saskatchewan, and Alberta, "separate" or dissentient schools exist in areas where either Roman Catholic or Protestant minorities prefer to set up and support, usually by extra taxation, a separate school, rather than patronize the one in existence which is predominantly of the opposite religious complexion. The problem of bilingualism has always been a serious one for French Canadians in Ontario, but a workable compromise in special instances allows French to be the language of primary instruction provided that proficiency in English is attained. Languages other than French and English are not granted special consideration.

In both primary and secondary public education, policies, standards, even textbooks and teacher training, are matters of provincial concern and uniformity to which the localities conform. Indeed, the four western provinces are in substantial agreement among themselves in these matters, so that a pupil moving, as western families have so often moved, anywhere westward from the Ontario-Manitoba boundary, would have little difficulty in taking up his education where he left off.

This conformity and standardization can be deadening to teacher and pupil alike, particularly when they are reinforced by similarly standardized examinations to mark the steps from primary to secondary and thereafter to university education.[2] Textbooks have a way of becoming containers for what a dominant group of teachers agrees are the "fundamentals" of a subject and within the grasp of average students in the prescribed grade. The tyranny of examinations set and marked by similar groups of teachers is revealed in excessive drilling of pupils in the regurgitation of the printed word, and fertilizing imagination or fanciful wandering into bypaths can be regarded as deleterious. Yet in a new country filled with a mixture

[2] It is not customary in English-speaking Canada (or in England) to differentiate between college and university levels of work as is done in French-speaking Canada and the United States,

of old and new citizens of the greatest variety in background and predilections, it is intelligible that provinces should risk a stultifying uniformity in the effort to stamp out illiteracy and to secure educable voters in their democracies. The percentage of illiteracy in persons ten years of age and over revealed by the census of 1921 was only 5.10 percent, and the increased interest in education since then is demonstrated by the reduction to 3.79 percent in 1931.

Primary and secondary education range from very bad to very good, roughly in correspondence to density of population. There have always been more rural than urban schools. Sparseness of population in frontier areas and the drift to the cities from worked-out ones mean that in an old province like Ontario (which contains about a third of the population) there are over a thousand schools with less than ten pupils, one teacher, and five or more grades represented in one room. Inasmuch as local school boards make up for their lack of control of educational standards and policies by selecting teachers and paying salaries, there is an inevitable tendency even in the larger rural schools for the post of teacher to be something of an economic favor, a petty political "plum," to swell some family budget before a young woman gets married. For this reason and from fear that the already heavy educational taxation would be increased, the movement for consolidated rural schools with provided transportation has met serious resistance. Even with provincial assistance and the enlargement of administrative areas, some regions cannot provide much beyond a bare minimum in the way of education.

Secondary education, therefore, is inevitably almost all urban, and there has been a remarkable increase in it during the last twenty years. Broader legal requirements for attendance, consolidation of settlement, and greater selectivity by employers have all played their parts in providing a vigorous response to nation-wide efforts to lengthen school life. Another clue can be found in the *Annual Survey of Education in Canada,* 1930, p. xii:

The secondary schools themselves have been changing in character to attract—or perhaps better, to serve—a wider range of students. Curricula have been altered and broadened in variety to include courses that it was previously not possible to obtain in the publicly controlled school systems. Technical and vocational courses have appeared in many quarters.

This democratic response to the practicality of taxpaying citizens is a factor in Canadian education to which more attention must be given later. The point to be observed here is that the growth in secondary education does not involve only the provision of vocational training, for in no Canadian schools is that divorced from secondary education in more "liberal" subjects.

Extensive technical and vocational secondary education has been largely a twentieth-century creation in Canada, beginning in large cities like Montreal and Toronto, but recently spreading with great rapidity in those cities and in the smaller industrial centres which grew with Canadian industrial expansion after 1914. During the last twenty years it has been a matter in which the Dominion government has concerned itself. In 1913 it voted ten million dollars to be granted over ten years to the provinces on a population basis, and in amounts equal to provincial expenditure, for the expansion of schools of agriculture. In 1919 another ten million dollars were allotted for technical education on the same plan. In 1931, seven hundred fifty thousand dollars a year for fifteen years were set aside for secondary agricultural and technical education. Coming late, these branches of education were able to profit greatly from the experience of Europe and the United States. On the industrial side such education proved very expensive, but on the commercial side it supplanted a large number of private business schools so that the taxpayer could be convinced that the secondary education which his children demanded was "practical" and therefore justifiable. In most cases, where it is financially possible, technical and vocational schools are separate institutions, but in other instances the ordinary high school or collegiate institute has been modified in sometimes extensive degree.

3. *Methods and Results of Educational Policies*

Before the twentieth century, the universities were expected to provide the technical and vocational education which could not be obtained either in industrial, agricultural, or commercial apprenticeship. Heavy public demands were laid upon the university faculties of engineering and they rose to the occasion sufficiently, first to make Canada almost independent of Europe and the United States, and later to export a surplus of engineers to other parts of the world. Indeed, during the last generation, Canada has produced far more engineers of university qualifications than could find employment in Canada appropriate to their training, and the present problem is that of stiffening engineering education to weed out the less able candidates and to equip the better more adequately for the highly competitive field which they now enter.

North America has for long nourished the tradition that universities, particularly on their technical sides, deserve state support, in return for which they should provide government with technical consultants. Agriculture provides a good example, but one could find others all the way from public health to public law. The earliest agricultural experiment stations in Canada were private establishments, but there gradually grew up a double structure of dominion and provincial stations, and provincial agricultural colleges. The last did a good deal of their early educational work in short courses during off seasons for agriculture, but degree courses were soon set up for more serious students, and the colleges became affiliated with the universities. A somewhat similar development in secondary and higher education might be traced for household science or forestry. This whole congeries of affiliations between the state and its educational institutions is an underlying determinant of education in Canada.

In the light of what has been said, it is natural to find that Canadian universities have had a very mixed development. In them three characters have struggled for expression: the French-Canadian idea of a classical and literary education to be pursued in a classical college affiliated either with Laval (Quebec) or with Montreal University, and then to be crowned in some cases by university studies for the professions; the English idea of a university composed of colleges for gentlemen, non-technical in character, to be supplemented by other professional institutions in the university or outside it; and the North American idea of a university largely technical, vocational, and professional, with respect paid to broader curiosities in the form of brief pre-professional courses of a "cultural" kind.

It can be said at once that French-Canadian education has been able to preserve the purity of its original French and Roman Catholic character most successfully. All institutions are subject to some ecclesiastical control. Most children go to the primary schools and thereafter about one-tenth of them go on to technical or vocational education in day or evening classes. Education in letters is available in some twenty-five classical colleges, where instruction begins in what elsewhere would be late primary grades and is carried to a bachelor's degree in arts in accordance with standards set by the Universities of Laval and Montreal. The normal attendance is from thirteen to twenty-one, with six years devoted to Latin, Greek, English, French, history, geography, and mathematics, and during the last two with philosophy and natural science as possible substitutes for the Latin and Greek. Other, less classical, secondary education is provided in what are known as complementary schools. Professional training, as in theology, medicine, and law, or advanced courses in arts, can be obtained at the universities by working toward a second degree. For French-Canadian students, education from bottom to top is kept in harmony with their religion. One notable result of the system of classical colleges is that the first degree is obtained at an earlier age than in a province like Ontario.

The English idea of a university can be best seen in its Canadian vicissitudes by taking the University of Toronto as an example. It was founded in 1827 as King's College, an Anglican replica of an Oxford or Cambridge college, much to the wrath of a colony in which the Anglicans were a minority. The critics used the new University College and University of London as examples in their campaign for secularization, and in 1853 succeeded in attaining their ends. King's College became non-sectarian University College and a University of Toronto was created as an examining body. The University has since served as the central apparatus for a remarkable federation of sectarian and professional colleges. In 1852, the Anglican Bishop of Toronto marked his disapproval of the approaching change by establishing a new separate college. Half a century later it was glad to federate with the University and it now has its buildings in the University grounds.

Toronto provides a series of neat illustrations of the conflict and compromise between English and North American ideas. Each of the four-year degree courses in arts, like an Oxford or Cambridge school or tripos, has been kept rigidly non-professional (for instance, the course in commerce does not lead to an arts degree). By separating the students into candidates for pass or honour degrees it has been possible to segregate the most gifted and allow them to pursue exacting, thorough, special courses of study, either in fields like classics or chemistry or in natural combinations such as English and history or mathematics and physics. Competition among honour students is keen, and the unsuccessful are rather ruthlessly relegated to the pass course or dropped altogether. Candidates for entrance into these courses spend a year beyond ordinary matriculation in the secondary school, as do candidates for immediate entrance into the professional schools of engineering and medicine. The existence of extra facilities for these students in the secondary schools also has its effect on candidates for the pass degree, many of whom find it less expensive to take the first year of university work as a last year in the secondary school.

Two basic processes are under way here. The University, still more than half master of its own standards, has allowed students from secondary schools to enter at once upon a professional training, but has forced the secondary schools to continue broader education for them for an extra year. At the same time, the University's own custody of the passman in what is a somewhat freely elective course has been diminished by one year. Perhaps the ultimate stimulus lies in a popular demand that students receive their first degrees at an earlier age than in the past. Ten years ago the average age of those receiving the first degree at Toronto was over twenty-three years. Since then, highly competitive economic conditions have made one group of Canadian youth crowd vocational training into the secondary school and ignore the University, and another slight the traditional education in arts in order to begin professional specialization at the earliest possible age. What has been said of Toronto applies with local modifications to Dalhousie, McGill, and Queens. It is not difficult to see herein the similarities to and differences from American education.

The American model of a university emerges most sharply in the Western Provinces or in the University of Western Ontario. The vocational and professional emphasis is strong. There is a good deal of free election of short courses for "credits" which can be added up to earn the degree. There is less compunction about giving degree credit for attainment in work belonging elsewhere to secondary or technical education. The idea of education as a process of self-cultivation almost divorced from utilitarian conceptions does not receive the same support as at Toronto, McGill, Queens, and Dalhousie. There is even some preference at these "American" universities for the instructor who has done graduate work in the United States over the one who has done the same thing in England. This frank North Americanism quite naturally is manifested in the parts of Canada where old French and British loyalties are weakest and where a European observer would find Canadians almost indistinguishable from Americans.

It should be recorded that Canadian professional education in at least two Canadian universities is of the very highest North American rank. This is particularly evident in medicine. Medicine was the first active faculty at McGill (1828) and there, even more than at Philadelphia or New York, the influence of Edinburgh was dominant. In the twentieth century, McGill and Toronto, having both had a hand in the education of Sir William Osler, refurbished the old Edinburgh model by extensive borrowings from Osler's Johns Hopkins. Both are formally ranked among the first six medical schools of North America. Toronto as a provincial university now feels that it must exclude wholesale the scores of candidates for admission from the United States. McGill, which is an independent foundation, admits a few by an informal quota system.

Reference has already been made to the high quality of engineering education. Theology is a special field, remarkable chiefly for the union in Canada of Presbyterian, Methodist, and Congregational churches. Law is another highly local pursuit, supervised by provincial bar associations, but it is notable in Canada as the usual ladder to politics. That is not to say that members of parliament are usually lawyers, but since before federation a few law offices scattered across the Dominion have played a highly disproportionate share in provincial and federal politics. The other professions have no remarkable or unique characteristics. Not all provinces provide all professional or graduate training and students move from one to another. In the Maritime Provinces there has always been some tendency to seek professional or advanced education in New England. There was a time during the nineteenth century when the same thing was true of English-speaking Quebec. Yet now it is on the whole true that Canadian institutions satisfy Canadian demands for professional education and that recourse to Europe or the United States is for work of a postgraduate sort. A variety of professional associations control the admission to practice of the professions under Dominion or provincial charters.

It is quite in keeping with Canadian conditions and ideas that university extension should have become a very important activity. This is particularly true in the form of lectures hitherto given over wide surrounding areas by teachers at the universities. The radio has in recent years seriously diminished the number of these lectures and perhaps it was just as well. In their place systematic adult education in the form of discussion groups and regular courses of reading and instruction has evoked remarkable response, not only in older provinces like Nova Scotia and Ontario, but also in the Western Provinces, where farmers have considerable periods of idleness and where recent immigrants want to sample the education their children are getting.

From the foregoing statements it should be apparent that in Canada, unlike England until very recent date, educational policies have to a large degree been democratically dictated by the people rather than aristocratically bestowed upon them from above. Some exception might be made for Quebec, but even there lay interests have forced religious educators to provide educational services of the sort which they thought necessary. The proposed new University of Montreal, whose physical creation has been delayed by economic difficulties, bore far more resemblance to Columbia University in New York than to the University of Paris, and the technical and commercial schools of Montreal are a far cry from the parish schools of a generation ago.

There is in Canada, however, a somewhat marked difference from much of the United States in the character of popular demand. It might be described as a greater concern to preserve the traditionally good. Because Canada absorbed fewer immigrants more slowly than the United States and because her eighteenth-century citizens found a substantial number of folk quite like themselves among the early newcomers, there has been a remarkable continuity of character in what might be described wholesale as the influence of home background. There have been several kinds of this background and the division between French- and English-speaking groups is a profound one, but whether it take the form of Scottish passion for self-improvement, English effort to preserve the concept of a gentleman, Irish love of history and romance, or French-Canadian pride in having made Canada a homeland, the Canadian child has behind him a slightly more stable and deeply rooted home background than his American cousin. Canada's digestion of new elements has not been so violently tested as that of the United States.

The two nationalisms, French and English, which mark Canadian education should not be surprising in a young democracy which has never stopped attracting the most various new citizens. The uneasiness which arises from having the colossal and ignoring United States as a neighbour is likely to keep those nationalisms alive. There seems little reason to believe that they will develop into British or French nationalism in the sense of strong European affiliation, and the recent slowing of the tide of immigration should permit them pretty thoroughly to permeate the population and perhaps to merge. The chief obstacle to a single nationalism has been the great linguistic and cultural bifurcation. Added to it are localisms and particularisms of many sorts. Time may moderate them, but they have a deleterious effect upon education in that Canada has too many of almost every kind of educational institution from universities and colleges to rural schools. "Fewer and better" might be a very good motto.

The commonest impression which the foreigner receives from educated Canadians is of great thoroughness in their training. He may also be struck by their conservatism, even narrowness, but the reception to educated Canadians in the United States bears witness to a gradually evolved respect for the Canadian's competence within almost any chosen and well-recognized field of intellectual enterprise. There is a strong Scottish strain of stubbornly won mastery, particularly in eastern Canadian education. It is unfortunate that Canadians do not yet feel sufficiently secure to be searchingly self-critical in education. It is more natural to look with pride (and on the whole justly) on what has been achieved, than painfully to hammer out a philosophy of education and build up to it. Yet preoccupation with what has been done in the past can, and does, breed some dangerous parochialism. Broader criteria come chiefly through university and secondary teachers who have studied in Europe or the United States. The effect of the latter country is reinforced by all sorts of imponderable infiltrations such as are carried by periodicals, international academic associations, visitors, and the radio.

In the field of non-utilitarian higher education Canada has something distinctive to her credit in the honour courses in arts such as have a history of about seventy years at Toronto. They represent a compromise between Oxford or Cambridge and North American conditions. They are selective, severely competitive, and productive of a small group of the intellectually distinguished who have been trained in self-education. They are sharply non-equalitarian except in the equality of opportunity. Thanks to the life of the English tradition in Canada there has been little objection to them on democratic grounds. The one serious threat to them is that completion of them qualifies a student to train to be a specialist secondary teacher at a higher than ordinary salary. This has tended to swell the numbers and introduce popular pressure for lowering of standards, but since standing is given in first, second, and third classes, the intellectual aristocracy is still easily distinguishable.

The quality of Canadian technical and professional education is high, and its predominance over non-utilitarian education is explainable. Education to assist specifically in making a living is natural in an exploitative country with an insignificant leisured class. This attitude is not so much intolerant of the arts and of self-cultivation as simply unreceptive to them. One odd result, characteristic of the United States as well as of Canada, is that North American scientists tend to be inventors and technicians rather than original theorizers. An Edison or a Banting is more characteristic and more acclaimed than a Willard Gibbs.

There are few signs of political curiosity, inventiveness, or activity in Canadian education. A generation ago undergraduate squabbles and rivalries were conducted behind the names of the Liberal and Conservative parties. Now that has largely passed, for Canadian students find it difficult to tell the political parties apart and they do not invent new ones. The Canadian student is about as unpolitical as the American. The universities teach political science, chiefly to intending lawyers, and economics, chiefly to intending business men. Sociology is barely recognized, disappointingly enough, for Canada herself provides an exciting field for sociological investigation. But such investigation would find its phenomena still pretty largely comprehended by conventional social and political institutions. There has been and is little social experimentation in Canada. Indeed, recent scholarship has revealed an overwhelming proportion of pure imitation of France, Great Britain, and the United States. Here differences from the United States, like Canadian respect for law and Canadian rejection of prohibition, should be kept in mind, but they also fall within the conservative category.

On the whole, the dominant trend of Canadian education and life should be sought in North American rather than in French or English terms. Canada will go on exporting her surplus of trained men and women to the United States, but will in turn accept a good deal of leadership from that lively republic. The time lag will continue to operate, sometimes advantageously, sometimes unfortunately, sometimes merely to postpone. Canada's appetite for amenities and services, whetted by American example, is likely always to be greater than her capacity to satisfy it. The only things likely to divert Canada from her present path would be Britain's subordination of her European relationships to her affiliations overseas or the swamping of English-speaking Canadians by the greater natural increase of the French-speaking Canadians. Until either happens, Canada will more and more consciously follow the North American way. The more she admits that she does so, the greater will her influence be in determining its character and in enriching it from her several cultural heritages.

INDEX

INDEX

Curricula (England)—*Continued*
tive unimportance of, in manly education, 78-80; university, 65-66
Curricula (France): elementary, 88-89,
113-14, 126; homogeneity in nation,
result of uniformity in, 106, 127; lack
of practical purpose in, 110-14; nationalism and, 111-14; secondary, 90-
96, 102, 111-13, 117-18, 126; university, 108, 116-17
Curricula (Germany): adapted by the
several states, 31; citizenship in, 33-
36; diversity of, 20; elementary, 16;
höhere schulen, 21, 34, restored to
pre-Republican basis, 21; international studies in, 36-37; religion in,
19; university, 23; vocational, 18, 25-
26
Curricula (Italy), nationalistic: elementary, 193-94; Fascist concept of,
190-91; secondary, 202; university,
205, 206. *See also* Textbooks
Curricula (Soviet Russia): as outlined
by Central Committee, 142-43; basic
principles of, 151; centering on nature, labor, society, 150; higher education, 163-64; Marxian, 151-58

Dalhousie University (Canada): influence of state university, 250; type of,
similar to that of Toronto, 256, 257
Dalton plan (Soviet Russia), 154; discarded, 150
Darwin, Charles Robert, 59
Degrees (Canada): classical, 255; economic pressure to grant at earlier
age, 256; in western universities, 257;
pass and honor systems of, 256
Degrees (England): general scheme of,
79-80; reading for, 75-76
Degrees (France): *baccalauréat*, 88, 89-
90, 94, 95-96, 99, 105, 112, 113, 118,
122, 123, failure in Latin endanger-
ing, 94, post-primary schools not
leading to, 89-90; bachelor's, average
age of attaining, 118; enablements of,
95-96; doctor's, required for professors
in higher education, 99; higher, requirements for, 99; of private institutions, honorary only, 86-87; university, criteria of, 118, granting of, reserved to state universities, 95-96,
requisites for, compared with those of
United States, 123

Degrees (Germany): deference paid to,
11; doctoral degree, required for
higher governmental posts, 43, for
teachers in secondary schools, 22
Degrees (Italy), university, 204
Delacroix, F. V. E., 124
Democracy, educational (France), 115,
118-24
Democratization of education (Germany): major objective of Republic,
29; overcrowding of universities by,
44; upsetting to social stability, 42
Denmark: and Danish tradition, 211-
19; area of, small, 211; comparison of,
with other countries, 211-14; "coöperative commonwealth," 214, 231-33;
democratic reform, sustained by
farmers, 234; distribution of wealth,
state control of, 213; England, fleet
lost to, 221; farmers, resourcefulness
of, 213; former political importance
of, 221-22; linguistic unity of, 211;
population of, homogeneous, 211-12,
rural, 212; Schleswig-Holstein, loss
of, 222, 223-24; social agencies, financed by state, 213; Social Democrats, rising political strength of,
234-35; state agencies, used for well-
being of people, 213; urban percentage of, 212
*Denmark, A Coöperative Common-
wealth*, 213
Department (France), 83; one lycée for
each, 90
Depression (Germany): middle class
destroyed by, 28; proletariat increased by, 46
Descartes, René, 133-34
Deutsche Oberschule, 17, 19, 20
Dewey, John, 154, 157, 175, 176
Dialectic materialism (Soviet Russia):
curricula permeated with, 151-53;
misapplied, 175, 176; the only outlook, 156
Diaz, Armando, 196
Dictatorship (Germany): constitution
set aside by, 14; demand of proletariat, 46-47; direct step to, from *Kaisertum*, 27; schools used by, to entrench,
12, 26; states deprived of self-government by, 16
Dictatorship (Soviet Russia): education
instrument of, 146; of proletariat,
connotes not only violence but re-

Dictatorship (Soviet Russia)—*Continued*
education, 140-41; vs. classless society,
171-72
Discipline (Germany), of feudal derivation, 9-10
Disraeli, Benjamin, 55
Doctorat, 96
Dominion status: Canada's contribution, 247; eventuation of, 244-45

Ebert, Friedrich, 27
Écoles libres, 85-86
Écoles normales supérieures, 120
Écoles primaires supérieures, 88
Economic conditions, educational influence of, 135-36
Economic poverty (Italy), educational
poverty caused by, 181-82
Economic program of Fascism, 188
Edinburgh University, Canadian borrowings from, 249
Edison, Thomas A., 261
Education (Canada): administration,
almost exclusive concern of provinces,
with state affiliations, 240, 251, 254;
attendance, 250; attendance, compulsory (Quebec excepted), 250; backgrounds, American, British, French,
239-43, 248-50, 251, 253, 254-57, 258,
260, 261; Catholic education, 248-49,
250-51, 254, 255; church and, 241,
248-49, 250-51, 255; classics, 248, 249,
254, 255, 256; curricula, 252-53, 255,
256, 261; degrees, 255, 256, 257; dissentient schools, 251; examinations,
standardized, 251; free (except for
dissentient school tax), 251; illiteracy,
252; nationalism (Canadianization),
248; objectives, vi, 248, 252, 257, 259-
61; private schools, 250; religion, 250-
51, 255, 257; students, democratic,
thorough, unpolitical, 258, 259-60,
261; system, elementary, 249, 250-53,
secondary, 248, 249, 250-53, 256, 258,
technical, 249, 253-54, 257, 258, 260-
61, university, 248, 249-50, 254-58,
260, university extension, 258, vocational, 253-54, 256, 257; teachers,
standardized, 251; textbooks, standardized, 251
Education (Denmark): administration,
by Ministry of Ecclesiastical Affairs
and Public Instruction, 215, 216, 226;
attendance, 214, 216, 217, 219; attend-

ance, compulsory, 214; church and,
215; classics in, 216, 217; communal
schools, 216; curricula, 215, 216-17,
218, 219, 226, 227, 233; degrees, 218;
examinations, 217, 228, 233; folk high
schools, unique contribution, 219,
221-29, 231-32, 235-36; free, 214; freedom, academic, 218; instruction,
methods of, 227-29; nationalism, 212-
13, 225, 227, 234; objectives, vi, 213,
214, 215, 222, 223, 225, 227, 233; private schools, 216, 226; religion, 215;
students, special provision for peasant, 213, 219, 222-23, 225-27, 229,
231, 232, 233, 234-35; system, elementary, 214-15, secondary, 216-17, 219,
221-29, 231-33, 235-36, technical, 218,
University of Copenhagen, 217-18, vocational, 218-20, 229-31; teachers, rôle
of, 215, 218, 228-29; women, schools
for, 219-20, 226, 227
Education (England), 50-80; administration, 72-73, 74, 77, 176; attendance,
compulsory, 71, 74; background, 52,
58, 62-80; church and, 58, 68-96; classics in, 63, 65-66, 70, 78, 110; curricula, 65-66, 70, 78-80; degrees, 75-
76, 79-80; Dissenters' schools, rise of,
71-72; examinations, 72, 75-76, 78,
79; ideals, 65-70, 71, 78-80; indoctrination, 69, 76, 77; private schools,
74; public schools, 64, 65-66, 68, 69,
70, 75, 77, 249; religion, 68-69, 71,
72; specialization, 76; students, aristocracy, education for, 65, 68, 77, 80;
system, 62-64, 65, 70-74, elementary,
71, 74, 75, professional, 74-80, secondary, 74, 75-76, 77, 78-79, technical,
69, 75, university, 54, 64, 65, 66, 68-
69, 72, 73, 75, 76, 77, 78-80, vocational, 72, 74-75; teachers, 68, 75
Education (France): academies, 84, 85,
96, 97, 125; administration, centralization under Minister of Public Instruction, basic principle of, 83-87,
90, 96, 97, 106, 115, 124-26; attendance, 89, 118-19; attendance, compulsory, 88; church and, 85-87;
classics, 91-92, 93-95, 102, 104-5, 110,
126, 127; curricula, 102, 110-14, elementary, 88-89, 113-14, 126, secondary, 90-96, 102, 111-13, 117-18,
126, university, 108, 116-17; degrees,
private institutions, 86-87, secondary,

Überfremdung, 31
Umschichtung, 42
United States: (Canada) disturbed by proximity of, 239, 240, 241-42, 244, 259; export from, of surplus Canadian scholars, 261; immigration to, 241, 244; tariff discriminations against, 245; (Denmark) grain exports of United States, disastrous to, 230; (Germany) Industrial Revolution of United States, borrowed by, 7
University (Canada): extension, 258; mixed development of, 254-58; of Alberta, 250; of British Columbia, 250; of Manitoba, 250; of Montreal, proposed, 258; of New Brunswick, 250; of Saskatchewan, 250; of Toronto, 250, 255-56, 257, 260; of Western Ontario, on American model, 257; professional training in, 257-58; provincial, 249-50; technical and vocational training in, 253-54, 257
University (England): aristocratic survival, 80; dependence on classics in, 65-66; introduction to education, 70; non-sectarian, rise of, 72; provincial, monopoly of aristocratic education broken by, 72; provincial, similarity between, and those of the United States, 54; traditions of, 64, 69, 75
University (France): autonomy of, 97; component parts of, 97; control over students not exercised by, 109; elections in, 111; faculties of, 97-98, 108; freedom of thought in, 108-9, 114-15, 126; not professional schools, 97-98, 108-9; relation of, to academy, 84, 97; theory taught in, 116-18
University (Germany): academic freedom of, 15, 23-24, 35, 38-39; destroyed under Nazi régime, 16, 22-24, 30-31, 38, 41; admission to, sharply restricted under Nazi régime, 31; democratization of, under Republic, 21, 30; entrance examination, 21, 30; professional bent of, 43-44
University (Italy), Fascist, 205-8; "by its very nature given a political task," 208; enrollment in, 203; scientific excellence, aim of, 188
University (Soviet Russia), scheme of, 147, 148, 149

University College, 72
University extension (Canada), an important activity, 258
University of Copenhagen, 219; faculties of, 217-18; nerve center of Denmark, 217
University of Edinburgh, influence of, on Canadian medical education, 257
University of France, a hierarchy, 83-85
University of London, 72; Canadian educational borrowings from, 249; University College of Toronto modeled on, 255
University of Lyons, 98
University of Perugia, Fascism at, 206
University of Toronto: development of, 250, 255-56; medicine at, 257; self-cultivation, aim of, 257, 260

Vaillant, Édouard Marie, 138
Vanity Fair, 59
Vatican Accord, 199
Veblen, Thorstein, 9
Vergil, 5
Victoria University, 72
Violence, dictatorship of proletariat committed to, 140-41
Vocational education: (Canada) 253-54, 256, 257; (France) in post-primary schools, 88-89, 100; (Germany) 40-46; required, 18; schools supplementary to, 26; (Soviet Russia) 162-69
Vocational schools (Soviet Russia), 147, 148
Voks, 166
Volk ohne Raum, 37
Volksschulen, 15, 16, 18, 21, 29, 30, 34, 36, 42
Volsunga Saga, 7
Voltaire, de (François Marie Arouet), 56, 124
Voyageurs, Canadian heritage from, 241
Vus, 147, 148, 149, 162-64
Vydvishenzy, 174

Wagner, Richard, 7, 10
Walpole, Horace, 53, 66, 69
War of 1812, 243
War of 1870, 12
Watson, J. B., 134-35, 175-76
Weber, Max, 27